EDUCATION AND PSYCHOLOGY OF THE GIFTED SERIES

James H. Borland, Editor

REVERSING UNDERACHIEVEMENT AMONG GIFTED BLACK STUDENTS

Promising Practices and Programs

DONNA Y. FORD

Teachers College, Columbia University
New York and London

Published by Teachers College Press, 1234 Amsterdam Avenue, New York, NY 10027

Library of Congress Cataloging-in-Publication Data

Ford, Donna Y.
    Reversing underachievement among gifted black students : promising practices and programs / Donna Y. Ford.
        p.   cm. — (Education and psychology of the gifted series)
    Includes bibliographical references and index.
    ISBN 0-8077-3535-3 (pbk. : alk. paper). — ISBN 0-8077-3536-1
(cloth : alk. paper)
    1. Gifted children — Education — United States.   2. Afro-American
students — Education. — 3. Underachievers — Education — United States.
I. Title. II. Series.
LC3993.9.F66 1996
371.95′6 — dc20   95-52527

ISBN 0-8077-3535-3 (paper)
ISBN 0-8077-3536-1 (cloth)

Printed on acid-free paper
Manufactured in the United States of America

03 02 01 00 99 98 97 96   8 7 6 5 4 3 2 1

Contents

Preface

On the fringes of most school environments gathers a shadow population of students whose motivation and achievement are stymied. These are the marginal students who are not being well served by our public schools. Precious little attention is given either to the needs of these young people or to their assets. They are viewed as deviants from the "regular" students, outsiders who are not productive members of the learning community. This persistent problem of increasing numbers of students who are not succeeding must be attacked because youth who fail on the margins are as deserving as those who thrive in the mainstream.

—Sinclair & Ghory, 1992, p. 33

The told and untold stories of many Black and minority students have not been positive in education. This is 1996, and although there are books and comprehensive treatises on underachieving students (including gifted students and minority students), there is no such work on *gifted, potentially gifted*, or *underachieving* Black students. This book is an ambitious undertaking, but not overly so. It was developed with multiple audiences in mind — educators, counselors, parents, administrators, researchers, and practitioners. It is comprehensive because it focuses on the psychological, social, and cultural factors that influence the achievement of Black youth who are gifted or potentially gifted. It focuses on the respective and collaborative roles that families, educators, peers, and students themselves must play in promoting the academic, psychological, and socioemotional well-being of these particular students.

Several premises guide this work. In defining giftedness, I have adopted the inclusive definitions espoused by the U.S. Department of Education (1993), Howard Gardner (1983), and Robert Sternberg (1985). These definitions and attendant theories contend that giftedness is a context-bound and multidimensional construct that requires multidimensional and multimodal assessment and identification strategies. They acknowledge the impossibility of a "one size fits all" intelligence test to capture this elusive and complex construct, and they recognize that tests are academic electric chairs for far too many students.

A second premise is that no group has a monopoly on giftedness, regardless of its form. It is illogical and statistically impossible for giftedness to be the prerogative of one racial, gender, or socioeconomic group. Nonetheless, gifted programs represent the most segregated programs in public school; they are disproportionately White and middle class, and they serve primarily intellectually and academically gifted students as opposed to students who are gifted in other areas of endeavor, such as creativity, visual and performing arts, and leadership. If all gifted and potentially gifted students are to receive an appropriate education, gifted programs must become desegregated.

Third, predicting potential is as problematic and difficult as predicting the weather. Despite sophisticated instruments (e.g., intelligence, achievement, and aptitude tests), mistakes are still made in identification and assessment. Some students score higher than we expect, others score lower. Tests touted to be highly correlated with achievement variables show huge discrepancies for some students. Students do well in college whose test scores predicted otherwise, and students with the highest test scores can and do drop out.

A fourth premise is that educators and counselors have a moral and ethical responsibility to help all children reach their potential in school; no child should sit on the margins, feeling either physically or socially isolated from the rewards of learning and educational challenge. A fifth premise is that family–school collaborations are essential to students' school success. Parents are children's first teachers; teachers are children's surrogate parents. Without family involvement, schools and children are less likely to succeed.

Finally, underachievement is not a sickness that can be cured; rather, underachievement can be prevented or reversed. Deficit perspectives and blaming children for their failures do little to resolve underachievement. The potential and motivation to achieve are inherent in all children. No talent or potential should be allowed to atrophy.

A preface permits the author to describe not only what a book is but also what it is not. Given this license, I shall end by dispelling any misconceptions about the goals and objectives of this book. The book does not cover the entire range of issues related to underachievement among gifted and potentially gifted Black students. The literature on this topic is too modest for this task. Nonetheless, it seeks to present a comprehensive and thorough discussion of the issues raised. The book discusses the educational plight of Black youth, but it is not an attempt to castigate or indict the educational system for these problems. In fact, finger-pointing would represent a significant waste of time and paper. Instead, I make a strong, consistent attempt to emphasize that underachievement is a multifaceted phenomenon whose etiology is equally multidimensional and complex. I hope to unravel some of its mystery.

Personally and professionally, I have witnessed Black children, many of them gifted but not formally identified, floundering in school. We all see events through the lenses of our personal ideologies, but only those with myopic vision can overlook the crises facing Black youth in both general and gifted education.

Racially and culturally diverse students are at the greatest risk of being forgotten in the context of both gifted and general education. Gifted Black students are a minority within a minority—an anomaly in gifted programs. As a gifted Black student, I walked in two worlds. Teachers had a difficult time understanding me, for I was gifted *and* Black—it was an oxymoron, just as gifted underachievement appears paradoxical. The gifted part of me was supposed to be conforming, hardworking, obedient, academically outstanding; the Black part of me was supposed to be disobedient, lazy, defiant of authority, and academically poor. No child should experience this hellish confusion. No human being should.

As a gifted Black student who *learned* to underachieve, I needed several things to ensure a healthy school experience. I needed teachers, counselors, psychologists, and other school personnel to acknowledge and appreciate the changing demographics of students, and to respond by:

(1) seeking substantive preparation in both gifted and multicultural education;

(2) changing curriculum and instruction to reflect and affirm diversity and my culture;

(3) understanding that racially and culturally diverse students have a number of battles to fight, including such social ills as poverty, racism, prejudice, and stereotypes that disrupt their motivation and inhibit equal and equitable learning opportunities;

(4) conducting more studies on the dilemmas confronting gifted underachieving Black students; and

(5) developing theories of giftedness that are sensitive to culturally and racially diverse students.

This book speaks to the poverty of research currently available on Black students (gifted and potentially gifted) and correlates of their underachievement. Without adequate research and subsequent prevention and intervention, many gifted Black students will continue to underachieve and, thus, fail to reach their academic potential. This book is offered as a contribution to the limited data available relating social, cultural, and psychological factors to underachievement among highly able Black students. Research that seeks to understand and then address such barriers to academic achievement is in great demand in our schools and gifted programs. The book, therefore, has several general objectives:

(1) to increase awareness and understanding of social, cultural, and psychological needs of gifted Black students, specifically those whose potential and talents are untapped;

(2) to provoke increased research and funding, as well as advocacy on behalf of underachieving and gifted Black students;

(3) to increase the support of broad and inclusive definitions and theories of both giftedness and underachievement; and

(4) to desegregate gifted programs by increasing the representation of Black children (and others of color) in programs and services for gifted students.

My ultimate goal is to decapitate the social inequities that rear their ugly heads in schools. I hope that this book will serve to revitalize national interest in gifted education, particularly the plight of underachieving and gifted Black students, and that it affords readers a broad understanding of how schools, families, and the social, cultural, and psychological matrix all interact to affect achievement. If this book contributes in any way to the discourse on educational equality and equity, it will have been well worth the effort.

Thanks with all my heart to my son Khyle, my husband John, and my mother for their encouragement and support. I am also in the difficult position of "thanking" gifted underachieving Black students, for without them, this book would not exist. This work is dedicated to those Black students who, for one reason or another, have failed or are failing to reach their potential in school and life. To all gifted Black children — diamonds in the rough.

REVERSING UNDERACHIEVEMENT AMONG GIFTED BLACK STUDENTS

Promising Practices and Programs

Chapter 1

Introduction

"Lee is such a social and active child; if only he'd calm down, talk less, and stay out of trouble, he would be one of our shining stars. He's a leader who uses his talents in nonproductive ways."

"Karen is one of my brightest students, but she has priorities other than school. She puts more effort into socializing and partying than into achieving in school."

"Patricia shows a lot of promise for becoming a medical doctor, but her grades in science and math are less than desirable. She seldom comes to class and when she does, she is not prepared. There are three other girls in chemistry this year, and they all seem to be struggling."

"John's performance is inconsistent. He makes a D as easily as he makes an A. I've noticed that he does poorly on tests, but his projects and ideas are outstanding."

These comments illustrate that underachieving students come in many guises, yet someone has recognized potential and promise, or untapped abilities in them. In the above scenarios, two stumbling blocks to academic success are apparent: test anxiety and priorities that do not include academic achievement. In other scenarios, self-esteem and self-concept issues, identity issues, the classroom climate, curriculum and instruction, teacher expectations, peer pressures and relationships, and family concerns inhibit students' motivation and achievement.

Underachieving students are not a homogeneous group. Some students have problems associated with poor peer or social relationships, identity issues, anxiety, defensiveness, or negative self-esteem. Other students may lack motivation and may be considered lazy, procrastinators, perfectionists, or nonconformists. A common perception is that students would not be underachievers if they would "just try harder," "pay attention," and "listen." However, overcoming or reversing underachievement is not that simple for many students, particularly those who have had little or no early intervention, those who lack basic skills to take advantage of educational opportunities, and those who have negative self-images. For gifted Black students, reversing underachievement may be especially difficult if it is related to social barriers, such as racism; to environmental barriers, such as poverty; or to educational barriers, such as inappropriate curriculum and instruction.

At some point, all children become at risk for underachievement. A portion of the student population in every school and gifted program consistently shows a lack of the academic, emotional, and social skills necessary to take full advantage of educational opportunities. Often, these children become "in-school dropouts" who are disillusioned or disenchanted with school, as reflected by poor motivation, disinterest, boredom, daydreaming, acting out, tardiness, or truancy. Such students are psychologically distanced from school. Other students physically reject schools, as reflected in the high national dropout rates. Describing students as lazy, unmotivated, or disinterested in school and learning fails to explain why some students flee, mentally and/or physically, from educational institutions and otherwise resist learning opportunities. Focusing on students in isolation from the conditions of their life circumstances provides a partial picture of their underachievement. This incomplete picture results in piecemeal, futile attempts at intervention.

Underachieving students fall into a gray area in education. Those students who manifest specific identifiable academic problems (e.g., learning disabilities, behavioral disorders, emotional problems) may qualify for special education programs and assistance. Students who manifest more subtle educational problems are likely to receive little or no meaningful assistance. Specifically, underachieving gifted students with subtle or nonspecific problems are seldom evaluated for learning problems and special services, primarily due to high intelligence test or achievement test scores. Subsequently, they may slip through gaps in standard diagnostic screening procedures and muddle through school.

Most descriptions of underachieving students focus on intellectual and academic underachievement. One is more likely to hear of a child who lacks motivation in math, reading, and the sciences, for example, than in creativity, leadership, and other areas of giftedness. Yet we all know people who are gifted in the art of persuasion and use this talent in nonproductive or socially unacceptable ways (e.g., gang leaders, computer hackers, corrupt politicians). We all know students who show great skill in the visual and performing arts but are too shy or anxious to perform for an audience.

Most descriptions of underachievers also support a deficit perspective;

students are said to "lack" or have "poor" study skills, task commitment, motivation, organization, memory, self-concept, self-esteem, and so forth. These characteristics, however, focus on the *symptoms* of underachievement rather than its etiology. The result of focusing on a child's perceived deficits, of blaming the victim, is that such students are considered less desirable, less salvageable than other students. Unfortunately, schools are unable to deal with students who deviate too much from the norm; schools are made for students who are independent learners — those who excel, achieve, and fulfill the expectations of teachers and parents.

Students who underachieve are not born lazy or unmotivated. Many students *learn* to underachieve (D. Y. Ford, Winborne, & Harris, 1991). For example, because of keen insight, an ability to note inconsistencies, and sensitivity to social injustices, many gifted Black students are aware of the contradictions between their academic learning and their lived experiences. They grow critical and wary of the meritocratic ideology promoted in schools, and they are cognizant of race, class, and gender discrimination in schools and the larger society. This constant feedback can demotivate gifted Black students and wreak havoc on their desire to participate in a system perceived as unjust.

Despite widespread problems associated with underachievement in schools, the study of gifted underachievers is relatively new. Terman (1925) contended that "circumstances that affect the fruition of human talent are questions of such transcendent importance that they should be investigated by every method that promises the slightest reduction of our ignorance" (p. vii). Yet resolving underachievement among gifted students does not appear to be a high priority in the educational arena, including gifted education. Comparatively speaking, few articles, books, and empirical studies have appeared in the professional and scholarly literature on gifted underachievers. Even fewer have appeared on underachieving gifted Black students.

PURPOSE

This book has several objectives, the foremost being to maximize learning opportunities and outcomes among Black students who have been formally identified as gifted but are failing to reach their potential, and among Black students whose potential is undiscovered, unrecognized, or ignored. Given their lack of formal identification and access to services for gifted Black students, undiscovered gifted students frequently become underachievers. Talent that is undiscovered or ignored will atrophy.

It is an unfortunate reality that many schools permit some degree of marginality among students—that is, a disconnection between students and the conditions designed for learning. In other words, schools allow individuals or subgroups to develop and sustain faulty, incomplete relationships with other school members and programs. Too many schools tolerate the existence of a fringe population that is not fully involved in the mainstream school life. These marginal[1] students learn and contribute only a fraction of what they can; they use only a portion of their potential at school (Sinclair & Ghory, 1987).

BLACK STUDENTS

Life on the margins is an all too familiar reality for Black students. More than other racially and culturally diverse students, Black youth face social problems that inhibit their achievement motivation and educational outcomes. Racism is alive and well in many schools, and negative stereotypes of Black students persist among teachers and school personnel. Such educational problems exacerbate and are exacerbated by social problems. When Black students fail to achieve at high levels, a vicious circle ensues. In the minds of some educators, these Black students fit into stereotypic roles assigned to Blacks; when they fail to achieve in school, they are destined to lives of economic disadvantage, unemployment, and underemployment. Society can avoid the costly problems associated with social and educational problems by investing now to develop the potential of all students. Although effective academic instruction serves as a primary and essential method for promoting students' success, there are other methods of maximizing learning opportunities and outcomes for gifted and potentially gifted Black students. These methods include controlling or eliminating the effects of factors—social, cultural, and psychological—that inhibit the learning and potential of capable and promising Black students. Ultimately, the cost of poor educational experiences and outcomes is significantly higher than the cost of equitable and excellent schools and schooling.

What are indicators of effective schools and educationally healthy students? Educationally healthy students achieve to their potential in school because their talents (be they academic, leadership, creative, artistic) are recognized and nurtured. They hold positive self-attitudes and self-images, as well as positive attitudes toward their families and schools. These students also have positive relations with teachers and peers.

Healthy schools adopt prescriptive and proactive measures to increase students' well-being. Students with diverse needs (academic, social, cultural, psychological) achieve at high levels. Teachers hold high expectations for and have positive attitudes about students, irrespective of their gender, race, or socioeconomic status (SES). There is consistent and substantive collaboration between the home and school. Student motivation and interests are high, and teachers are prepared to work to meet students' academic and nonacademic needs. Administration, faculty, and staff are respectful and accepting of individual differences. The curriculum is pluralistic, and assessment is comprehensive and dynamic. Essentially, the degree to which schools work to reduce or eliminate impediments to achievement is a barometer of a school's wellness. Contrary to popular opinion and practice, test scores are not necessarily the most important indicator of school wellness. As described later, too many Black students do not demonstrate key characteristics of educationally healthy students. Research consistently shows that Black students are overrepresented in educational and social situations that place them at risk for educational and economic disadvantages, and underrepresented in educationally and socially advantaged situations.

Areas of Underrepresentation

Numerous studies and reports have described the dismal educational status of Black students in schools. For instance, Black students, particularly males, are three times as likely as White males to be in a class for the educable mentally retarded, but only half as likely to be placed in a class for the gifted. Not only are Black students underenrolled in gifted education programs, they are underrepresented in academic tracks, high-ability groups, and academic programs at all educational levels — kindergarten through grade 12, baccalaureate degrees, and graduate degrees. Moreover, the higher the level of education, the greater the degree of underrepresentation and the lower the graduation rate (G. Gay, 1993). In terms of high-level academic courses, Black students are less likely than White students to be enrolled in math, physical sciences, and social studies; if Black students are enrolled in higher-level classes such as calculus, algebra, trigonometry, and geometry, they are unlikely to have as many years of such course work as White students. Similarly, in terms of college studies, Black students are underrepresented in the *vast majority* of degree areas — math, business, engineering, biological science, the physical sciences, and other science-related areas (College Entrance Examination Board, 1985).

Areas of Overrepresentation

Black students are overrepresented in special education, in the lowest ability groups and tracks, and among high school and college dropouts, the underemployed and unemployed, and, accordingly, the economically disadvantaged. In terms of college enrollment and degree areas, Black students are underrepresented in *all* fields of study *except* the social sciences and education (College Entrance Examination Board, 1985).

In the case of low-track and low-ability classes, research has consistently found a poor quality of curriculum and instruction and a negative classroom climate, as well as poor teacher interaction and low student expectations. Lower-track classes foster lower self-esteem, lower educational aspirations, lower levels of cognition (e.g., thinking critically, processing information, making inferences, synthesizing material), and, ultimately, few opportunities for economic mobility among students.

The collective results suggest that even gifted Black students are less likely to be educated for self-determination, independence, and social empowerment than are White students; they are more likely to be prepared for vocations that promise a life of dependency in the economic and social underclass (College Entrance Examination Board, 1985; G. Gay, 1993).

Many factors contribute to the poor participation of Black students in gifted education programs and services. Without increased attention and substantive commitments to redress these issues, gifted programs will continue to be racially and socioeconomically segregated; Black students will continue to be underserviced educationally.

This book seeks to encourage equity in access to educational opportunities for Black students who have been formally identified as gifted, who are potentially gifted, or who are underachieving. Despite the landmark decision *Brown v. Board of Education* (1954), Black students still find themselves at an educational disadvantage in many schools, and gifted programs continue to be racially and economically stratified (D. Y. Ford & Webb, 1994).

NOTE

1. Such students have also been called underachievers, low achievers, economically disadvantaged students, dropouts, and so forth. Irrespective of the term used, these students are educationally disadvantaged, and their educational needs are not being met. These students are failing in school, and schools are failing these students.

Chapter 2

Gifted Students: Definitions, Theories, and Assessment

> If the definition of giftedness is not a useful one, it can lead to unfavorable consequences of many kinds, both for society and its individuals. If the definition of giftedness is not useful or valuable, talents may be wasted, and less valuable ones fostered and encouraged.
> —Sternberg & Davidson, 1986, p. 4

Definitions of giftedness reflect the attitude of the times. In a Stone Age society, giftedness would probably have included the ability to hunt effectively; in ancient Greece, it might have been defined as skill in rhetoric; and in modern society, giftedness often involves mastering the skills demanded by advanced technology (Freeman, 1983).

The concepts of achievement and intelligence and, by extension, giftedness have been assigned a number of definitions in psychology, education, and related fields. Over the years, theorists have debated, for example, whether giftedness is primarily a cognitive entity or a function of some other construct such as experience or insight. More recently, it has been suggested that giftedness is a multidimensional concept and that educators should identify, promote, and nurture students who are gifted in creativity, leadership, and the visual and performing arts as well as those who are intellectually and academically gifted (D. Y. Ford & Harris, 1991; Frasier & Passow, 1994, 1995; Harris & Ford, 1991). If potential is to be fostered, it must first be located. These contemporary definitions suggest that it is naive and fruitless to homogenize gifted students.

This chapter discusses conceptualizations of giftedness and presents an overview of both traditional and contemporary definitions. It draws implications of these definitions for underachieving and gifted Black students. Theories of giftedness are also described, along with a brief overview of social, cultural, and psychological factors that influence identification practices. These factors emphasize the importance of moving beyond decontextualized definitions and conceptions of intelligence and giftedness. The chapter concludes with promising and equitable practices relative to increasing the representation of Black students in gifted programs.

WHAT IS INTELLIGENCE?

> We have all too often behaved as though intelligence is a physical substance, like a house or an egg crate composed of rooms or cells; we might better remember that it is no more to be deified than attributes like beauty or speed or honesty. (Wesman, 1968, p. 267)

Historically, the terms *gifted* and *intelligent* have been used interchangeably, especially in educational and psychological settings. When students are referred to gifted education, it is most often because they are viewed as "intellectually" gifted students. What is intelligence, and how does it differ from giftedness?

Despite the vast volumes of research on intelligence, there is little consensus on a defensible definition. In their book, Sternberg and Detterman (1986) presented two dozen definitions of intelligence. In general, the definitions were categorized based on the notion that (a) intelligence resides within the individual (e.g., biological, motivational), (b) intelligence resides within the environment (e.g., cultural, societal), or (c) intelligence is an interaction between the individual and the environment.

Samuda, Kong, Cummins, Lewis, and Pascual-Leone (1991) also examined definitions of intelligence. Included in their examination are definitions espoused by test developers, such as Binet and Simon, Weschler, and Vernon. Binet and Simon defined intelligence as the capacity to judge well, to reason well, and to comprehend well; Weschler defined intelligence as the aggregate or global capacity of the individual to act purposefully, to think rationally, and to deal effectively with the environment; and Vernon defined intelligence as the outcome of the interplay of innate potentiality and such conditions as good emotional adjustment and appropriate educational stimulation.

At least three themes emerge from the various definitions just described. First, intelligence is the ability to adapt to the environment and to changing situations and contexts. That is, many of the definitions relate to social competence or practical intelligence. Second, intelligence is the ability to reason abstractly. Third, intelligence is culture or context bound and socially determined. Thus, two different cultures may have different definitions of intelligence, and the value of different abilities varies from setting to setting. Given such diverse definitions, one is left to wonder what intelligence tests *really* measure. Do they measure social intelligence—the ability to use intelligence to facilitate interactions with others, or to facilitate understanding of self? Do they assess practical intelligence—the ability to perform one's job effectively, cope with daily aspects of living and surviving, adapt to adverse life circumstances? Do intelligence tests measure schoolhouse intelligence or the kind of intelligence needed to succeed in the real world?

DEFINITIONS OF GIFTEDNESS

The definition of giftedness also eludes consensus. Since Terman (1925) presented his unidimensional definition of giftedness, traditional definitions of giftedness have been operationalized primarily in two ways: by high scores on IQ tests (130+) or by high scores on achievement tests (90+ percentile). Terman believed that gifted students were in the top 1% on the normal distribution curve of the Stanford-Binet intelligence test, and his cutoff score for giftedness was an IQ of 140. Terman's definition is grounded in the assumptions that giftedness is synonymous with intelligence and that intelligence can be measured by standardized tests. Both of these assumptions ignore the difficulty of defining such a complex term as intelligence.

As reflected in Figure 2.1, the federal government has adopted five definitions of giftedness since 1970. The respective definitions have been both promising and harmful to the successful identification of underachieving, potentially gifted, and gifted Black students. The 1970 definition is very vague and general. It offers little guidance to states and school districts and mentions intellectual and creative giftedness only. Schools that accept and implement the definition at face value are likely to ignore other areas of giftedness. The Marland definition (1972) helped rectify this problem; it specifically lists six types of giftedness: general intellectual, specific academic, creative or productive thinking, leadership, visual and performing arts, and psychomotor. It also mentions *potentially* gifted students. However, in the most commonly adopted definition (1978), psychomotor giftedness is not specifically listed. The 1988 definition strongly resembles the 1978 definition, with the exception that emphasis is also placed on gifted "youth." The latest definition (1993) addresses two historically ignored issues specific to Black and other minority students: (1) students must be compared with others of their age, experience, or environment; and (2) outstanding talents are present in individuals from all cultural groups, across all economic strata, and in all areas of human endeavor.

FIGURE 2.1. Federal definitions of gifted and talented students.

1970	The term "gifted and talented children" means, in accordance with objective criteria prescribed by the Commissioner, children who have outstanding intellectual ability or creative talent, the development of which requires special activities or services not ordinarily provided by local education agencies (USDE, 1970).
1972	Gifted and talented children are those identified by professionally qualified persons who by virtue of outstanding abilities are capable of high performance. These are children who require differentiated educational programs and/or services beyond those normally provided by the regular school programs in order to realize their contributions to self and society. Children capable of high performance include those with demonstrated and/or potential ability in any one of the following areas, singly or in combination: (1) general intellectual ability; (2) specific academic aptitude (grades in a particular subject area(s)); (3) creative or productive thinking; (4) leadership ability; (5) ability in the visual or performing arts; and (6) psychomotor ability (Marland, 1972).
1978	The term "gifted and talented children" means children and, whenever applicable, youth identified by professionally qualified persons and who, by virtue of outstanding abilities, are capable of high performance. These abilities, either potential or demonstrated, include (1) general intellectual ability, (2) general and specific academic ability, (3) creative or productive thinking, (4) leadership ability, and (5) ability in the performing arts (USDE, 1978).
1988	The term "gifted and talented" students means children and youth who give evidence of high performance capability in areas such as intellectual, creative, artistic, or leadership capacity, or in specific academic fields, and who require services or activities not provided by the school in order to fully develop such capabilities (USDE, 1988).
1993	Children and youth with outstanding talent perform or show the potential for performing at remarkably high levels of accomplishment when compared with others of their age, experience, or environment. These children and youth exhibit high performance capacity in intellectual, creative, and/or artistic areas, and unusual leadership capacity, or excel in specific academic fields. They require services or activities not ordinarily provided by the schools. Outstanding talents are present in children and youth from all cultural groups, across all economic strata, and in all areas of human endeavor (USDE, 1993).

A Closer Look at the Federal Definitions

Cassidy and Hossler (1992) found that most states use either the 1978 federal definition outright or a modification of it, and no states reflected the more contemporary definition advanced by Sternberg (1985) and Gardner (1983). They added that 30 states had made no definitional revisions in at least a decade, and only 15 had made revisions in the last 5 years. Given that the federal definitions, particularly the 1978 definition, tend to guide school practices more than other definitions and theories of giftedness, a closer examination of their implications for Black students is in order.

Intellectual ability. The student demonstrates or shows potential for high levels of abstract reasoning, advanced vocabulary, advanced academic performance, excellent memory, and an accelerated rate of learning. Other characteristics include abstract and logical thinking, the ability to store and retrieve a wide range of information, the ability to deal with complex and abstract problems, and resourcefulness in managing the environment.

Individual or group intelligence tests are usually administered for identification or assessment purposes. Based on IQ scores, there are several levels or categories of intellectual giftedness. An IQ score of 130 (top 2%) is usually required for formal identification or further placement consideration. Highly gifted students are those with IQ scores of 145 to 159, and students of superior intelligence score 160 or higher.

General and specific academic ability. The student demonstrates or shows potential for high levels of academic achievement (e.g., mastery of content area or subject matter), particularly in an area or areas of interest. These students learn quickly, are curious, have long attention spans, and enjoy challenging schoolwork. Contrary to popular opinion, these gifted students are not always identified as gifted in every subject area.

Achievement and aptitude tests are most often used to assess general and specific academic ability. Achievement tests presumably assess students' knowledge and skills acquired as a result of school experiences, specifically instruction. Aptitude tests are also considered to be measures of achievement; however, they are used to assess ability in specific areas and the test taker's ability to learn something in the future.

Creativity. The student demonstrates or shows potential for high levels of performance in such areas as divergent thinking, elaboration, originality, and fluency. These students perform above average on divergent rather than convergent thinking activities and exercises. They may be proficient in solving problems using such skills as finding facts, generating ideas, identifying multiple solutions and alternatives, and evaluating solutions and outcomes. Creative students tend to be probing, highly imaginative, and independent; they are experimenters and risk takers. Creative students are also considered nonconformists and nontraditional; they may be uninhibited in their opinions and are sometimes radical and spirited in disagreement.

Leadership. The student demonstrates or shows potential for high levels of performance in organization and management, persuasion, communication and public speaking, interpersonal relations, and intrapersonal skills. Sternberg and Kolligian (1990) refer to leadership as a component of social intelligence, whereas Gardner (1983) considers leadership ability to come under both interpersonal and intrapersonal intelligence. Socially gifted students have positive interpersonal relationships, are sensitive to the feelings of others, and can effectively manage everyday problems. Other students look to them for ideas and decisions; they are frequently sought after by peers. They interact easily with others and participate in clubs, especially as officers and decision makers. Students who are gifted in leadership exude vision, confidence, charisma; they inspire, initiate, and mobilize others. Persons with such strengths include those in sales, public relations, communications, teaching, and other human and social service professions.

Visual and performing arts. The student demonstrates or shows potential for high levels of performance in such areas as dance, music, and drama and for self-expression through the visual modality. Students who are gifted in music are often identified by an unusual sense of pitch or a singing voice; others can play a melody almost flawlessly without formal training. Dancers may be identified by the fluidity of their movement, whereas students with strengths in the dramatic arts tend to express themselves with unusual energy and emotion. Artistically gifted students have an unusual ability to communicate visually through sculptures, paintings, sketches, and photography, for example. For these students, a picture may indeed be worth a thousand words.

Implications for Gifted and Underachieving Black Students

The 1978 federal definition is often misinterpreted and misused by practitioners who give primary consideration to specific academic and general intellectual giftedness and who treat the five areas of giftedness as if they are exhaustive. In actuality, the definition merely lists potential areas of giftedness, as indicated by the phrase "such as." Equally problematic is the fact that most programs retrofit students to the gifted program rather than develop programs based on students' needs.

The 1978 definition eliminated psychomotor ability as an area of giftedness. Yet, as Gardner (1983) indicates, psychomotor ability is a legitimate type of intelligence. It is an area in which many students excel, and they require special services outside of those normally provided by the schools to develop their talent. These students are unusually well coordinated and capable of athletic feats such as world-class figure skating, gymnastics, dance, basketball, and other physical tasks requiring a combination of dexterity, sensory acuity, and intellectual ability. How would the gifts of such persons as Arthur Ashe, Jackie Joyner-Kersee, Pelé, Michael Jordan, and Florence Griffith-Joyner have developed without nurturance and special guidance? One can only wonder whether their abilities would have atrophied.

The most encouraging aspect of the 1978 federal definition is its inclusion of the "potentially" gifted. It recognizes the critical need to serve those students who have, for various reasons, yet to manifest their gifts — that is, students who might otherwise go unrecognized. The contemporary definition (1993) acknowledges that giftedness is not an absolute condition that is magically bestowed upon a person. There is no golden chromosome for giftedness (Renzulli, 1978). Potentially gifted students include underachievers, minority students, economically disadvantaged students, students with learning and behavioral disorders, and physically disabled or challenged students. The emphasis on potential represents a progressive, future-oriented definition by denoting students' capacity to become critically acclaimed performers or exemplary producers of ideas in spheres of activity that enhance the moral, physical, emotional, social, intellectual, or aesthetic life of humanity (Tannenbaum, 1983, p. 86).

This most recent federal definition (U.S. Department of Education [USDE], 1993) offers much promise for increased equity in identifying gifted Black and other minority students. As Feldhusen (1994) noted, the 1993 federal definition moves beyond the monolithic academic definition that has been embraced for so long. It also recognizes a broad range of ability and, for the first time, specifically mentions that no racial, ethnic, or socioeconomic group has a monopoly on giftedness.

Irrespective of one's definition, emphasis on the cognitive and academic aspects of giftedness prevails. "Intellectuality" dominates our conceptualization of giftedness. Students who score low on standardized intelligence and achievement measures are not likely to be placed in gifted programs. A national survey by VanTassel-Baska, Patton, and Prillaman

(1989) revealed that only 12 districts reported using definitions of "disadvantaged" gifted students. Of those, nine districts reported a definitional construct, and four included the culturally different, minority, and poor. One definition reported by the researchers follows:

> Those children regardless of race or ethnic group who may have language patterns and experiences, cultural backgrounds, economic disadvantages, educational disadvantages, or differences that make it difficult for them to demonstrate their potential using traditional identification procedures. (p. 10)

CONSIDERATIONS OF CULTURAL DIVERSITY IN THE MANIFESTATION OF GIFTEDNESS

The strengths that Black students bring into the classroom too often become weaknesses in school settings. To desegregate gifted programs by recruiting and retaining Black students, educators, counselors, and other school personnel must recognize, affirm, and address the strengths of minority students.

Gifted students from all cultures share certain characteristics of giftedness, including the ability to meaningfully manipulate some symbol system held valuable in the subculture; the ability to think logically, given appropriate information; the ability to use stored knowledge to solve problems; the ability to reason by analogy; and the ability to extrapolate knowledge to new or novel situations (Gallagher & Kinney, 1974). In addition to these characteristics, gifted minority students learn quickly through experience, and they retain and use ideas and information well. They are adept at generalizing learning to other areas, at seeing relationships among apparently unrelated parts, and at solving problems in resourceful ways (Baldwin, 1989, 1994; Borland & Wright, 1994; Frasier & Passow, 1994, 1995). Other characteristics include persuasive language, language rich in imagery, humor rich with symbolism, creativity, social intelligence, resilience, psychosocial sensitivity, and sensitivity to movement and action (Horowitz & O'Brien, 1985).

Torrance's (1977) list of creative positives captures many of the strengths that gifted Black students bring into learning and assessment situations: unusual ability to express feelings and emotions; ability to improvise with common materials; articulateness in role playing and storytelling; enjoyment of and ability in music and rhythm, performing arts, creative movement, dance, and dramatics; expressive speech and sense of humor; and expressive body language, including responsiveness to kinesthetic experiences.

J. E. Gay (1978) noted that manifestations of giftedness in Black students include the ability to quickly pick up racial attitudes and practices, effectiveness at reading behavioral cues and their implications, independence, originality, large vocabulary, and multiple interests. Gifted Black students may also ask questions that teachers consider "wrong" or inappropriate and use language that is considered inappropriate for school. They are experiential, perceptual, and concrete learners; however, these strengths may be hidden due to substandard educational experiences.

In general, Black students prefer to respond with gestalts rather than atomistic responses; they prefer inferential reasoning to deductive or inductive reasoning; they focus on people rather than things; they have a keen sense of justice and are quick to analyze perceived injustices; they lean toward altruism; they prefer novel approaches and freedom (particularly relative to music, clothing, speaking); and they favor nonverbal communication modalities.

Simply stated, gifted Black students share many of the strengths of gifted students in general — they retain and recall information well; enjoy complex problems; can tolerate ambiguity; are creative; are extremely curious, perceptive, evaluative, and judgmental; and are interested in adult and social problems. These various characteristics and those described earlier serve as general guidelines for identifying and assessing gifted and potentially gifted Black students. To truly understand and appreciate the strengths of these students, however, educators and other school personnel must get to know them as individuals as well as use students' strengths for prescriptive and proactive educational purposes. To do otherwise allows these strengths to become weaknesses in the classroom and contributes to the persistent underrepresentation of Black students in gifted programs and to racially segregated gifted programs.

CONTEMPORARY THEORIES OF GIFTEDNESS: IMPLICATIONS FOR BLACK STUDENTS

Numerous theories of giftedness exist and have been described in detail elsewhere in books on gifted education (e.g., B. Clark, 1992; Colangelo & Davis, 1991; G. A. Davis & Rimm, 1994; Silverman, 1993). Three contemporary theories of giftedness, however, are in the forefront of efforts designed to develop equitable and culturally sensitive perspectives of giftedness (Gardner, 1983; Renzulli, 1986; Sternberg, 1985).

Three-Ring Conceptualization of Giftedness

According to Renzulli (1986), interaction among creativity, above-average ability, and task commitment results in giftedness. It is advised, therefore, that educators give equal attention to all three variables in the identification process and that giftedness be assessed in a natural setting, a real-life situation.

Renzulli contends that students with well above-average ability constitute 15 to 20% of the school population. These students serve as a talent pool from which to further assess giftedness and potential. General ability is the capacity to process information, to integrate experiences that result in appropriate and adaptive responses in new situations, and to engage in abstract thinking. Specific ability is the capacity to acquire knowledge and perform in one or more activities in a specialized area (e.g., chemistry, ballet, photography). Each specific ability can be divided into more specific areas (e.g., portrait photography, photojournalism).

Renzulli asserts that task commitment is not equated with motivation. Task commitment represents energy brought to bear on a particular task or specific performance area. Related terms include perseverance, hard work, dedicated practice, and endurance. Task commitment is reflected in Edison's statement that "genius is 1% inspiration and 99% perspiration." Task commitment, therefore, represents academic hunger for one's particular area of interest. Creativity represents the third and final cluster of giftedness. Creativity is evident in nonconformity and divergent and original thinking, as well as other characteristics discussed earlier.

Implications. Renzulli has continuously advocated for inclusive rather than exclusive definitions of giftedness. Inclusive definitions and identification practices avoid the omnipotent cutoff scores and do not adopt simple solutions to complex problems. Renzulli's theory broadens the identification net from the traditional 3 to 5% of the population to 15 to 20%. Talent pools support the notion of potential and talent development. Talent pools acknowledge that lower test scores do not automatically equal lower intelligence or ability, and that many talents are resistant to formal testing. Talent development is a contemporary view of giftedness that is dynamic and relative rather than static and absolute.

The inclusion of task commitment in the definition of giftedness has many implications for underachieving students. Although Renzulli's theory has been criticized on this component, he does not contend that task commitment is synonymous with motivation, that it is global, or that students are gifted in all areas. The theory focuses on what fuels students in their areas of giftedness. Thus, underachieving students may show task commitment in one area but not in another.

Triarchic Theory of Intelligence

Sternberg's triarchic theory of intelligence (1985) posits three kinds of intelligence: Componential intelligence, most valued in schools, is characteristic of students who routinely achieve high test scores and take naturally to analytical thinking. Experiential intelligence describes creative thinkers who can combine disparate experiences in insightful ways without necessarily achieving high test scores. Contextual intelligence is apparent in students who possess common sense and practical intelligence; they are "street-smart" but may not test particularly high. Further, the theory proposes that (1) intelligence cannot be understood outside of a sociocultural context and what is "gifted" in one culture or environment may not be gifted in another; (2) intelligence is purposeful, goal-oriented, relevant behavior consisting of the ability to learn from experience and adapt to one's environment; and (3) intelligence depends on information-processing skills and strategies.

Implications. Unlike other theories, Sternberg's focuses on social intelligence and competence. According to the theory, gifted individuals shape their environments but do not necessarily boast high IQs and achievement test scores. The theory acknowledges that schoolhouse giftedness does not guarantee success in the real world. By focusing on intelligence both inside and outside of schools, Sternberg recognizes that talent comes in different forms and is context specific. Low socioeconomic status, minority, and underachieving students may demonstrate their abilities best or more often in nonschool settings. They are often socially competent and aware. These students may not perform well *in* school, but they are proficient *outside* of school. In the real world, they excel in an area of interest. These students know how to adapt to the environment, which is a key characteristic of intelligence. In essence, the knowledge and experience of many Black students cannot be measured by standardized tests.

Theory of Multiple Intelligences

Gardner's theory of multiple intelligences (1983) contends that intelligence resembles a constellation of at least seven discrete competencies:

(1) *Musical intelligence* is an unusual sensitivity to pitch, rhythm, and timbre. These students understand and appreciate the power and complexity of music. They are rhythm and melody oriented.

(2) *Bodily kinesthetics* requires cognitive intelligence and problem-solving skills. These students exercise great control over their bodies and over objects; they are aware of and sensitive to timing, and behaviors in their particular talent areas are reflexlike. They are able to control their body movements and to handle objects skillfully; they excel in fine-motor activities and crafts and achieve self-expression through body action and touching things to learn about them. They are physically oriented.

(3) *Logical-mathematical intelligence* is a remarkable ability to solve problems; it is the archetype of "raw intelligence." This type of intelligence has been heavily investigated by traditional psychologists and is found ad nauseam on traditional standardized intelligence tests. Logical-mathematical students are proficient at abstract thought, organization, logic, and problem solving.

(4) *Linguistic intelligence* is held in high esteem by traditional psychologists and is also measured extensively on standardized intelligence tests. These students are sensitive to language and the various meanings of and relationships among words; they are sensitive to the sounds and rhythm of words and to the different functions of language. They are strong in oral and written expression and understanding. In essence, they are word oriented.

(5) *Spatial intelligence*, such as the visual arts, employs intelligence in the use of space. For example, spatial problem solving is crucial for playing chess, navigating, and performing surgery. Such students have a keen sense of observation and are visual thinkers who learn best using mental images and metaphors. They also are holistic learners who often see the forest before the trees.

(6) *Interpersonal intelligence* requires a capacity to notice distinction among others, particularly in their mood, temperament, motivation, and intentions. These individuals are adept at reading both the overt and the covert intentions of others. Social competence, empathy, solidarity, leadership, organization, persuasion, and communication are important elements of interpersonal intelligence. These students are socially oriented.

(7) *Intrapersonal intelligence* requires access to one's own feelings and emotions and the capacity to discriminate among various affects. These gifted students draw upon affect as a way of understanding and guiding their own behavior. Self-knowledge, awareness, and sensitivity to one's own values, purposes, shortcomings, and feelings are important qualities of intrapersonal intelligence. These students appear wise and philosophical; they are intuitively oriented.

Implications. Gardner maintains that a person can be gifted in one area but average or below average in others. The theory opposes the prevailing belief that students are globally gifted, that they achieve in all areas. Further, intelligence in the "noncognitive" domains is just as valuable as competencies in traditional notions of intelligence. For example, among the Puluwat Islanders in the South Seas, spatial intelligence is critical for navigating canoes (Gardner, 1983); in Third World countries, moral intelligence and social intelligence are highly valued. Hundeide (1992) contended that culturally different students live in unique cognitive worlds, and they seem to have developed those aspects of intelligence that are relevant for social survival. In other societies, interpersonal intelligence is valued in literary endeavors. Nonetheless, the ability to write poetry, to play sports, to present a convincing argument, or to lead others is not reflected on standardized tests. Yet, as Hundeide asks: How relevant is our conception of deductive-analytic ability to the pragmatic challenges of their everyday life at the subsistence level (p. 62)? The theory of multiple intelligences is culturally fair, that is, it does not appear to discriminate against racially and culturally diverse students.

The theory can help decrease the misplacement and mislabeling of behaviors. For instance, bodily kinesthetic students are likely to be (mis)-labeled as "hyperactive" and unjustly medicated. Male and Black students are overrepresented among those identified as hyperactive. Similarly, spatially oriented students who require vivid pictures and images for optimal learning may be mislabeled as "dyslexic." Historically, musically inclined students and students with strengths in the visual and performing arts are likely to be labeled "talented" rather than gifted. Accordingly, they are less likely than logical-mathematical and linguistic students to be placed in academically rigorous programs. Similarly, interpersonally and intrapersonally gifted students are unlikely to be placed in gifted education programs.

The intelligences just described — bodily kinesthetic, spatial, intrapersonal, and interpersonal — represent important strengths of Black students. For example, more Black students than White students are social, spatial, visual, and active learners (Shade, 1994). Many Black students demonstrate social intelligence; they prefer to focus on people rather than things and to focus on the social aspects of learning. According to Damico's (1983) research, the people in school are more important to Black students than the concept of school. Similarly, Eato and Lerner (1981) found that Black students are better able to recognize faces and emotions than are other racial groups, and they are extremely sensitive to social nuances.

A PROPOSED DEFINITION OF GIFTEDNESS

A crisis exists in the psychoeducational assessment of minority group students (Jones, 1988). However, the definitions of giftedness described earlier offer some assurance that giftedness among Black students can be identified. Their collective perspectives suggest that:

> Gifted children and youth demonstrate or show potential for high levels of accomplishment when compared with peers of their age, racial, and cultural groups; experience; and environment. Demonstrated or potential giftedness can be assessed using reliable, valid multidimensional and multimodal instruments and strategies. Areas of giftedness include, but are not limited to, social ability (including leadership, interpersonal, and intrapersonal skills), intellectual ability, general or specific academic ability, creative ability, and visual and performing arts ability (including spatial, psychomotor, and bodily kinesthetic skills). These students require services not ordinarily provided by schools to more fully develop and nurture their potential. Giftedness is present in children and youth from all cultural groups, across all economic strata, and in all areas of human endeavor.

IDENTIFICATION AND ASSESSMENT PRACTICES: PITFALLS AND PROMISES

Giftedness is multifaceted, as Figure 2.2 illustrates. Some students demonstrate their giftedness, and others show potential giftedness but may not be formally identified due to low test scores, cultural differences, or some other factor. The model also acknowledges the heterogeneity of giftedness and its contextual nature. Two students, described below, place the model into perspective.

> Student A: Jackie is an 8-year-old Black student whom teachers describe as very gifted in creativity, based primarily on her performance outside of school. On the Renzulli-Hartman Creativity Subscale (a teacher checklist), Jackie received a 48 (out of 50). She has written several books of poetry (two of them published). In language arts, however, Jackie consistently earns Cs.
>
> Student B: Myron is an 8-year-old Black student whom teachers describe as very gifted in creativity, based primarily on his performance in school. On the Reuzulli-Hartman Creativity Subscale, his language arts teacher rated Myron 48 out of 50. He has never written

FIGURE 2.2. A proposed multidimensional model of giftedness.

MANIFESTATION	LEVEL	TYPE	CONTEXT
Potential	Above-average	Visual and Performing Arts	School
Demonstrated	Gifted	Intellectual	Home
	Very Gifted	Academic (general; specific)	Community/ Environment
		Creative	
		Social (leadership; interpersonal; intrapersonal)	
		Other	

a book and shows no interest in poetry but consistently earns As in language arts.

The abilities of Jackie and Myron are reflected in their creativity scores; whereas Jackie demonstrates her abilities outside of school, Myron demonstrates his ability in school. Given this information, which student is likely to be admitted to a gifted program? Which student appears to require special services not ordinarily provided by the school? Is an intelligence or achievement test needed before a placement decision can be made for either student?

Standardized Tests

Neill and Medina (1989) reported that U.S. public schools administered 105 million standardized tests (an average of 2.5 tests per student) to 39.8 million students during the 1986–87 school year. This figure includes more than 55 million standardized tests of achievement, competency, and basic skills. Not counted are the 30 to 40 million tests administered to students in compensatory and special education programs and the 2 million used to screen prekindergarten students. Nor does it include tests for the General Education Development Program, the National Assessment of Educational Progress, and admissions to college and secondary school, which total an additional 6 or 7 million tests annually. Finally, these figures do not include tests used to identify students with limited proficiency in English, tests administered by private and parochial schools, or tests used to identify students for gifted programs.

Public Law 94-142, the Education for All Handicapped Children Act, requires that students be evaluated using instruments that are not racially or culturally biased. A major impetus for the law was the overrepresentation of minority students in special education classes. Other legal battles have been fought based on equity (or the lack thereof) in testing practices for Black and other minority students (e.g., *Hobson v. Hansen*, 1967; *Diana v. California State Board of Education*, 1970; *Larry P. v. Wilson Riles*, 1979). These court cases were brought because of legal, ethical, or social concerns related to students of color (see the appendix).

Identification techniques discriminate against Black students because they rely on tests that are designed to measure the values generally espoused by White middle-class students. Sternberg and Kolligian (1990) found that standardized intelligence tests measure analytic abilities but ignore synthetic abilities. The tests do not describe in toto intelligence, personality, and achievement because they explain only 10 to 25% of performance outside of school (Sternberg, 1985). Sternberg and Wagner (1985) reported moderate correlations (0.4 to 0.7) between school achievement and ability, and other work has reported correlations of 0.7 between intelligence tests taken in early and later years (Bloom, 1964; Tannenbaum, 1992). Essentially, IQ scores account for only 16 to 50% of school achievement (Pelligrini & Glickman, 1990) and assess only a minute fraction of the 100 or more kinds of intelligence that actually exist (C. W. Taylor & Ellison, 1968).

In essence, traditional standardized tests show little criterion validity relative to Black students, and their utility for making consequential decisions about Black students' futures is questionable. Academic and intelligence tests predict the results a person will obtain on other tests of the same kind. Nonetheless, testing is big business, and massive standardized testing in schools and gifted programs persists. Educators seem not to have heeded the sage advice of Tannenbaum (1992) and others: "IQ in itself is far from a totally valid sign of any kind of giftedness, no matter how giftedness is defined" (p. 18).

Sources of Poor Test Outcomes for Black Students

> Care should be taken not to attribute the biases in our society to the instruments that report their cumulative effects. In many respects, our tests are only a mirror that reflect the educational results of cultural bias; shattering the mirror will not solve the problem. (Worthen, Borg, & White, 1993, p. 38)

Many factors inhibit the performance of Black students on standardized tests of intelligence and achievement, specifically, environmental factors, psychological variables, cognitive styles, and problems with the tests themselves.

Environmental factors. McCall, Applebaum, and Hogarty (1973) found that students' Stanford-Binet scores increased an average of 28.5 points between the ages of 2 1/2 and 17, with the largest change being 40 points (almost 3 standard deviations). However, for economically disadvantaged students, scores tended to *decrease* with formal schooling. McCall and colleagues attributed the decrease primarily to the effects of environmental factors. Low SES students have qualitatively different and quantitatively fewer educational opportunities than middle and high SES students. Because a disproportionate number of Black students live in poverty, they are especially vulnerable to low test scores and poor educational outcomes.

My own assessments of several intelligence and achievement tests reveal that many items assess moral rather than cognitive development and are biased against low SES students (D. Y. Ford, Harris, & Winborne, 1990). For example, on one popular standardized intelligence test, students are asked what they "should" do if they find a wallet containing money. Students must choose between returning and keeping the money. For economically disadvantaged students, this may be a very difficult decision that is based on economic need and survival rather than cognitive or moral development. Similarly, on a popular achievement test, students are asked to choose common items found in a restaurant. Some poor students have never been to a restaurant; therefore, the particular items listed are irrelevant and inappropriate. The degree to which such questions predict academic success is questionable.

Psychological factors. A large database exists regarding the influence of motivation and test anxiety on test outcomes. Students who have poor internal motivation and an external locus of control and are disinterested in tests, easily distracted, and excessively concerned about test outcomes tend to have lower standardized test scores than students who have an internal locus of control and are intrinsically motivated, interested, and less anxious about taking tests or being evaluated. These same concerns regarding poor test scores hold true for students with low academic self-concept, low self-esteem, an external locus of control, and other indices of low self-confidence.

Cognitive styles such as attention to global versus analytical features of stimuli (also referred to as field-dependent and field-independent perceptual styles, respectively), the division of stimuli into large rather than small or discrete categories, intuitive and inductive thinking compared with deductive thinking, and impulsiveness versus reflexiveness also affect test results in terms of speed, precision, and quality. For example, impulsive students are likely to make errors because they take less time to understand the questions, or they focus on irrelevant information when responding to items.

Decades of research demonstrate that Black students are likely to be field-dependent learners (relational, social, holistic, global learners) who approach learning situations intuitively rather than logically (Boykin, 1986, 1994; Hale-Benson, 1986; Shade, 1994). Field-dependent students tend to have difficulty separating the stimuli from the background, are less analytical, and are more socially inclined (e.g., prefer group over individual learning experiences). Field-independent students (which include many gifted and White students) tend to be analytical, independent learners, and intrinsically motivated. Because these are the values espoused in schools, field-independent learners (gifted and White students) have a greater chance for school success than field-dependent students (underachieving and Black students). Further, field-independent students often favor mathematics and the sciences, thus they are likely to do well on intelligence tests that measure abstract reasoning and analytical abilities.

Instrumentation issues. The most important aspect of any test is the degree to which it is valid and reliable. These two characteristics determine the usefulness of a test — an instrument that provides inconsistent and invalid results lacks usefulness. As McLeod and Cropley (1989) stated, no identification instrument acts like a crystal ball; it does not predict the future without a reference point.

Sources of error affecting test reliability include trait instability, sampling error, administrator error, scoring error, and the test takers' health, motivation, degree of fatigue, and luck in guessing. Other factors also influence the reliability of tests, including test length (the greater the number of items, the higher the reliability), group heterogeneity (the more homogeneous the group, the higher the reliability), and the spread of scores (the wider the range, the higher the reliability).

Arguments against using standardized tests have proliferated in recent years on the grounds that minority students are consistently assessed by tests that do not indicate the value of the reliability coefficient for their particular group. The tests indicate only how reliable the results are according to sample groups upon which reliability was first established. In essence, high reliability coefficients are high only for the reference group and those groups that approximate it. To illustrate, if a test is normed on a sample of predominantly White and middle or upper SES students, it will be less reliable for Black and/or low SES students. Specifically, because the life experiences and educational opportunities vary considerably between Black and White students, the reliability of the test may be questionable for Black students, including middle and high SES Black students.

Factors affecting test validity are also problematic in terms of using standardized tests with Black students. In terms of content validity, it is assumed that the test taker has been exposed to and is familiar with the information from which the tests are drawn, and that the language of the test (or test maker) is the language of the test taker. The emphasis placed on the definition of abstract words, sentence completion, analogies, and so forth in the Stanford-Binet and other standardized intelligence tests presupposes a certain mastery of the comprehension and usage of standard English. Perhaps the most obvious example is that we continue to give students tests in English when their primary language is not English; or we test students on their command of standard English when they communicate best in other dialects (e.g., Black English). Although this latter example is rather controversial, too many educators equate command of the English language with level of intelligence and the potential to achieve.

Other tests lack cultural sensitivity relative to format and presentation. For example, how valid are the results if a Black student takes a pictorial test in which none of the people represented in the pictures is Black? The same question holds when females take tests in which males consistently play dominant roles and females have passive roles. What impact do the race and gender of the examiner have on students' test performance? How important is the rapport between the student and the test administrator? How important is students' familiarity with the test format? How important are the quality and presentation of instructions (e.g., oral, written, both)? How do students' test-taking skills affect their test performance and attitudes toward evaluation?

Snyderman and Rothman (1987) found that more than half of the 661 measurement experts who responded to a 1984 survey on intelligence and aptitude testing still believe that genetic factors contribute to Black–White differences in IQ scores. A major reason for concern about bias in mental testing is that it involves the specter of biological determinism; that is, differences in test scores are attributed largely to inherent differences. A second reason for concern is that tests play a pivotal role in the (mis)classification of students, particularly relative to special placements such as tracking, ability grouping, special education services, and gifted education services. A third reason is that standardized test scores are highly correlated with family income (Nairn, 1980); thus, tests are a major institution for preserving the status quo.

Grading Practices

Grades serve many practical purposes in school and identification practices. However, they lack standardization and are influenced significantly by students' motivation, classroom behavior, personal appearance, and study habits. Further, teachers' knowledge of students' IQ scores, socioeconomic status, area of residence, and family structure contributes to stereotypes characterized by low expectations.

The validity of grades is also questionable given that grading practices vary by the particular teacher, school district, and scales used. For example, my son has attended five school districts with three different grading scales. In one school district, the lowest grade for an A is 90%, at another it is 93%, and at the third it is 95%. Similarly, 50% is failing at one school, whereas 69% is failing at another. One school district has a 10-point scale, the second has a 7-point scale, and the third has a scale that varies (e.g., an A has a 5-point range, a D has a 7-point range). These practices make evaluation of students' performance quite confusing and arbitrary.

Grades are also influenced by course difficulty and the quality of the school and district. For instance, honors courses and higher-track or higher-ability-group courses are more difficult than other courses. Grades received in courses that are less academically rigorous are quite different from those received in more academically rigorous courses.

Teachers as Nominators and Identifiers

Tuttle, Becker, and Sousa (1988) and Cox, Daniel, and Boston (1985) noted that the most prevalent method of identifying gifted learners is teacher recommendations, a method that they and others have found to be inadequate. Archambault et al. (1993) also reported that teachers are among the most highly used sources of referral and identification. Yet teachers are not necessarily effective at identifying gifted students.

Specifically, Pegnato and Birch (1959) found that junior high school teachers not only failed to nominate over 50% of the gifted students in their schools but also identified many average students as gifted. Jacobs (1971) found that primary teachers could identify only 10% of the students who had scored high on individual IQ tests. Cox, Daniel, and Boston (1985) found that almost 38% of the third- and fourth-grade teachers in their study reported unidentified gifted students in their classrooms; yet 90% of school districts used teacher nominations for identification purposes.

A primary factor in the successful identification of gifted Black students is teacher attitude. D. Y. Ford (1995) reported that racially and culturally diverse students were less likely than White students to be referred by teachers for gifted programs. This lack of referrals was attributed to teachers' attitudes and expectations. For example, teachers frequently emphasize such behaviors as cooperation, answering correctly, punctuality, and neatness when identifying gifted students. These may not be the behaviors demonstrated by Black and underachieving gifted students. Similarly, there is often a mismatch between the learning characteristics of gifted Black students and those included on many checklists completed by teachers. A perusal of several nomination forms and checklists indicates that (1) characteristics of underachieving and minority students are noticeably absent; (2) they frequently lack national and (perhaps more importantly) local normative data; and (3) they focus almost exclusively on academic and cognitive characteristics of giftedness.

To more effectively identify gifted Black students, checklists and nomination forms should gather information on students' special hobbies and interests, special talents, preferred activities when alone, and relationships with others, including older students and adults. Information on developmental and special needs (e.g., learning styles, medical problems, physiological difficulties) as well as learning opportunities provided by parents and other family members should also be gathered by school personnel. Opportunities play a significant role in the development of talent. A child who has the "good fortune" to come from a home (or school) where certain skills are modeled, where special resources are available, where interests and achievement are greeted with enthusiasm and support, and where self-esteem is fostered has the optimal opportunity to distinguish himself or herself.

Given the consistent findings regarding the difficulties teachers have in identifying gifted Black students, teacher nominations must be interpreted and used with considerable caution. By focusing on the model student (cooperative, well dressed, English speaking, teacher pleasing, White, and middle class), many gifted students will be overlooked, specifically underachievers, nonconforming students, creative students, and minority students. Stated differently, the subjectivity of nomination forms and teacher biases represents a threat to the successful identification of gifted, potentially gifted, and underachieving Black students.

Davis and Rimm's (1994) recommendation that schools develop their own teacher nomination forms must be taken with caution. The forms must have respectable levels of reliability and validity, local norms must include a sizable portion of minority and low SES students, and they must include characteristics of giftedness among Black and underachieving students.

Counselors and School Psychologists as Identifiers

School counselors and psychologists are also heavily relied upon for identification and placement decisions. Several studies have explored public school counselors' awareness of issues confronting gifted students, as well as their training to work with this student population. Findings indicate that few school counselors or psychologists are formally trained to work with gifted learners (D. Y. Ford & Harris, 1995a, 1995b; Klausmeier, Mishra, & Maker, 1987). They feel inadequate relative to identifying gifted students and even less competent at identifying gifted minority students. Further, Frantz and Prillaman (1993) found that only 11 states required at least one course in special education for certification as a school counselor, 17 were changing certification requirements, and the remaining states neither required any courses nor were in the process of considering changes in certification. This lack of training among school counselors and psychologists can contribute to the misinterpretation of information gathered from tests and teachers. This lack of experience must contribute to the underidentification and poor enrollment of Black students in gifted programs.

Parents as Identifiers

Because Black parents impart cultural values to their children and share those values with them, they represent effective sources of information. Parents are generally an excellent and reliable source of information about their children's strengths and weaknesses, yet they are seldom utilized in the identification process, even though P.L. 94-142 requires parent participation. Ryan (1983) found that parents were more effective than teachers at identifying intellectually gifted Black students. Carroll, Gurski, Hinsdale, and McIntyre (1977) noted that:

> Parent involvement in assessment and programming adds a new dimension to the concept of assessment and accountability in education — the direct access of educators to the parents whose child they shape. In the context of culturally appropriate assessment, this accountability to parents is particularly meaningful since it implies accountability to the child's cultural and linguistic heritage as well. (p. 323)

Although parents represent important and reliable sources of information, nomination forms and checklists themselves may be unreliable. Parental nomination forms and checklists suffer from the same shortcomings as teacher nomination forms and checklists — poor or lack of reliability and validity data, no local norms, inattention to characteristics of gifted and or underachieving Black students, and an exclusive focus on the intellectual or academic characteristics of giftedness. Forms must also be sensitive to reading levels. Parents who have difficulty understanding the forms are likely to over- or underestimate their children's ability or refuse to complete the forms altogether. Information from grandparents or other extended family members should also be accepted in lieu of or in addition to nomination information from parents. For instance, if children are reared primarily by grandmothers or aunts, these family members may be in a better position to describe gifted behaviors in Black children.

Peers as Nominators

Many articles extol the virtues of peer nomination for identifying gifted students. Cox, Daniel, and Boston (1985) found that 25% of the school districts they surveyed used peer nominations for identification purposes. Gagne (1989), however, reviewed 13 studies that used peer nominations and concluded that the scientific foundation for peer nominations is fragile. For instance, peer nomination forms tend to be monothematic; all the items assess one ability. When nominations are plurithematic, decision makers often combine the different subscales into a global score. This practice cancels out or neutralizes the information gained from specific subscales. Further, peer nominations are often normed on a small sample; reliability data (such as interjudger reliability, pre–post test reliability) and data on construct and criterion validity are often lacking. When construct validity data are provided, the nomination data are compared with IQ scores!

Although peer nominations are not sociograms, one must consider the extent to which they are appropriate for Black students who attend predominantly White gifted programs. The lack of heterogeneity in gifted programs calls into question the quality and quantity of peer relations and cross-cultural awareness and understanding. Further, to what extent are White students sensitive to the many cultural strengths of Black students? What perceptions do White students hold of Black students? To what extent are peer nomination forms culturally sensitive or biased? To what extent do they contain characteristics of underachievers?

Self-Nomination

Self-nomination represents an important opportunity for unrecognized gifted Black students to be considered for identification and assessment. However, as discussed in the next chapter, some gifted underachievers and

Black students may not wish to be identified. For any student who wishes to hide his or her abilities, self-nominations are impractical. These students are not likely to nominate themselves.

RECOMMENDATIONS

There is no "one size fits all" test of intelligence or achievement. Hence, to optimize the identification of and learning opportunities for gifted Black students, particularly underachievers, assessment must be comprehensive, dynamic, and culturally sensitive. Equally important, teachers and other school personnel must have substantive training in both gifted and multicultural education. There is also a critical need to progress from a culture of testing to a culture of assessment, as well as to close the gap between research and practice.

From a Culture of Testing to a Culture of Assessment

The imperative to move from a culture of testing to a culture of assessment is long overdue. Given the magnitude of testing, educators must be ever mindful of the important distinctions between identification and assessment. The purpose of identification is not a mere categorization of gifted abilities that are already fully manifest; it is a needs assessment for the purpose of placing students into educational programs designed to develop their latent potential. Identification is designed to confirm one's perception that a child needs special services (e.g., is gifted or underachieving), whereas assessment is prescriptive or diagnostic. Assessment gives more specific information on the areas in which a student is gifted, as well as the student's strengths and shortcomings.

Assessment requires making an evaluation or estimation of development, the end product being a decision about what intervention would be appropriate to facilitate a student's development. Because of its prescriptive nature, assessment conveys expectations about what is important for students to learn, provides information for students and parents about the students' progress, and helps guide and improve instruction. Because of its emphasis on multiple and diverse measures, assessment also provides information relative to accountability, guides policy decisions about school improvement and reform, and provides information for program evaluation.

Teachers must examine their evaluation practices and self-constructed tests relative to shortcomings. Such tests, according to Fleming and Chambers (1983), consist mostly of short-answer and matching items but may also include true-false and multiple-choice items. Dorr-Bremm and Herman (1986) found that although teachers may use tests to report results to parents, to identify students' strengths and weaknesses, to group and place students, to assign grades, and to plan instruction, they are more likely to use their own opinions when judging student performance.

Despite the widespread use of teacher-made tests, few data exist regarding their quality. K. Carter (1984) and Gullickson and Ellwein (1985) reported that, too often, items are ambiguous and teacher-made tests place a heavy emphasis on simple recall of facts and information. Further, the tests are often too short to produce reliable scores, and teachers seldom conduct item analyses to improve the tests.

Ideally, assessment reflects the goals of the gifted program and activities, mirrors the philosophy of the program, and actively involves students and their parents in the process. Assessment should not be used to filter out minority and low SES students from gifted programs and services. And, as discussed below, assessments should be conducted by well-trained personnel who understand not only the instruments and their intended purposes but also their shortcomings. All these variables affect the quality and outcome of assessment practices, and they call for comprehensive, dynamic, and culturally sensitive assessment.

Comprehensive, Dynamic, and Culturally Sensitive Assessment

The goal of comprehensive assessment is to generate an accurate profile of students' current level and mode of functioning within the context of their backgrounds and experiences. Comprehensive assessment provides information on students' specific learning needs such that it is diagnostic or prescriptive. Assessment should examine and gather data on students' culture, language, SES, self-concept, racial identity, and learning styles, for example. At the same time, information should be gathered on students' strengths and weaknesses. Methodology includes surveillance — ongoing and consistent information gathering — that consists of qualitative data and observations, school and anecdotal records, personality assessments, and maturational and developmental information from parents and teachers. Key objectives of comprehensive and dynamic assessment also include examining students' abilities when dealing with familiar or novel tasks and situations and observing the strategies that Black students use to perform and understand tasks. Practices that do not acknowledge the complexity of assessment cannot be considered comprehensive.

To repeat, valid and reliable instruments must be utilized in the assessment process. One must consider the purpose of the instrument, the target population, and the limitations of the instrument. These considerations are necessary to help ensure equity and to avoid exploiting and invading students' right to privacy based on thoughtless employment of dubious measurement devices. The considerations listed in Figure 2.3 are essential for both formal and informal instruments. Accordingly, nomination forms and checklists for parents and teachers must be sensitive to all reading and educational levels and include characteristics of Black students and underachieving students. Parents and educators who are unable to understand the items on the checklist will have a difficult time responding accurately. It would be informative if teachers and parents used the same or similar checklists so that decision makers could explore consistencies or discrepancies in the responses of parents and teachers. If discrepancies were significant, educators could examine the nature and extent of the differences. What do parents see that teachers do not (and vice versa)? Are there certain items in which inconsistencies are evident?

Culturally sensitive assessment is essential for identifying and assessing gifted Black students. What are the strengths and weaknesses of assessment materials used for identification and placement decisions? What formal and informal mechanisms are used to assess, place, and determine programming for gifted Black and underachieving students? What barriers adversely affect the assessment and placement opportunities of students because of race, culture, ethnicity, and language? Is the underrepresentation of gifted Black students related to low teacher expectations, low student expectations, ethnocentric curriculum, discrimination or hostile school and/or classroom climate, a mismatch between teaching and learning styles, lack of support services, inappropriate assessment practices? To what extent are test instructions presented in students' preferred mode of learning? Do students have opportunities to ask questions and clarify instructions? Has a good rapport been established between the test administrator and student? Other questions appear in Figure 2.4.

Multidimensional and Multimodal Assessment Practices

Numerous options exist for assessing Black students for placement in gifted programs; the most promising of these practices rely on multidimensional and multimodal assessment strategies. Such unidimensional instruments as intelligence and achievement tests do not reliably measure a multidimensional construct like intelligence, but multidimensional assessment can increase the probability of doing so. These assessments take different forms, but the essential components include both quantitative and qualitative assessment strategies. Using such strategies ensures that gifted programs and identification practices are inclusive rather than exclusive for potentially gifted students, underachievers, minority students, and other his-

FIGURE 2.3. Checklist of guidelines for selection of valid and reliable tests and instruments.

I. Define the goals of the identification process.
A. List the major goals of the gifted program.
B. List the areas of giftedness to be served.
C. Determine how all types of giftedness will be served.

II. Assess the relevance of the instrument.
A. What does this instrument purport to measure?
B. Is this instrument relevant to the intended purposes?
(e.g., Does it measure behaviors listed in the goals of the identification process?)

III. Be familiar with the technical components of the instrument.
A. Is the instrument reliable?
   1. What types of reliability coefficients are reported?
   2. What are the reported reliability coefficients?
   3. What are the demographic characteristics of the population on which the instrument was normed?
B. Is the instrument valid?
   1. What types of validity evidence are presented?
   2. What are the reported validity coefficients?
   3. What are the demographic characteristics of the population on which the instrument was validated?

IV. Use a variety of assessment strategies.
A. What other evidence is available that can measure the constructs or behaviors of interest and their relevance for identification of gifted students?
B. Are both quantitative and qualitative measures, methods, or practices used?
C. Is information gathered from multiple sources?

V. Identify practical considerations.
A. Is the test efficient in terms of:
   1. Scoring?
   2. Administrative time?
   3. Cost?

VI Assess the limitations of the instrument.
A. What are the limitations of the instrument (e.g., biases relative to gender, race, type of giftedness, format, instructions)?
B. Is the instrument acceptable in terms of community values?

FIGURE 2.3. Continued.

VII. Determine the potential benefits of using the particular instrument.
   A. Are the data already available from existing sources thus, eliminating the need for standardized tests?
   B. What are the advantages and disadvantages of one particular instrument over another?

VIII. Interpretation of results.
   A. Is there someone on the staff who is knowledgeable about psychometrics and can appropriately interpret and use test results?
   B. Are recommendations based on the results made by one individual or a panel of professionals (familiar with testing) and concerned citizens?
   C. Are the results interpreted in isolation from other data?
   D. Are standardized test results weighed more heavily than other data?
   E. Are results interpreted in a culturally sensitive manner?
   F. How will test results be explained to the parent or guardian, both before and after testing? Is the parent or guardian aware of potential risks to the child?

IX. Determine the risks associated with the instruments and results.
   A. What are the chances or risks of students' suffering from embarrassment or emotional and psychological damage from taking the test? from the results?
   B. To what extent will tests serve as gatekeepers?

X. Determine how confidentiality will be ensured.
   A. How will students' rights to privacy be ensured? Who will have access to the results?
   B. Has parent or guardian consent to testing been obtained?

---

torically underrepresented groups. As Figure 2.5 suggests, quantitative identification instruments include both traditional and nontraditional instruments.

Qualitative identification strategies include portfolio assessments; reviews of students' transcripts; observational or performance-based assessments; nominations by parents, teachers, peers, or students themselves; interviews; and biographical inventories. Portfolios and biographical inventories represent two promising qualitative indices for identifying gifted Black students. Such practices and educational programs are currently under way in many of the Javits projects and at the four National Research Centers on the Gifted and Talented (see Chapter 10).

FIGURE 2.4. Multicultural and diversity considerations in gifted education programs and services.

I. What is the school district's philosophy of gifted education and definition of giftedness?

A. In what ways are the philosophy and definition inclusive? exclusive? To what extent are the strengths of Black (and other minority) students represented in the definition?

B. Does the gifted education program reflect community needs? Are students retrofitted to the program or is the program reflective of student needs?

C. Have contemporary definitions of giftedness been adopted and/or modified for use with racially and culturally diverse students?

II. Is the gifted program reflective of community demographics?

A. To what extent is diversity evident relative to gender, race, and SES?

B. What, if any, discrepancies exist among the community, school, and gifted program demographic characteristics?

C. Is there evidence of increasing diversity among professionals and students in the gifted program?

III. Are there opportunities for continuing professional development in gifted and multicultural education?

A. Are faculty and other school personnel encouraged and given opportunities by administrators to participate in workshops, conferences, university courses, and so forth? Do administrators attend such professional development training? Do personnel seek or willingly take advantage of these opportunities?

B. What are the indications of multicultural commitment? For instance, does a library exist for teachers and students that contains up-to-date multicultural resources (e.g., newsletters, journals, books)?

IV. Are assessment practices equitable?

A. Are the measures used valid and reliable for the student population?

B. What biases exist relative to the selection process?

C. How are instruments administered (individually or in a group)?

D. Which instruments appear to be most effective at identifying the strengths of minority students?

E. Is a combination of qualitative and quantitative assessment practices used? If so, is one type given preference or higher weight than the other?

F. What are the primary purposes of assessment?

G. Are personnel trained to administer and interpret test results?

H. In what ways are students' learning styles accommodated relative to test administration and instructions?

I. To what extent are students' home language, culture, and background reflected in the tests?

J. Are tests biased in favor of verbal students, higher SES students, White students?

FIGURE 2.4. Continued.

V. What, if any, mechanisms are in place to assess and address affective or noncognitive needs among students (i.e., social and emotional needs, environmental and risk factors)?
   A. To what extent are support personnel and test administrators trained in gifted education?
   B. To what extent are support personnel and test administrators trained in multicultural education?
   C. How diverse is the professional staff (teachers, counselors, administrators) relative to race, gender, and SES?

VI. To what extent are families involved in the formal learning process?
   A. In what ways are parents and families encouraged to become and remain involved?
   B. How diverse are the parents and families involved?
   C. Are extended family members encouraged to participate?

VII. Does the curriculum reflect a multicultural orientation?
   A. Is multicultural content infused throughout the curriculum?
   B. Is the content pluralistic (i.e., does it reflect diversity relative to gender, race, and other sociodemographic variables)?
   C. To what extent are learning style preferences and differences accommodated?
   D. Are all students are exposed to multicultural content, regardless of school or program demographics?
   E. Does the curriculum provide genuine options for minority and White students to understand pluralism?
   F. Are students encouraged to seek greater understanding of multiculturalism and pluralism through reading, writing, additional courses, and so forth?

VIII. What policies are in place to support multiculturalism and diversity?
   A. To what extent are there published policies regarding multiculturalism?
   B. If specific policies exist, to what degree are they observed in the school?
   C. In what ways do policies and procedures about grouping, scheduling, and student assignments promote or inhibit interaction among White and minority students?

The ultimate method of achieving equitable assessment is to adhere to ethical standards of testing, advanced by such authors as Sax (1989) and such professional organizations as the American Educational Research Association, American Psychological Association, and National Council on Measurement in Education (1985), and the American Federation of Teachers, National Council on Measurement in Education, and National

FIGURE 2.5. Sample identification instruments: A multidimensional and multimodal framework (D. Y. Ford, 1994c).

QUANTITATIVE

Traditional
Weschler Intelligence Scale for Children—Revised (1)
Stanford-Binet Intelligence Test (1)
Otis-Lennon Mental Ability Test (2)
Iowa Tests of Basic Skills (2)
Comprehensive Test of Basic Skills (2)
Peabody Individual Achievement Test—Revised (2)

Nontraditional
Raven's Coloured, Standard, and Advanced Progressive Matrices (1)
Kaufman Assessment Battery for Children (1, 2)
Matrix Analogies Test—expanded and Short Form (1)
Torrance Test of Creative Thinking (3)
Torrance Creativity Tests for Children (3)
Tests of Creativity in Movement and Action (3)
Vineland Social Maturity Scale (4)
California Preschool Competence Scale (4)
Basic Motor Ability Test (5)
Developmental Test of Visual and Motor Integration (5)
Purdue Perceptual Motor Survey (5)

QUALITATIVE

Portfolios and performance-based assessments (e.g., writing samples, artwork, audio or visual taping of classroom discussions, journals, projects) (1–5)
Biographical inventories (1–5)
Nomination forms and checklists (completed by parents, teachers, peers, self) (1–7)
Transcripts (e.g., to explore strengths in certain subjects and areas or look for inconsistent performance) (1–5)
Learning styles inventories (6)
Motivational and attitudinal measures (7)

Promising instruments for developing profiles:
Baldwin Identification Matrix
Frasier Talent Assessment Profile
Potentially Gifted Minority Student Project
Program of Assessment Diagnosis and Instruction
System of Multicultural Pluralistic Assessment

Note: 1 = intellectual; 2 = academic; 3 = creative; 4 = leadership; 5 = visual and performing arts; 6 = learning styles; 7 = socioemotional (e.g., motivation, self-concept, self-esteem, attitudes toward school, anxiety, peer relationships).

Educational Association (1990). Specifically, any educator who uses or advises others in the use of standardized tests should:

(1) Possess a general understanding of measurement principles.
(2) Understand the limitations of tests and test interpretations.
(3) Understand clearly the purposes for which a test is given and the probable consequences of scores resulting from it.
(4) Be knowledgeable about the particular test and its appropriate uses.
(5) Receive training necessary to understand the test, its uses, and its limitations and how to administer, score, and interpret it.
(6) Possess enough technical knowledge to evaluate technical claims (e.g., validity and reliability claims).
(7) Know the procedures necessary to reduce or eliminate bias in test selection, administration, and interpretation.
(8) Advise examinees in advance that they will be tested and tell them the purposes and nature of the test.
(9) Keep all standardized test materials secure at all times so as not to invalidate present or future uses of the test.
(10) Provide examinees with information about correct procedures for filling out answer sheets (the mechanisms, not the substance, of responding).
(11) Keep test scores confidential (see Worthen, Borg, & White, 1993).

Other ethical considerations include monitoring the test-taking conditions for academic dishonesty, examining barriers to students' performance (e.g., high noise level, poor light, student illness, distractions), and having personnel who are trained to work with minority students to interpret test results in a culturally sensitive manner.

Consideration of Noncognitive Factors in Assessment

Davis and Rimm (1994) assert that "the chief index of actual ability is test scores. Despite all the faults and problems related to testing, despite unreliability and measurement error, and despite all the biases that need to be considered related to low test scores, it seems apparent that children cannot score extremely high on tests purely by accident" (p. 281). If students *consistently* score high on standardized tests, there may be some truth to this assertion. But what is the likelihood that a child with an IQ of 130 or higher will be asked to repeat the test because the results may be inaccurate? Reasoning by analogy, just as low test scores can be attributed to test bias, measurement error, and test unreliability, so too can high test scores. Test scores are affected by countless and complex variables.

School Personnel Training to Increase Identification and Assessment Skills

As indicated earlier, few teachers and counselors receive formal, consistent, or comprehensive training in either gifted education or multicultural education. Further, textbooks in gifted education often include only a perfunctory chapter on gifted underachievers and minority students (e.g., B. Clark, 1992; Colangelo & Davis, 1991; G. A. Davis & Rimm, 1994; Silverman, 1993); articles and research discuss and treat gifted students as a homogeneous group, which is a naive practice. Seldom does discussion of gifted Black students permeate books and articles in gifted education. Although Maker and Schiever's (1989) edited book represents a departure from the norm in this respect, it contains derogatory and stereotypical information about Black and low SES students. For instance, several tables list "absolute characters of giftedness" in comparison to the values and behaviors of various racially and culturally diverse groups. For the most part, this format supports an either-or model of giftedness, and the absolute characteristics presented are frequently in opposition to characteristics of Black students. For example, Black students are described by such negative stereotypes as "manipulative behavior," "immediate or short-term gratification," "mastery of minimum academic skills," "acting out," and "leadership in gangs" (p. 210).

The lack of integration in training and research, as well as attention to stereotypes about gifted Black students, significantly hinders teachers' referrals of Black students for identification and assessment. This lack of attention to the positive characteristics of Black students in general supports a "cultural deficit" perspective that contributes to or exacerbates the underrepresentation of Black students in gifted programs. To avoid miseducating themselves and Black students, teachers and counselors must seek substantive rather than superficial training and preparation in both gifted and multicultural education.

In terms of gifted education preparation, Karnes and Whorton (1991) recommended a minimum of four courses in the psychology of the gifted, the assessment of gifted students, the counseling of gifted students, curriculum development for gifted students, strategies and materials for teaching gifted learners, creative studies, program development and evaluation, parent education and advocacy, and the special problems of gifted students. Finally, they recommended at least three courses in graduate-level research methodology, a minimum of three courses in an approved content area designed to develop specialization, and a practicum in gifted education under the supervision of a university faculty member. Beyond these recommendations, course work in multicultural education is essential, and the practicum should occur within a racially or economically diverse school community. Teacher education training must espouse a culturally responsible and responsive pedagogy for gifted Black students by using state-of-the-art research and practices based on racially and culturally diverse groups:

(1) Preservice teachers should gain classroom experience with Black students (e.g., during practicums or internships).
(2) Teachers should be trained to understand and respect students' cultural heritage and knowledge base, their worldviews, values, and customs. This training includes studying the history and culture of Black students.
(3) Teachers need to understand students' communication skills and behaviors (e.g., body language, facial expressions, eye contact, silence, touch, public space).
(4) Teachers must understand and decrease their stereotypes, apprehensions, fears, and overreactions to Black students, particularly males.
(5) Teachers need to learn outreach skills—how to work effectively with Black students, their families, and their community.
(6) Teachers must gain a greater respect for individual and group differences in learning, achievement, and behavior.

The Need for Consistency—Matching Practice and Research

Teacher nominations are most often used for identification, followed closely by achievement tests and IQ tests. Archambault et al. (1993) surveyed over 3,000 third- and fourth-grade teachers regarding identification practices. Results indicated that most of the public school teachers used achievement tests (79%), followed closely by IQ tests (72%) and teacher nominations (70%). Although the percentages or rankings appear to have changed over the years, the three primary identification sources remain the same.

The negative educational outcomes from relying heavily on tests to identify giftedness among Black students have been described at length in earlier sections of this chapter. Given the numerous and urgent calls to find more comprehensive and equitable identification strategies and instruments, Gubbins, Siegle, Renzulli, and Brown (1993) conducted a study about educators' assumptions underlying the identification of gifted students. More than 3,000 educators from 47 states responded to a survey distributed at the 1992 National Association of Gifted Children conference. Respondents also included Consultant Bank members of the National Research Center. There were five major findings. First, results indicated that educators disagreed that identification should be based on *restricted* identification practices (i.e., services provided for identified students only, based on achievement and IQ tests, precise cutoff scores, and restricted percentages, without teacher judgment or subjective criteria). Teachers of the gifted were more likely to disagree with restricted identification practices than were regular classroom teachers. Second, both educators of the gifted and those in regular classrooms agreed that identification practices should be *responsive and sensitive* to students' ability to express their talents and gifts through various measures or observations (e.g., case studies, student-selected tasks, multiple formats, and such non-intellectual factors as creativity and leadership).

A third finding was that educators in both settings tended to agree that *ongoing assessment* was important in the identification process. They agreed that regular, periodic reviews, alternative identification criteria, judgment by qualified persons, and programming informed by identification information were essential factors in designing and implementing an effective and flexible identification system. Fourth, educators agreed that *multiple criteria* were important in the decision-making process. The respondents acknowledged that students express their abilities in diverse ways, that development can affect the expression of abilities, and that multiple types and sources of information should be gathered to ensure an effective identification plan. Finally, teachers of the gifted agreed more strongly than other teachers that students' *cultural, experiential, and environmental backgrounds* provide important data on students' performance and, thus, for the identification process. They acknowledged that locally developed methods and criteria should be used, and that services and activities should be informed by context-bound information.

The findings indicate a clear need for more consistency between research and practice. Evaluation and follow-up studies are needed to explore the match between research and practice. Key questions focus on the school district's philosophy of gifted education and definition of giftedness; the degree to which the gifted program is reflective of community demographics; the opportunities for continuing professional development in gifted and multicultural education; whether assessment practices are equitable; the mechanisms in place to assess and address affective or noncognitive needs among students (e.g., social and emotional needs, environmental and risk factors); the extent to which families are involved in the formal learning process; and the extent to which the curriculum reflects a multicultural, pluralistic orientation.

SUMMARY

Psychologists, psychometricians, and educators are obsessed with standardization and intelligence testing. Standardized tests are frequently used to identify and assess students for achievement or lack thereof. These tests are given enormous credibility in educational institutions; they are essentially reified, a state of grace that is only a little less gained by being deified (Hargis, 1989). In essence, there is a dogged insistence that standardized tests be relied on as the ultimate arbiter of educational value and success. Hargis likened practices associated with standardization (e.g., norm-referenced tests and curriculum) to Procrustes'[1] bed — we force and squeeze students in various ways to make them fit the norm. Black students are too often casualties of Procrustean methods of dealing with students who vary from the educational norm.

The well-documented biases of standardized tests in predicting academic success among Black students have had little effect on educational policy and decision making. Black students have always been an enigma to educators because of their seeming unresponsiveness to standard measures of intellectual and academic performance — yet educators know that they have substantial intellectual and academic ability and potential. This blind faith in tests and their use as the only (or even primary) criterion for giftedness is educationally harmful, unjust, and inequitable; such scores can reduce any chance Black and underachieving students have for placement in gifted programs and, thereby, contribute to or guarantee their underenrollment in such programs.

The problems associated with defining intelligence and achievement are made complex by several factors: First is the value judgments placed on these constructs. That is to say, both achievement and intelligence per se are ubiquitous and relative terms; what is considered gifted or an achievement to one person (or culture) may not be judged the same in another. Second, one's potential is frequently determined by some cutoff criteria on standardized tests. Test scores frequently determine who is "gifted" or not and who has failed, achieved, or underachieved. In some schools, gifted Black students go unidentified because little, if any, consideration is given to the possibility that they may be highly capable students who are poor test takers. Further, no one instrument is adequate to identify gifted students. Gifted students are a heterogeneous group with a wide range of individual differences. Although educators are urged to be sensitive to such differences and the special characteristics of individual gifted students, most programs still persist in using traditional methods of identification that rely on popular notions of giftedness.

Perhaps the most educationally relevant individual differences relate to cognitive styles — the way individuals perceive and process information, and the strategies they use to carry out tasks. In essence, *how* underachieving and gifted Black students use and process information is as educationally informative as *how well* they do so. To more effectively identify and assess giftedness, potential, and underachievement among Black students, educators must personalize testing and provide for diversity. This means moving toward less standardization and more individualization. Included in this recommendation is the need for educators to adopt broader and more inclusive theories, definitions, and assessments of giftedness, underachievement, and potential. Theories espoused by Renzulli, Gardner, and Sternberg embrace the ideology of inclusiveness and acknowledge the influence of cultural and contextual variables on educational outcomes. In the final analysis, school personnel must work diligently to recruit and retain gifted and potentially gifted Black students — that is, to desegregate gifted programs.

NOTE

1. Procrustes was a legendary scoundrel from Attica who had an iron bed in which travelers were forced to sleep. Travelers who were too tall were shortened with an axe to fit the bed; those who were too short were stretched.

Chapter 3

Underachievement: Definitions, Theories, and Assessment

Einstein failed in language, Schubert in mathematics; George Bernard Shaw could not spell properly and Tolstoy displayed a severe learning disability during his school years. Delius, Ghandi and Nehru showed no promise in school. Edgar Allan Poe and Einstein were actually expelled for serious misbehavior, while Edison was taken out of school after three months, on the grounds that he was "unstable."

—McLeod & Cropley, 1989, p. 119

Scholars have always been intensely interested in those factors that motivate and demotivate students. Certainly, no situation is more frustrating and perplexing for parents and educators than rearing or teaching a child who does not perform as well academically as his or her potential indicates. Alarmingly, cases of underachievement are becoming more common than ever, with estimates that some 15 to 50% of students fail to reach their potential.

In a letter to presidential candidates, David T. Kearns, chairman of Xerox Corporation in 1987, charged America's public schools with turning out a product with a 50% defect rate. Kearns argued that of the students the public schools are supplying to the workforce, 25% have dropped out and another 25% have graduated with such minimal skills that they can barely read their own diplomas. Kearns added that Xerox expects defect-free parts from its suppliers, and although it gets 99.9% perfection, it is still trying to correct that last tenth of a percent (Hargis, 1989).

School failure, dropping out, and underachievement are too familiar in schools. Students of all ages and from all backgrounds and racial groups are wrestling with issues that threaten to promote or exacerbate under-achievement—cultural differences, gender issues, learning difficulties, learning style differences, negative peer pressure and poor relationships, family difficulties, fiscal problems, and conflicting goals and priorities. In

44

essence, the phenomenon of underachievement is as complex and multifaceted as the students to whom this label is applied.

This chapter discusses the concept of achievement in its various manifestations—low achievement, nonachievement, overachievement, and underachievement. The chapter concludes with recommendations for the identification and assessment of underachievement among gifted Black students. It is worth repeating that no student or group is totally exempt from poor educational outcomes. Middle-class and White students, however, are least likely to have negative school experiences. In contrast, life on the margins is an all too familiar reality for Black students in classrooms today. It is unfortunate that far too many Black students are overrepresented among poor achievers, dropouts, and push outs, in the lowest ability groups and educational tracks, and among the otherwise educationally disenfranchised and disillusioned. In essence, too many gifted Black students are falling victim to educational suicide (Renzulli, Reis, Hebert, & Diaz, 1994). Mounting evidence indicates that economically disadvantaged and minority students are first and foremost victims of "defects" both inside and outside of the schools. Curricular and instructional issues, testing practices, teacher-student relations, classroom climates, cultural differences, and social and environmental factors all take their toll, either in isolation or collectively, on the educational, psychological, and affective (socioemotional) well-being of Black students, including gifted and potentially gifted Black students.

CONCEPTUAL DEFINITIONS

No concept can be applied without some attempt to define it, and the more complex the concept, the more difficult the task of defining it. Similarly, the more complex the concept, the more likely it is that one definition will not satisfy all who ponder it. Such is the case with most terms in education and related fields. The following section presents definitions of achievement and its various manifestations—low achievement, underachievement, nonachievement, and overachievement.

What Is Achievement?

When students are referred to as "achievers," it usually means that they have accomplished a task or tasks. When performance is commensurate with predicted potential, students are said to be achieving to their potential. Often, this judgment is based on standards and opinions external to the student, for example, test scores and the opinions of teachers and parents. In this regard, the extent to which one has "achieved" is relative. The expectations set by parents may differ from those set by teachers. A child identified as intellectually gifted who brings home a B− on a test may get different reactions from her mother, father, and teacher, depending on the expectations of each. A linguistically gifted student whose teacher encourages him to submit a poem for publication will learn first-hand that people have different expectations for achievement. An academically gifted child whose grade point average (GPA) is less than 3.0 may find that her teachers are satisfied with her school performance but her parents are not. Similar concerns relate to students whose talents are in creativity, leadership, visual and performing arts, and other areas of giftedness.

Intrinsic motivation is touted as one of the primary factors that distinguishes achievers from underachievers. For example, when asked to describe "good" students, teachers typically list characteristics such as hard-working, cooperative, interested, and motivated. Gifted students who lack motivation are as problematic for their teachers as nongifted students who lack motivation. If given the choice of working with hardworking, motivated students who are not formally identified as gifted or working with gifted students who are unmotivated, teachers would probably choose the former. Of course, motivation alone does not guarantee that students will achieve to their potential. Other important factors include students' learning styles, study skills, work ethic, and attitudes toward school and the quality of the classroom climate or learning environment.

Low Achievement Versus Underachievement

Low achievement is a failure to meet minimum standards of performance (e.g., the student is below average relative to grade level or group norm data). Sinclair and Ghory (1987) indicate that 23 to 40% of the student population are low achievers. From a statistical perspective, low-achieving students represent those who rank at the 50th percentile or lower on the normal curve. Thus, half of students are destined to being labeled as low achievers.

In some cases, underachieving students are also low-achieving students. For example, if a gifted student ranks at the 39th percentile on an achievement test (or some other measure of achievement), he would be not only an underachiever but also a low achiever. A gifted student who ranks at the 79th percentile would not be described as a low achiever but may very well be an underachiever.

Nonachievement Versus Underachievement

Kessler (1963) distinguished between nonlearners and nonproducers, with the latter term being different from Delisle's (1992) description of nonproducers. According to Kessler, nonlearners are students with identifiable learning disabilities (e.g., dyslexia, attention deficit disorder) who score substantially better on standardized tests than their class performance indicates. Nonproducers have no discernible learning disabilities or problems, yet they perform lower than expected in school. Seemingly, nonproducers have difficulties resulting from motivational issues, which can be personal, familial, or school related.

Delisle (1992) also distinguished between underachievers and nonproducers. Underachievers, he argued, are psychologically at risk, dependent, reactive, withdrawn, and perfectionistic and have poor academic self-concepts. They have persistent achievement problems such that reversal and change are difficult (but not impossible). Nonproducers are described as mentally healthy, independent, and proactive students with positive self-concepts of ability. Their poor performance is situation-specific or temporary, and their prognosis for intervention is more positive. For nonproducers, poor achievement is a conscious decision—students are unwilling to do the work. However, regardless of whether underachievement is or is not within one's control, the results are the same—students are not working to their potential.

Learning Disabilities Versus Underachievement

Despite federal regulations, the definition of learning disabilities remains controversial and debatable. Hammill (1990) reviewed 28 articles and found 11 different definitions, all of which emphasized that a child with a learning disability is an underachiever. According to P.L. 94-142, a specific learning disability is:

> a disorder in one or more of the basic psychological processes involved in the understanding or in using language, spoken or written, which may manifest itself in an imperfect ability to listen, think, speak, read, write, spell, or to do mathematical calculations. . . . The term does not apply to children having learning problems which are primarily the result of visual, hearing, or motor handicaps, of mental retardation, or emotional disturbance, or of environmental, cultural, or economic disadvantage.

Some 1.5 to 4.6% of individuals have a learning disability (Mercer, 1986). Berk (1983) described gifted learning disabilities as a subcategory of underachievement, and Silverman (1993) appears to use the terms interchangeably. Learning disabilities are apparent in such areas as oral expression, listening comprehension, written expression, basic reading skills, reading comprehension, mathematics calculations, and mathematics reasoning.

Like underachievers, gifted learning disabled students are identified by an aptitude-achievement discrepancy. Learning disabled students may also have intracognitive discrepancies and intra-achievement discrepancies (Aylward, 1994). Intracognitive discrepancy occurs in students who have a specific type of cognitive dysfunction (e.g., auditory processing, short-term memory, visual processing). Such students may have difficulty retaining information presented verbally by teachers but can adequately recall information that is presented visually. All students may have a preference for a specific mode of instruction, but students who are *unable* to perform adequately in one area compared with another may have a learning disability. An intra-achievement discrepancy reflects divergence or inconsistency in educational achievement performances. This particular discrepancy may occur between academic areas or within an academic area (e.g., between reading decoding and reading comprehension) (Aylward, 1994).

Berk (1983) proposed the following typology of learning disabilities: students have (a) at least normal intelligence (more specifically, the child is not mentally retarded); (b) ability-achievement discrepancy; (c) academic disorder (in reading, writing, spelling, math); and (d) psychological processing disorders (i.e., learning problems associated with memory, perception, modality, sequencing, and closure). These factors inhibit or interfere with students' ability to process information effectively.

Gifted Underachievement Versus Nongifted Underachievement

Traditionally, gifted underachievers have been defined as students who possess high or superior mental ability but lower performance than expected or predicted. In comparison, nongifted underachievers tend not to have high intelligence or achievement test scores. The term *nongifted underachievement* is problematic for many students who do not score well on standardized intelligence and achievement tests. There are many gifted students, particularly Black students, who have not been formally identified because of poor test performance.

What Is Overachievement?

Overachievers are often defined as students whose academic achievement performance is higher than predicted on the basis of their intelligence test scores. The independent variable (intelligence test score) is compared with the dependent variable (e.g., achievement test score, GPA). If the intelligence test score is low but academic performance is high, the student is said to be an overachiever. Mandel and Marcus (1988) highlighted the difficulty inherent in defining overachievement:

> The term "over-achievement" contains perhaps the greatest logical inconsistency. How can one achieve above one's actual "ceiling" level of ability? How can one incapable of a certain activity nevertheless achieve above his or her actual potential for performing that task? Ordinary common sense tells us that "you cannot do what you cannot do," i.e., you cannot do what, in fact, you are not capable of doing, and yet the term "over-achievement" is applied on an everyday basis, and with a great deal of face validity. (p. 4)

The term overachievement places much faith in the validity of standardized tests in identifying ability and potential (or the lack thereof). For example, it places greater emphasis on the value of the test results than on students' school performance.

A CLOSER LOOK AT UNDERACHIEVEMENT

Operational definitions of poor achievement vary extensively, but many focus on motivation. Theorists have debated whether achievement motivation (or the lack thereof) is a learned behavior based on experience, personality factors, or both. Notwithstanding definitional difficulties, it is generally accepted that underachievement (manifested by poor grades, lack of effort, dropping out of school, or otherwise not reaching one's academic potential) is a serious problem among students in our schools, particularly among those in urban areas. The statistics on the number of students who drop out of school are mind-boggling, and they highlight the malaise in the educational milieu. Some schools report epidemic numbers—dropout rates from 30 to 80%, especially in inner-city and urban school districts.

Contrary to popular opinion, educational disengagement is also experienced by formally identified gifted students. In *A Nation at Risk* (National Commission on Excellence in Education, 1983), it was reported that as many of 20% of students who drop out are gifted or highly able. Although Black students are overrepresented in the ranks of dropouts, the number of these individuals who may be gifted is not calculated. However, D. Y. Ford (1992, 1993b) found that 80% of formally identified gifted Black students were underachieving, primarily due to lack of effort.

In a different study, D. Y. Ford (1995) found that 35% of gifted Black students were underachieving according to regression analysis. Underachievers had GPAs that were one or more standard deviations below the predicted level, as determined by achievement test scores. Further, Smith, LeRose, and Clasen (1991) reported that 30% of gifted Black students who had been identified in high school had dropped out of college.

Myriad definitions of underachievement can be found in the educational and psychological literature, with a few focusing specifically on gifted underachievers (e.g., Butler-Por, 1987; Raph, Goldberg, & Passow, 1966; Supplee, 1990; Whitmore, 1980). Generally, underachievement is defined as a discrepancy between some expected level of achievement and students' actual performance on one or more designated indices. This gap can result from high scores on standardized tests, with academic performance that is comparatively low. Underachievement can also be defined as a gap between teachers' expectations and students' performance. That is to say, when teachers hold high expectations of Black students but their performance is low or does not match the expectation, students may be labeled "underachievers," "learning disordered," or "educationally handicapped."

Methods of operationally defining academic underachievement can be placed into three broad categories: arbitrary absolute splits, simple difference score, and regression method (McCall, Evahn, & Kratzer, 1992). Researchers adopting the arbitrary absolute splits method define underachievers as those having higher than a certain minimum on a measure of mental ability but lower than a certain maximum on a measure of school performance. This definition is most often adopted relative to gifted students. For example, Saurenman and Michael (1980) defined gifted underachievers as students with IQ scores of 132 or higher on the Stanford-Binet and percentile rankings of 75 or below on the California Test of Basic Skills. Finney and Van Dalsem (1969) defined gifted underachievers as students who were in the top 25% of the Differential Aptitude Battery (DAT) on the verbal-numerical subscale but whose GPAs were below the mean for all students at the DAT level. In one of the most recent studies of gifted underachievers, Colangelo, Kerr, Christensen, and Maxey (1993) defined underachievers as students with composite scores at or above the 95th percentile of the American College Test (ACT) and GPAs less than or equal to 2.25.

There are several limitations associated with the arbitrary absolute splits definition of underachievement (McCall et al., 1992). First, this definition lacks generalizability and comparability across studies because absolute values of scores or rankings are totally dependent on the instrument, the sample, or both. Second, there is no consensus on the particular instruments or splits to use, particularly given that identification and placement criteria for giftedness can vary considerably from one school to another.

The simple difference score method requires a common metric for ability and achievement, such as standard scores, grade level, or percentiles. Curry (1961) defined underachievement as a discrepancy of 10 or more points between scores on the California Test of Mental Maturity and scores on the California Achievement Test. According to McCall et al. (1992), statistical problems associated with regression to the mean can influence interpretations of underachievement based on this method. For instance, students who score high on one instrument are not likely to score as high on the other. In addition, if the measures correlate strongly, a student who scores high on one instrument is not likely to score low on the other. A third problem relates to the unreliability of difference scores. If the reliabilities for the two instruments are 0.8 and 0.9, and their correlation is 0.7, the difference scores will have a reliability of 0.51, which is relatively low or unstable (see McCall et al., 1992; Thorndike, 1963).

The most common and simplest method of conceptualizing underachievement is the regression method. One calculates the regression of the achievement instrument on the ability measure and then calculates the deviation of each student's score from the regression line. Students with a large negative deviation (most often 1 standard deviation or more) are considered underachievers. Regression models, which attempt to correct problems inherent in the discrepancy models, are used in 13 of 30 states that have set specific criteria for determining a severe discrepancy (Aylward, 1994). A major benefit of the regression model is the equal probability that a discrepancy will be identified across all IQ levels. Given that the majority of referrals for poor school achievement involve students with lower IQs, use of discrepancy models results in underidentification of underachieving and learning disabled students; however, use of regression equations may increase the identification rate by as much as 10% (Aylward, 1994, pp. 96–97).

The regression method has limitations. First, it assumes that the standard error of estimate is a constant value across the entire range of ability (McCall et al., 1992). Second, using 1 standard error is arbitrary and lacks empirical justification. At what point, for example, should 1 standard error rather than 1 1/2 or 2 standard errors of measure be used? Third, this method will always produce a given percentage of underachievers in a sample. Utilizing the statistical bell curve, 16% of students will automatically fall 1 standard deviation below the regression line. Despite these limitations, several researchers perceive it to be the most user-friendly method (e.g., Farquhar & Payne, 1964; Gowan, 1957). They contend that the discrepancies between expected and actual scores are independent of the predictor variable (such as mental ability); thus, the method can be applied across the entire range of abilities. The regression approach can be applied regardless of the particular instruments used, and deviations from a regression line have better reliability than simple difference scores.

Exclusive Versus Inclusive Definitions of Underachievement

As described below, definitions of gifted underachievement can be categorized in at least two ways: narrow and exclusive, and broad and inclusive. Depending on which definition a school district adopts, many gifted and potentially gifted Black students will be missed (Figure 3.1).

Narrow and exclusive definitions. Several problems are associated with narrow and exclusive definitions of underachievement. First, narrow definitions refer to gifted students as those who demonstrate well-above-average scores on standardized intelligence and achievement tests but fail to develop or demonstrate their abilities. For instance, Raph, Goldberg, and Passow (1966) defined such a student as one who ranks in the upper third of the population in ability but does not graduate from high school, does not attend college, or drops out of college.

Second, narrow definitions rely primarily or solely on standardized tests to identify and characterize underachievement among gifted students. For example, a discrepancy exists between an intelligence test and an achievement test. Third, narrow definitions rely on a discrepancy between intelligence test scores and students' school performance. For example, the intelligence test score is high (e.g., at or above 130) but a student's GPA is lower than expected (e.g., 1 or 2 standard deviations below the level predicted). As with the previous example, other variables affecting achievement are not considered in this type of definition.

These definitions place great faith in intelligence tests' ability to identify both giftedness and underachievement. In these examples, intelligence tests are used as the independent variable—if the intelligence test score is high, then the achievement level should be high. The aforementioned definitions ignore the impact of personal, cultural, and social variables on test performance. Other variables—affective, noncognitive—are also ignored in such definitions.

Overall, exclusive definitions result in an elite group of students being identified as gifted underachievers. By defining gifted underachievement from a psychometric basis only, and by limiting the definition to those with "high" test scores, many Black students (and other students who tend not to perform well on standardized tests) will be overlooked. Thorndike

FIGURE 3.1. Exclusive definitions of underachievement among gifted students.

Type I—Intelligence Tests as Independent Variable

A child whose day-by-day efficiency in school is much poorer than would be expected on the basis of intelligence tests (Bricklin & Bricklin, 1967).

Students who rank in the top third of intellectual ability but whose performance is dramatically below that level (Fine, 1967).

One who evidences a long-standing pattern of academic underachievement not accounted for by learning disabilities, and giftedness appears only through intellectual testing or from remarkable discrepancies in reading and math (Fine & Pitts, 1980).

A child achieving significantly below the level statistically predicted by his or her IQ (Newman, Dember, & Krug, 1973).

A child whose achievement score is lower than his or her ability score (Kowitz & Armstrong, 1961)

Those individuals who demonstrate well above-average intellectual or academic ability on intelligence and aptitude tests but fail to perform in school-related tasks at an equally high level (Hall, 1983)

A student whose language or nonlanguage IQ scores are 116 or above his or her predicted potential and whose achievement test scores are at least one grade level below the achievement level expected and whose grades are B or less (Ohlsen & Gazda, 1965).

A student with a Stanford-Binet IQ of 132 or above and a percentile ranking of 75 or below on the California Test of Basic Skills (Saurenman & Michael, 1980).

Students for whom a gap exists between achievement test scores and intelligence test scores or between academic grades and intelligence test scores (Gallagher, 1979).

A student scoring in the upper 25% of the population on the Pinter General Ability Test (IQ greater than 110) and who earned a GPA below the mean of his or her class in grades 9 through 11 (M. C. Shaw & McCuen, 1960).

Type II—Aptitude and Achievement Tests as Independent Variable

A student who was in the top 25% of the Differential Aptitude Test in verbal-numerical and whose GPA was below the mean for all students at the DAT level (Finney & Van Dalsem, 1969).

A student with a composite score at or above the 95th percentile on the American College Test (ACT) and a GPA less than or equal to 2.25 (on a 4.00 scale) (Colangelo, Kerr, Christensen, & Maxey, 1993).

Students who demonstrate exceptionally high capacity for academic achievement and are not performing satisfactorily for their levels on achievement tests (Whitmore, 1980).

(1963) questioned the legitimacy of the concept of underachievement based on both psychometric and statistical bases, primarily because such measures are less than perfect predictors of potential and ability.

Finally, regardless of whether one adopts a definition of underachievement based on intelligence tests, achievement tests, school performance, or teacher expectations, the above definitions are exclusive because they focus only on academically and intellectually gifted underachievers. How is underachievement defined among gifted students whose strengths are in creativity, leadership, and the visual and performing arts, for instance? This issue is discussed later in this chapter.

Broad and inclusive definitions. Perhaps the broadest definition of underachievement includes those students who have failed to develop and demonstrate their potential. The overreliance on psychometric assessment and on high test scores and the primary focus on academic and intellectual giftedness are absent from inclusive definitions. Broad definitions support the notion that if five gifted students of the same age and gender have the same IQ score and socioeconomic status, they may achieve differently. One student may perform less than satisfactory in the sciences, another in language arts, the third in music, the fourth in mathematics, and the fifth in physical education. In a different scenario, two of the five students may have the same GPA, the third student may be retained, the fourth student may have failed history, and the fifth student may have decided that school is a waste of time.

Broad definitions reflect a qualitative orientation that considers the extent to which motivation is present and effort is exerted. Moreover, emphasis is placed not so much on the discrepant test scores but on the *nature* of the discrepancy. For example, a student's achievement test score is lower than her intelligence test score because the student exerted little effort or did not understand the directions, the tests were administered in a large group, the tests were biased, the student was distracted or disinterested, and so forth. Broad definitions are based on a comprehensive, holistic assessment of intelligence, achievement, motivation, self-concept, anxiety, and test-taking skills. Information is also gathered from parents (checklist, interview), teachers (observations, interview, checklist), and the child. In brief, broad and inclusive definitions support the notion that underachievement is a multidimensional construct that cannot be assessed with unidimensional instruments.

Perspectives on Underachievement

Most descriptions of underachievers support a deficit perspective — "poor" study skills, task commitment, motivation, organization, memory, self-concept, self-esteem, and so forth. These characteristics, however, focus on the child and the symptoms rather than on the etiology of under-achievement. The result of focusing on the child, of blaming the victim, is that these students are considered less desirable and less salvageable than other students. Schools are unable to deal with students who deviate too much from the norm; schools are made for students who excel, achieve, and fulfill the expectations of teachers and parents. A more productive approach to understanding underachievement is to look at what contrib-utes to low intrinsic motivation and high extrinsic motivation. It is little wonder that Terrell Bell stated that there are three things to remember about education: motivation, motivation, and motivation.

Underachieving students are a heterogeneous group. Some have prob-lems associated with poor peer or social relationships, lack of insight, depression, anxiety, defensiveness, and a negative self-image, for example. Other students may lack motivation; they may be considered lazy, pro-crastinators, perfectionists, or nonconformists. A common perception is that these students would not be underachieving if they would "just try harder," "pay attention," and "listen." However, overcoming or reversing underachievement is not that simple for many students, particularly those who have had little or no early educational intervention, those who lack basic skills to take advantage of educational opportunities, and those who have negative self-perceptions. For Black students, reversing under-achievement may be especially difficult if it is related to social barriers such as racism, environmental barriers such as poverty, and educational barriers such as inadequate school experiences.

THEORIES OF UNDERACHIEVEMENT

Academic underachievement is often described in one of three ways—undifferentiated, specific, and hidden. *Undifferentiated* underachieve-ment is general in nature. For instance, the student is not performing as well as her assessed aptitude would predict in all or most subject areas. With *specific* academic underachievement, the student does poorly in one or two specific or broad content areas (such as language-based, science-based, or math-based subjects). *Hidden* underachievement is perhaps the most difficult type to assess. For example, one student's performance on aptitude and achievement measures is consistently low; this student's abili-ties remain hidden because he is functionally untestable. A second stu-dent's underachievement can be hidden by satisfactory performance when teachers have little evidence that the student is capable of much higher performance.

Roth (1970) categorized underachievement as follows: (1) *neurotic anxiety* — because the student is preoccupied with relationships with parents and is suffering from substantial anxiety and guilt over it, the student is paralyzed by concerns and cannot produce; (2) *nonachievement syndrome* — the student chooses not to make an effort and is failing or achieving below his potential; and (3) *adolescent reaction* — a developmental issue characterized by extreme independence seeking whereby the student works diligently to do everything her parents, teachers, and other adults oppose.

Whitmore (1980) studied underachievement specifically among gifted students and reported that types of underachievement can be categorized as: (1) *aggressive* — the student is disruptive, talkative, clowning in class, rebellious, and hostile; (2) *withdrawn* — the student is uninterested, bored, and does not try to participate; and (3) a *combination* — the student is erratic, unpredictable, and vacillates between aggression and withdrawal.

Educators should also consider the duration of underachievement. Is it temporary, situational, or chronic? Situational underachievement results from a temporary period of disturbance (e.g., family problems, illness, new interests, moving to a new school, and personality conflicts with teachers). Chronic underachievement is characterized by an established pattern; the student is usually below average in all subject areas, and there are no indications that underachievement is being created by a temporary situation.

Underachievement in Other Areas of Giftedness

There is a sizable body of literature on underachievement among academically and intellectually gifted students but comparatively little information on other types of gifted underachievers.

Underachievement in leadership. Although we know that gifted leaders can and do use their abilities in socially unproductive and unacceptable ways, we know little about such students. Adolf Hitler, Charles Manson, and Jim Jones were gifted leaders. Inside traders, industrial and military spies, and computer invaders and "virus" spreaders are described in the media as talented, intelligent persons. Before their downfall, most such leaders have been respected for their abilities. Underachievers in leadership choose unethical and expedient solutions to problems; they go with the group rather than against it; they compromise their values; they lack commitment to principles and causes; they do not identity with humanity; they do not feel compassion; they cannot admit to their shortcomings; and they are unwilling to accept societal norms.

According to Seeley (1984), most of the literature on delinquency and giftedness centers on students with high IQ scores. Mahoney and Seeley (1982) found that many students in the juvenile delinquency system were gifted, but their giftedness was not necessarily associated with high academic achievement. Many of the students scored poorly on tests that assessed fluid intelligence but performed well on achievement tests.

Although gifted students generally are rational thinkers who have highly developed consciences and are often concerned about world and adult issues, they are not immune from using their gifts in nonproductive ways. Seeley (1984) explained the relationship between gifted students and delinquency in two ways — the vulnerability thesis and the protection thesis. The vulnerability thesis proposes that gifted students, because of their greater perceptual acuity and ease of learning, are more sensitive to environmental factors than are other students. Subsequently, they are affected more by unfavorable environments. For instance, a gifted Black student may be vulnerable because he feels different from his classmates and feels less able to fit in. To strengthen peer relations, this gifted student may do what is expected by peers to fit in. This thesis suggests that gifted students are more likely than other students to become delinquent because they are adversely affected by negative environments at home and in school.

The protection thesis, however, views giftedness as a protection against delinquency. Gifted students have greater insight into their actions and those of others and are better able to evaluate the long-range consequences of their behaviors than are nongifted students. Consequently, gifted students are better able to understand and cope with environmental problems. As the antithesis of the vulnerability thesis, this perspective holds that gifted students are less likely to succumb to delinquent behaviors. Gifted students become delinquent only when environmental conditions are exceptionally unfavorable. This latter statement carries important implications for Black students, who are more likely than other students to confront racial discrimination, to experience low teacher expectations, and to live in conditions that place them at risk for underachievement (e.g., poverty). (Chapter 4 focuses specifically on social and environmental factors that contribute to underachievement among gifted Black students.)

Underachievement in creativity. Creative underachievers may have high test scores on measures of creativity yet demonstrate few of the characteristics of creativity — divergent thinking, elaboration, fluency, originality, and so forth. Such students may produce ideas but lack initiative or follow-through, which results in a failure to generate products needed to evaluate their creativity. Similarly, underachievers can demonstrate creative behaviors, but standardized tests fail to capture their strengths or particularly creative abilities. Specifically, with their emphasis on convergent thinking and paper-and-pencil evaluations, intelligence and achievement tests are antithetical to creative and divergent thinking. Personality characteristics of nonconformity, resistance to adult domination, independence, risk-taking, and indifference to rules can also hinder creative students' performance. Similarly, if these students are considered "weird" and too nonconforming, neither teachers nor classmates may nominate them for identification and placement.

Underachievement in the visual and performing arts. Public speaking is one of the most common fears held by children and adults. It comes as no surprise, therefore, that many gifted students who are introverted, shy, or have low self-esteem may have difficulty performing for an audience, going to an audition, or submitting work for contests and competitions. Also, low SES students may not have the resources to seek professional training, mentors, and other experiences to develop and nurture their confidence and abilities. Without formal training, students who are gifted in art, drama, music, dance, and other areas have less probability of being identified and served. Further, males may be discouraged from pursuing interests in these areas due to societal expectations and misperceptions that dance, for example, is a feminine (a)vocation.

IDENTIFICATION AND ASSESSMENT

Predicting underachievement is as difficult as predicting the weather. The burden of proof for designating students as underachievers is on educators and researchers. They must have confidence in the instruments chosen and be cautious in interpreting the results. Intelligence, aptitude, and achievement tests have been used to operationalize definitions of underachievement. The same instruments that are used to identify gifted students are used to identify underachieving students. Yet the legitimacy of defining underachievement based on both psychometric and statistical bases is questionable, particularly as measurement criteria are less than perfect. Further, underachievement, like giftedness and intelligence, is not a unidimensional construct and should not be assessed with unidimensional instruments. Because of its multidimensional nature, underachievement may be better understood using noncognitive and qualitative information.

Noncognitive Measures

Measures of noncognitive variables provide more educationally relevant data than do standardized test scores of intelligence and achievement. Assessments of self-perceptions, attitudes toward school and courses, motivation, test anxiety, test-taking and study skills, and learning styles further increase our understanding of the reasons gifted Black students may underachieve, the difficulties of identifying gifted Black students, and the reasons for poor test scores. Numerous instruments are available that provide quantitative data on motivation, self-perceptions, learning styles, and so forth. However, student achievement depends on the extent to which educators use both quantitative and qualitative indices to better understand underachievement. Educators and school personnel are encouraged to rely on interviews with and observations of students for assessment purposes.

Self-perceptions. Central questions regarding Black students' perceptions focus on their self-concept (academic and nonacademic) and racial identity. How do Black students compare themselves with other students intellectually, academically, and socially? Are they aware of their own strengths and shortcomings? Are they overly concerned with certain aspects of self, and do these preoccupations interfere with their school performance? The research of Diener and Dweck (1980) provides important information regarding self-perceptions and achievement. Poor achievers tend to have negative perceptions of their intelligence and ability compared with high achievers. Specifically, poor achievers (1) hold negative self-attributions — they attribute failures to personal inadequacy, such as deficient intelligence; (2) rely heavily on emotion to explain away failures (e.g., they were bored, tired, worried); (3) avoid difficult tasks in order to "look smart"; and (4) become frustrated and do not persist in the face of failure.

Relative to racial identity, how comfortable do Black students feel in diverse settings (predominantly White, predominantly Black, integrated)? Do they show pride, shame, or discomfort about their racial heritage? Do they seek greater self-understanding and cultural awareness? How effectively do Black students cope with racial injustices and misunderstandings?

Attitudes toward school and courses. Students who hold negative feelings about school or their courses are unlikely to work to their potential. Through interviews and observations, teachers and counselors gain a better understanding of students' educational engagement. Do they seem eager to learn? To be in school? Do their on-task behavior, punctuality, and attendance vary relative to different courses and teachers? What do students like and dislike about school and specific classes, and why? D. Y. Ford (1995) interviewed gifted Black achievers and underachievers, the majority of whom held positive attitudes about school subjects. However, underachievers were significantly less positive than achievers about school climate factors. For example, underachievers did not perceive their classrooms to be supportive and nurturing, they reported less positive relationships with teachers, and they wanted more time to understand material presented in class than did achievers. Further, underachievers were less positive about math, science, reading, and English than were achievers.

Motivation. To what extent is the underachiever intrinsically motivated? Extrinsically motivated? Is the student an independent or a social learner (motivated by peers, teachers, parents)? Does he or she perform best in a competitive or a cooperative setting? Does the student perform best during individual or group assignments? What social, cultural, and psychological factors impede achievement motivation?

Test anxiety. Test anxiety is a special form of general anxiety that consists of phenomenological, physiological, cognitive, and behavioral responses related to fear of failure (Sarason, Davidson, Lighthall, Waite, & Ruebush, 1960). When test anxiety occurs, many cognitive and attentional processes interfere with task performance. Students with high levels of test anxiety experience both worry and emotionality. Worry concerns the cognitive aspect of consequences. Those who worry about tests fear the consequences of evaluation. Emotionality is characterized by stress-evoked autonomic arousal prior to or during evaluative situations. Further, test anxiety is often accompanied by negative self-evaluations, attention to irrelevant information, distraction, poor self-esteem, few peer relations, and low estimates of cognitive ability. Thus, repeated failure on tests lowers one's sense of self-efficacy.

Test anxiety develops early in life and exists without regard to ability. Such anxiety is a common source of emotional distress in school-age children, especially among students in upper elementary grades (Sarason et al., 1960); it persists throughout schooling and in other settings that are social and evaluative. Children's social learning history and sociocultural background determine the cues that elicit anxiety in evaluative situations. For instance, a child may be tuned through child-rearing practices to interpret a wide range of environmental cues as evaluatively stressing; equally important, one traumatic experience with a specific teacher and a specific stressful examination may predispose an individual to react with self-devaluing cognitions, which transfer to high emotionality in other similar situations.

Further, Sarason et al. (1960) considered test anxiety to be a personality characteristic resulting from unrealistic or excessive parental expectations. That is, parental criticism when children fail or do not perform to expectations is internalized by children, who become more sensitive to failure. These feelings take the form of guilt, anxiety, grief, pain, shame, and other emotions. Parents' failure to provide emotional support to children in evaluative situations, and the failure to reinforce children's self-evaluations, results in lower performance (Dusek, 1980).

When children enter school, their concerns are reinforced by teachers and school practices. Such practices as minimal competency testing, for example, have important consequences for test-anxious students. Test performance assumes a more important role in school and children's lives when the results determine whether a child is promoted to the next grade or receives a high school diploma. Hill (1984) noted that children experience strong apprehension about this type of evaluation and, consequently, may not do well.

Similarly, the increased use of test scores to evaluate school and program effectiveness and greater public demands for high levels of skill learning and achievement in schools create a more pressure-laden atmosphere (Hill & Wigfield, 1984). Because test scores are the major indicator of school effectiveness, students and schools are under pressure to increase standardized test scores. Given the heavy reliance on test scores and comparative evaluations by schools, reformers, and policy makers, it is little wonder that test anxiety is the most researched of anxieties. There appears to be a never-ending loop in which test performance is increasingly hindered by rising levels of test anxiety.

Few studies have focused specifically on test anxiety among Black students. Such research is particularly important, given that Black students have some of the lowest standardized test scores nationally. Several researchers have attributed the lower performance of minority students on standardized tests to test anxiety. Hembree (1988) and Clawson, Firment, and Trower (1981) found that Black children had significantly higher test anxiety than White children. Crocker, Schmitt, and Tang (1988) examined the relationship between test anxiety and performance on the Metropolitan Achievement Test. Results indicate that Black students had significantly higher levels of test anxiety than White students. Willig, Harnisch, Hill, and Maehr (1983) found a strong negative relationship between test anxiety and performance among White, Hispanic, and Black students in upper elementary and junior high school. Payne (1984) found racial differences as well, with Black students reporting more text anxiety than

White students. Similarly, Beidel, Turner, Marquette, and Trager (1994) examined the presence of test anxiety and other anxiety disorders among Black and White elementary school students. Results indicated significant differences relative to race, with more Black students having anxieties. Finally, Turner, Beidel, Hughes, and Turner (1993) studied test anxiety, self-concept, achievement, and social functioning among Black students. Results indicated that 41% of the students suffered from test anxiety. These students had lower levels of achievement, lower self-concepts, and a lower sense of self-worth than students not reporting test anxiety.

Whereas the studies just cited relied on test anxiety scales to determine the nature and extent of test anxiety, teachers and counselors can use qualitative assessments of test anxiety to note students' concerns, frustration, and discomfort during evaluative situations. They can also observe students' test-taking strategies. An extensive list of recommendations is provided by Hill and Wigfield (1984).

Learning and cognitive styles. School achievement is influenced significantly by one's learning style; hence, what contributes to school failure is not only *what* is taught but also *how* it is taught and learned. Dunn, Beaudry, and Klavas (1989) defined learning styles as a biologically and developmentally imposed set of personal characteristics that make the same teaching method effective for some students and ineffective for others. In other words, students are products of family and community settings that predispose them to patterns of behaviors that are more or less functional in school settings (Sinclair & Ghory, 1992). Dunn, DeBello, Brennan, Krimsky, and Murrain (1981) defined learning styles as the way individuals concentrate on, absorb, and retain new or difficult information or skills. Style, they added, comprises a combination of environmental, emotional, sociological, physical, and psychological elements that permit individuals to receive, store, and use knowledge or abilities. Saracho (1989) described learning styles as a distinctive pattern of apprehending, storing, and employing information or, more simply, as individual variations in methods of perceiving, remembering, and thinking. All these definitions suggest that learning is based on the way students manipulate and process information as the material is being taught. In essence, they reflect a learner's mode of selecting, encoding, organizing, storing, retrieving, decoding, and generating information, all of which influence learning and performance (Frederico & Landis, 1980).

Learning styles are significantly influenced by culturally induced cognitive styles related to communicating, interacting, perceiving, and acquiring knowledge (Saracho & Gerstl, 1992; Shade, 1994). When there is an incompatibility between Black students' learning styles and the instructional preferences of schools, which generally favor field-independent, abstract, and analytical styles of learning, academic failure may result.

Research suggests that the learning styles of gifted, White, and achieving students are different from those of Black and underachieving students. In general, gifted, White, and academically successful students prefer formal learning classroom designs, less structure in learning materials, and auditory modes of presentation; they are reflective, tactile, kinesthetic, and field-independent learners; they are responsible for their own learning, persistent, motivated, and task oriented. Black students, however, are likely to be field-dependent, holistic, relational, and visual learners; they learn best in social and cooperative settings, are socially or other oriented, and prefer tactile and kinesthetic learning and teaching experiences. Underachievers also tend to be impulsive, low-task-oriented, nonconforming, creative, visual, and tactile and kinesthetic learners.

In essence, the learning style preferences of gifted students and Black students appear oppositional, and the styles of Black students and underachievers appear similar, which must certainly pose a dilemma for gifted Black students by hindering their school performance. Black students do not fail in school because of learning style differences but because schools fail to accommodate these differences. Figure 3.2 presents a checklist designed to assist teachers in identifying factors that contribute to or exacerbate school problems for gifted Black students. Teachers are encouraged to examine school factors, peer relations, familial factors, personality factors, and academic factors. All these issues are given greater attention in later chapters.

STRATEGIES FOR REVERSING UNDERACHIEVEMENT

In general, strategies for reversing underachievement must address academic skills deficits (such as test-taking and study skills) and include curricular changes (such as multicultural education) and instructional changes (such as accommodation of learning styles). They should also include increased training among school personnel in gifted and multicultural education and increased family involvement.

Academic underachievement. Whitmore (1980) recommended three types of strategies that empower underachieving students to become more self-sufficient, mastery-oriented learners: supportive strategies, intrinsic strategies, and remedial strategies (Figure 3.3). Supportive strategies are facilitative; they affirm students' sense of worth, convey the message that success is possible, and provide positive learning experiences. Intrinsic

FIGURE 3.2. Checklist for identifying indices of underachievement among gifted Black students.

Social Factors

____ Student's primary social group is outside of the school or gifted program

____ Student participates in few or no extracurricular activities

____ Student socializes with delinquents and/or students who have poor achievement orientation

____ Student's need for peer acceptance and relations outweighs his or her academic concerns about school and achievement

____ Student has one or more risk factors (e.g., poverty, single-parent family, poorly educated parents)

Family Factors

____ Student's home life is stressful

____ Parents have a low educational level

____ Student has only one parent in the home

____ Student has relatives who have dropped out of school

____ Student has little parental or family supervision; poor family relations

____ Parental expectations for student are too low or unrealistic

____ Family is low SES

____ Communication between home and school is poor

School Culture and Climate Factors

____ Teachers and school personnel have low expectations for minority students

____ Morale among teachers, school personnel, and/or students is low

____ Classroom environment is unfriendly or hostile

____ Gifted program lacks cultural and racial diversity relative to students

____ Gifted program lacks cultural and racial diversity relative to teachers

____ Little attention is given to multicultural education

____ Teachers and other school personnel lack substantive training in gifted education

____ Teachers and other school personnel lack substantive training in multicultural and urban education

____ Student feels alienated and isolated from teachers

____ Student feels alienated and isolated from classmates

____ Minority students are underrepresented in gifted program and services

____ Teaching, administrative staff, and other school personnel lack racial and cultural diversity

---

FIGURE 3.2. Continued.

Psychological and Individual Factors

_____ Student motivation is consistently low

_____ Student has negative attitude toward school

_____ Student cannot tolerate structured and/or passive activities

_____ Student relates poorly to authority or adult figures (e.g., teachers, parents, school administrators)

_____ Student has low academic and/or low social self-concepts

_____ Student has poor racial identity (e.g., pre-encounter, immersion–emersion)

_____ Student has health or medical problems

_____ Student attributes failure to lack of ability; attributes success to luck or easy task

_____ Student consistently seeks immediate gratification

_____ Student's learning style preferences are inconsistent with teaching styles

_____ Student suffers from test anxiety on standardized and/or nonstandardized tests

Student Achievement Behaviors

_____ Student has low standardized test scores

_____ Student has low grades or GPA

_____ Student exerts little effort on school tasks

_____ Student avoids challenging work

_____ Student bores easily; dislikes drill work and rote practices

_____ Student disrupts the classroom

_____ Student procrastinates on school assignments

_____ Student has poor study and/or test-taking skills

_____ Student resists participating in gifted program and services (e.g., resource room)

---

strategies help students develop self-initiation, independence, and self-efficacy. These strategies communicate the importance of internal rather than external motivation. Remedial strategies are designed to improve students' academic performance in specific areas of difficulty.

Underachievement in creativity. Creative underachievers may need to be taught critical thinking, convergent thinking, and test-taking skills and strategies. They should be given opportunities to learn independently and to take risks. Time management skills may also help these students cope with multiple problems, ideas, and products. These students also need opportunities to demonstrate their abilities and mastery of material in alternative formats, such as portfolios, that provide opportunities to dem-

FIGURE 3.3. Strategies to enhance academic achievement among gifted Black students (adapted from Whitemore, 1980).

Strategy	Goal/Objective	Recommended Strategies
Supportive strategies	To affirm the worth of students and convey the promise of greater potential and success	Consistent opportunities to meet with teachers to discuss concerns Accommodate teaching and learning styles (e.g., provide students with options to demonstrate mastery of material; teach students to be bi-cognitive) Mastery learning Cooperative learning Positive reinforcement Nonauthoritarian learning atmosphere; affective and student-centered classrooms High teacher expectations Multicultural counseling Mentors, role models, internships
Intrinsic strategies	To help students develop self-initiation, independence, and intrinsic motivation	Mentorships and role models Positive reinforcement, with constructive and consistent feedback Personally meaningful and relevant coursework Increase metacognitive skills and self-awareness Independent study projects Accommodate learning styles to various situations, courses, and teachers Multicultural and urban education Flexible, nurturing classrooms
Remedial strategies	To improve students' academic performance in the specific area or areas or difficulty	Academic counseling (e.g., tutoring, study skills, test-taking skills) Small-group instruction Learning contracts, written contracts (daily, weekly, or monthly)

onstrate divergent thinking, inventiveness, originality, and other creative behaviors.

Leadership underachievement. Students who use their leadership skills in socially unacceptable and harmful ways should be provided opportunities for empathy and introspection — looking inward so that they can see how their behavior affects others. Counseling, mentorships, and internships represent important opportunities for guidance and support, but students can also be exposed to theories of moral development. Older students can take courses in philosophy, social psychology, child development, and law, for example.

Underachievement in the visual and performing arts. These gifted underachievers may need access to scholarships, internships, and mentorships to develop their abilities, particularly low SES students. Shy students may also need to work with counselors to increase their self-concepts and for assertiveness training and help in public speaking and performing.

Strategies for reversing underachievement must be multifaceted and comprehensive. They must also be tailored to a student's individual situation and type of underachievement. Students may require personal, academic, and family counseling; they may require assistance with developmental and racial identity issues; others may need to explore conflicts between the need for achievement and the need for affiliation; some students need greater attention to affective or social and emotional needs. The strategies employed also depend heavily on the type, intensity, duration, and nature of underachievement. For instance, although cooperative learning may be effective for some students, it may not be necessary for others. Similarly, some students need personal counseling for poor racial identity, self-concept, and self-esteem; others do not.

Perhaps the most common recommendation for improving students' achievement is to enhance their learning skills — study habits, time management, and stress reduction, as well as listening skills, goal setting, and self-concepts. Rathvon (1991) found that enhancing underachievers' study habits (at home and in school), test-taking skills, and attitudes facilitated achievement. Campbell (1991) and Ruben (1989) found that group guidance was helpful with students who were at risk of underachieving. Guidance techniques (such as guided fantasy, positive affirmation, and visualization) can increase students' self-concepts and provide them with new, alternative behaviors. Guided fantasies that focus on successful experiences such as making friends, getting along with teachers, or being successful on a test or in a class are important exercises for gifted Black students. After such exercises, counselors can invite students to debrief — to explore their feelings, attitudes, and behaviors. Homework assignments in which gifted Black students practice role playing and other exercises can help reinforce the desired and mutually agreed upon behaviors.

Positive affirmations help eliminate self-defeating thoughts and behaviors. Gifted and underachieving Black students need help identifying specific goals, recognizing negative self-messages, and rephrasing or reframing those messages into positive thoughts and realistic goals. Visualizations can be used to capitalize on gifted Black students' imagination and to foster feelings of empowerment.

It is recommended that one behavior at a time be targeted, even though gifted Black students may be experiencing multiple problems. These students need to identify and then prioritize their concerns. Counselors need to model the behaviors they wish students to adopt; similarly, using diagrams, pictures, and other visual teaching aids can facilitate the counseling process, which focuses on learning style preferences and strengths.

Counselors should explain the relationship between thinking and feelings; they should help gifted Black students realize that their intense feelings are not (necessarily) caused by negative events but by the manner in which they personalize, perceive, and interpret those events. That is, the negative event (stimulus) generates thoughts (perceptions and beliefs) that lead to negative emotions (response). It is therefore important to focus on gifted Black students' cognitive strengths by teaching them how positive thinking can reduce their emotional upsets. By focusing on current events, gifted Black students can be taught how to cope with similar or related events in the future. Important techniques include role playing, role modeling, and homework assignments that give students opportunities to practice newly discussed or acquired behaviors and thinking skills.

SUMMARY

Perceptions about gifted students have been shaped by stereotypes and myths of these students as motivated learners, with outstanding school performance and leadership. Gifted students are seldom perceived as unmotivated, lazy, procrastinators, or emotionally immature. Although the idea of gifted underachievers seems contradictory, it is a logical concept based on the reality that gifted students are represented among school dropouts. The concept is further supported by the fact that numerous definitions and several theories of gifted underachievement have been advanced.

Motivation is not synonymous with achievement, and student motivation cannot be inferred by examining achievement test scores. Test scores are determined by a variety of factors. When we evaluate students' success by how well they achieve in school and on standardized tests, we lose sight of other factors affecting their achievement and test outcomes. Teachers must develop an understanding of why student motivation is lacking.

Underachievement is a ubiquitous term, and little consensus exists regarding the definition that promises to capture the greatest number of youth who fail to reach their potential in school. Whereas many definitions support a behavioral, qualitative perspective of achievement and underachievement, studies of gifted underachievers have traditionally supported a psychometric or quantitative definition. These definitions describe gifted underachievers as having a discrepancy between some standardized test score and school performance, or a discrepancy between two test scores (such as intelligence and achievement). Too often, however, tests fail to consider students' level of test anxiety, test-taking skills, level of motivation or task commitment, interest, learning styles, and the many risk factors impacting their performance. Further, tests fail to explore students' self-concepts, fear of failure, fear of success, perfectionism, locus of control, lack of skills, and rebellion against authority figures. They fail to consider the reality that ability does not always determine performance.

Caution is essential when interpreting and defining achievement and underachievement in narrow and exclusive terms. For example, how logical is it to assume that IQ scores are immune to the effects of nonacademic factors that are frequently associated with poor school performance (e.g., motivation, task commitment, interest, test anxiety, self-concept, self-esteem)? To what extent do total battery scores obscure the presence of specific types and areas of underachievement? How valid and reliable are results in which a single measure of intelligence is used to predict school performance? How are grades affected by teachers' bias, experience, or special interests or by students' attitudes, behavior, and work habits? These same questions were raised by Thorndike (1963) over 3 decades ago. Assuming that children come to school with well-developed self-systems and intrinsic motivation, future research must examine the nature and etiology of underachievement.

Underachievement is a dangerous, downward spiral resulting from many factors, and it seldom occurs in a simple, unidirectional fashion. Although underachievement is a complex, multifaceted concept that remains elusive to definition, we cannot abandon the concept. We can define it in more specific and more comprehensive ways, however. Future research must focus on the etiology of underachievement among gifted Black students, including its nature, scope, duration, and intensity. When definitions of underachievement are psychometrically driven to the exclusion of noncognitive and affective factors, many underachievers will go unidentified.

Chapter 4

Social Factors as Correlates of Underachievement

All the men of genius that we have ever heard of have triumphed over adverse circumstances, but that is no reason for supposing that there were not innumerable others who succumbed in youth.

—Bertrand Russell

This chapter focuses on the many social factors that place gifted Black students at risk for underachievement and underrepresentation in gifted education programs. It is contended that, because of societal forces, an individual does not necessarily choose to underachieve. He or she may have no choice. In essence, children are put at risk because of various external disadvantages.

Bowles and Gintis (1976), Bourdieu (1977), and Giroux (1983) described how social class inequality passes from one generation to the next. More specifically, Ogbu (1983, 1988, 1994) attributed the poorer school performance of Black students to structured inequality — racism, discrimination, and other social injustices. He postulated that injustices, including job ceilings and unequal power relations, reproduce class and social inequality such that those at the bottom of the socioeconomic ladder remain at the bottom, which undermines the realization of potential among highly able students.

Several social factors place Black students at risk for educational disadvantage on a consistent basis — poverty, residing in a single-parent family, mother's low level of education, racial minority status, and English as a second language. These environmental risk factors, described below, along with a welter of other social injustices, further exacerbate the educational problems of Black students.

RISK FACTORS

Although definitions of what it means to be "at risk" vary, there is consensus that many students lack the home and community resources to benefit from schooling. That is, differences in learning outcomes result from the two-sided interaction between students and the environment (Sinclair & Ghory, 1992). Risk factors can limit the school achievement and motivation of Black and other minority students who are disproportionately represented in at-risk conditions (Garcia & Walker de Felix, 1992; Levin, 1990; Walker de Felix, 1992). Thus, for some Black students, survival takes a strong precedence over educational achievement and developing gifts and talents.

Race and Ethnicity

For numerous reasons, minority students are less likely to complete high school or be placed in upper tracks and ability groups (including gifted programs), and they are more likely to have lower standardized test scores, be retained, or be placed in special education than are White students. For example, Black students represent 16% of the public school population but constitute 27% of all students classified as trainable mentally retarded or seriously emotionally disturbed, 8% of students in gifted programs, 30% of all students expelled, and 31% of those who have received corporal punishment (National Coalition of Advocates for Students, 1985, 1988). These data and others indicate that Black students face unique problems related to race. The color of one's skin is a powerful determinant of oppression in the United States and its schools.

Educators who hold a cultural deficit hypothesis reinforce this cycle of low achievement and poor representation of Black students in gifted programs. This paradigm was commonplace during the 1960s, à la Moynihan (1965) and J. S. Coleman et al. (1966), when the poor school achievement among Black students was explained by their "culture of poverty" and inadequate socialization practices. Jensen (1969) believed that race and inherited intellectual inferiority explained the poorer school performance of Black students.

Poverty

Twenty-four percent of children under the age of 18 live in poverty; children represent 40% of the total population of people in poverty (Bempechat & Ginsburg, 1989; W. E. Davis & McCall, 1990). Poor students have less access to educational opportunities that nurture and sustain both potential and abilities. Thus, poverty is a circumstance, not a measure of inherent worth. Poverty limits potential. Singly or in unison, poverty and the various other risk factors wreak havoc on *any* student's achievement and motivation.

Edelman (1985) reported, as have numerous other researchers, that Black students face staggering obstacles to achieving decency, dignity, and success in America. These children suffer disproportionately from downward trends in the economy and from the lack of commitment toward alleviating problems in health, education, housing, and employment. The poverty rates for Black families and children in America have been high, both historically and currently. For example, in 1967, 50% of Black families were poor, compared with 20% of the general population; in 1980, 70% of Black families had family incomes of less than two times the poverty level (U.S. Bureau of the Census, 1982); and in 1982, 51% of Black children under the age of 3, and 48% of those between 3 and 13, lived in poverty (U.S. Bureau of the Census, 1983). Equally troubling is that the median income of Black families is 51% that of White families.

Children in impoverished conditions have fewer resources and less access to formal learning opportunities; more and greater health problems and psychological difficulties; and more handicapping conditions that affect educational outcomes, namely, learning disabilities, speech impairment, mental retardation, emotional disturbance, and other health problems (U.S. Department of Education, 1993). A report by the Council for Exceptional Children (1994) indicated that Black students constituted 24.2% of youth with disabilities in 1986. Students with disabilities have poor graduation rates. In 1991, for instance, a study found that 36.1% of students with learning disabilities did not complete high school, compared with 24.4% of students in general (Wagner, 1991).

Single-Parent Families

Some 26% of children under the age of 18 live in single-parent families; of these, 13 million live with their mothers and 1.6 million with their fathers (Bempechat & Ginsburg, 1989; W. E. Davis & McCall, 1990). In 1982, more than half (53%) of all Black children were born to single mothers, and 60% overall did not live with both parents (National Center for Health Statistics, 1983). Single-parent families are often characterized by poverty, and a disproportionate percentage are minorities. Data indicate that 53% of Black single-parent families were poor in 1985 (U.S. Bureau of the Census, 1985b).

Role conflict and strain, differential priorities, and struggles to meet basic needs often take precedence over academic needs for these families. Strained parents may hold high and positive achievement orientations but have difficulty meeting the academic needs of their children, as described in Chapter 9.

Educational Level of Mother

A little more than 20% of children have mothers who have not graduated from high school (Bempechat & Ginsburg, 1989; W. E. Davis & McCall, 1990). A little more than one-third (36%) of Black high school graduates (class of 1982) attended college in 1982, a significant decrease from the 50% that was reported in 1977. Relative to the 43% of Black mothers who have not graduated from high school, 44% were never married, 27% were separated, 6.9% were widowed, and 20.3% were divorced (U.S. Bureau of the Census, 1983). Major educational issues for mothers include less personal contact with school personnel and less knowledge about schooling, both of which contribute to less parental involvement. Consequently, children of parents who have low educational levels tend to have low achievement levels and high dropout rates.

Limited English Proficiency

For approximately 10% of students, English represents their second language (Bempechat & Ginsburg, 1989; W. E. Davis & McCall, 1990). Language barriers contribute to social isolation from peers and teachers due to lack of communication, understanding, and sensitivity. Other educational issues include inappropriate assessment tools and curriculum, as well as cultural and learning style differences.

Black English is the primary language of many students. Professionals frequently consider Black English inferior to standard English. When teachers hold this perspective, students who speak Black English may be at risk for educational problems. Allington (1980), Brophy (1988), and others have found that teachers' negative attitudes regarding Black English contribute to underachievement in Black students. Specifically, students who speak Black English are likely to be seated farthest away from the teacher, be called on less frequently, be given less time to respond to questions, receive more negative criticism, get less praise for correct answers, and have responses interrupted more frequently. J. B. Taylor (1983) also found a significant relationship between negative attitudes toward Black English and lower teacher evaluations of students' reading comprehension.

Black English is considered by many linguists to be a legitimate, rule-governed, and fully developed dialect. Black English speakers are highly competent language users when speaking their vernacular (Bowie & Bond, 1994; Labov, 1985; Smitherman, 1983). Modification of teachers' attitudes toward the dialect of their students and increased understanding of diverse linguistic backgrounds should be a primary concern of the education profession.

The risk factors just described cannot be viewed in isolation. For example, almost half of Black students fall into one or two risk categories: 43% live in poverty, and 67% in single-parent homes (Waxman, 1992). The various risk factors take their toll, as reflected in the fact that Black students drop out at a 40% higher rate than White students (Garcia & Walker de Felix, 1992). Logically and statistically, gifted Black students must be present in situations and environments that place them at risk for underachieving, exhibiting low motivation, dropping out, and otherwise not reaching their potential as students and adults.

SOCIAL INJUSTICES: RACISM AND PREJUDICE

At least three reasons help explain the negative school experiences of Black students in education: chance or random occurrence, deficit theories, and racism. Chance explanations assume that there are no compelling forces that cause or contribute to the negative educational outcomes experienced by Black students. These outcomes are believed to occur as natural phenomena that are relatively free of outside influences. This perspective assumes that the underrepresentation and underachievement of gifted Black students have little to do with the student or the school specifically. This argument is analogous to "being at the wrong place at the wrong time." Tannenbaum's (1983) theory of giftedness is the only one to include the notion of chance variables. It appears that being White and upper SES, living in a two-parent family, and having highly educated parents increase one's chances of being identified as gifted. Statistically, however, the persistent underrepresentation of Black students in gifted education programs and services cannot be a function of chance alone. This impossibility calls for other explanations.

Deficit hypotheses and theories, described in greater detail later, also explain the educational and achievement outcomes of Black students. These hypotheses maintain that there are predetermined deficiencies among Black (and other minority) students that relegate them to an inferior status. One aspect of the deficit hypothesis claims that Blacks are genetically inferior. It is contended that biology plays the primary role in determining intelligence and potential. Another perspective holds that

Blacks have personality deficits that cause abnormalities in character and behavior. This view is more common in the mental health profession (Ridley, 1989).

The third explanation holds that racism, prejudice, and stereotypes significantly affect the educational outcomes of Black students. Jackman (1977) defined prejudice as negative generalized beliefs or stereotypes about a group, a feeling of dislike for that group, and a predisposition to behave in a negative way toward that group, directly as well as vicariously. Prejudice is an attitude that grows out of stereotypes or generalizations about a group of people. Stereotypes are overgeneralizations that are both inaccurate and resistant to new information and change.

Racial attitudes and preferences are learned early in life. As early as age 3 or 4, children become aware of their racial and ethnic backgrounds. From this age until about 7 or 8, children demonstrate increasing competence in perceiving similarity to their own group. Specifically, children at this age can accurately categorize different groups based on perceptual cues, and they understand the notion that race and ethnicity are unchangeable (Ponterotto & Pedersen, 1993). Gifted Black students may note social injustices much earlier than other students.

Allport's (1979) seminal work indicates that prejudice takes various forms and expressions, which range from mild and overt to harsh and covert. His five-phase model of "acting out prejudice" is based on a continuum from least to most energetic: antilocution, avoidance, discrimination, physical attack, and extermination. *Antilocution* is the mildest form of prejudice. It is characterized by prejudicial talk among persons who hold similar beliefs. It is a rather controlled expression of antagonism that is limited to small circles. For instance, White parents may express concern that the gifted program is becoming "too integrated" and "watered down," such that the quality of their child's schooling will decrease. Or White students might express concern about sitting next to Black students in class.

Avoidance occurs when individuals move beyond lip service or talking about minority groups to deliberate efforts to avoid them. In an attempt to avoid contact with gifted Black students, parents may transfer their children to another school or program. Such inconvenience is self-directed, and no overt harm is directed against the group being avoided. White flight is common when schools, programs, and communities are ordered to desegregate (D. Y. Ford & Webb, 1994).

Discrimination occurs when individuals take active steps to exclude or deny minority students entrance or participation in an activity, for example, a gifted program. Discriminatory practices can extend to educational programs, employment practices, social privileges, and recreational opportunities. For example, a member of the identification and placement panel votes, without justification, against the admittance of a Black student seeking entrance into the gifted program. Or the identification and placement committee indicates that efforts should not be focused on affirmative action because "we've already admitted two Black students." Or a teacher refuses to refer *any* Black student for identification and assessment.

Physical attack represents one of the more extreme forms of prejudice. It is most likely to occur under tense or emotionally laden conditions and during economically stressful times. *Extermination* represents the final phase of prejudice, according to Allport (1979). Extermination involves the systematic and deliberate destruction of minority groups because of their race. Lynchings and massacres are two forms of extermination that have been aimed specifically at Blacks.

Racial discrimination is any behavior that systematically denies one group access to opportunities or privilege while perpetuating privilege for members of another group (Ridley, 1989). Racism is a ubiquitous social problem; its cause is hidden, but the result is known. Black and other minority groups continue to suffer racism, discrimination, and oppression, which are the root of many of today's social problems.

The racial attitudes of White Americans have changed over the years (National Opinion Research Center, 1980). Yet data indicate that prejudice is still evident among some Whites who unabashedly dislike Blacks. In 1942, approximately 70% of White respondents did not believe that Black and White students should attend the same school. In 1985, approximately 90% believed that it was acceptable. Nonetheless, in 1991, the National Opinion Research Center found that Whites were more likely to see Blacks as lazy, violence prone, less intelligent, and less patriotic (see Tran, Young, & Di Lella, 1994).

In contemporary America, most racism is subtle rather than blatant (Dovidio & Gaertner, 1986; Kinder, 1986); it is camouflaged by a more "pleasant" exterior, yet few people are immune to subtle prejudice. Manifestations of racism can appear at either the individual or the institutional level and are overt, covert, or unintentional. According to Ridley (1989), institutional racism includes the intentional and unintentional manipulation or toleration of institutional policies that unfairly restrict the opportunities of targeted groups. Figure 4.1 presents examples of individual and institutional racism in schools offering gifted programs or services.

Whether it is overt or covert or at the individual or the institutional level, racism interrupts the normal development of those persons subjected to it. It hinders their ability to function at their full potential as both children and adults and increases their levels of stress. Leveled aspirations are all too common in urban and Black communities, where effort, hard

FIGURE 4.1. Possible manifestations of racism in gifted education.

	Individual Racism	Institutional Racism
Overt/intentional	A teacher believes that all Black students lack motivation. On this basis, he or she requests that Black students be assigned to low ability groups or tracks without assessment information.	School personnel openly deny admittance of Black students into the gifted program for fear of flight by White students to other schools[*]
Covert/intentional	A school psychologist interprets high test scores received by Black students as a fluke and requests that students be retested.	School personnel deliberately set the test score criterion for admission above the range scored by the majority of Black students nationally or in the school district. This practice excludes them from the gifted program and otherwise limits the number of identified Black students.
Unintentional	A school counselor misinterprets Black dialect as an inability to understand standard English or to communicate effectively. The student is referred to speech therapy or placed in remedial language classes. Despite high verbal skills, the student is not considered gifted in this area.	Admission to gifted program and services is based on standardized tests without consideration of group differences and biases in the tests.

[*] This practice is now illegal

work, and support for the achievement ideology do not always reap positive outcomes. D. Y. Ford (1992, 1993b, 1993c) and D. Y. Ford and Harris (in press) found that gifted Black underachievers represented a paradox of underachievement; although they supported the *ideals* undergirding the achievement ideology, they were troubled about the *reality* of social injustices. For instance, while believing that Blacks could become successful if they worked hard, spoke standard English, and so forth, some gifted Black underachievers feared that such success would be tempered with racism and other social barriers; thus, only those Blacks who were "lucky" would succeed. Black students at all ability levels may question the integrity of the achievement ideology.

SOCIAL SELF-CONCEPT: NEED FOR
ACHIEVEMENT VERSUS NEED FOR AFFILIATION

Students' affective, psychological, and educational problems often relate to an inability to fulfill their basic needs. One of our basic needs is the desire to belong and to feel loved (Glasser, 1986; Maslow, 1954). Schools have great difficulty fulfilling Black students' need for self-esteem and their need to belong. Further, although educators and counselors acknowledge the interrelation of the psychological, socioemotional, and cognitive domains of development, programs for gifted students appear to have largely neglected such needs and subsequent development. The primary focus of gifted programs is on meeting academic and vocational needs.

Many studies purporting that gifted students have higher self-concepts investigated only the general domain rather than specific domains such as social self-concept, in which gifted students frequently score poorly (Janos & Robinson, 1985; Li, 1988). Winne, Woodlands, and Wong (1982) and Whitmore (1980, 1986) noted the feelings of difference and isolation that gifted students experience due to their unique gifts and talents. M. A. Ford (1989) reported that gifted elementary students expressed embarrassment, guilt, and even confusion about their academic success, which had negative effects on their peer relationships. Gifted children surveyed by Galbraith (1985) had numerous concerns, two of which were that they felt different and alienated and that they were often teased by peers.

Educators must understand that being placed into programs with students and teachers who look, speak, and behave differently can negatively influence Black students' academic and social self-concepts. This phenomenon is best explained by the social comparison theory, first posited by Festinger (1954) and expounded upon by M. J. Coleman and Fults (1985):

> In the absence of objective standards of comparison, people will employ significant others in their environments as bases for forming estimates of self-worth and, given the choice of relatively similar or dissimilar others, they are more likely to select similar others as the bases for social comparison. (p. 8)

As a cultural group, Black students are socially oriented, as reflected by strong kinship networks and large extended families (McAdoo, 1988, 1993). There is a strong need to belong and for affiliation, as well as a need to bond with others who share similar concerns and interests. In many ways, groups represent a mechanism for self-preservation. This need for group affiliation, however, can have unfortunate ramifications when an anti-achievement ethic is espoused by the peer group.

Social injustices represent important sources of vulnerability for Black youth. Black youth who are confronted with racism and respond with anger and rebelliousness may develop an *oppositional social identity* (Ogbu, 1988). They may deliberately perform poorly in school, rebel against teachers and school administrators who are perceived as agents of oppression, and shun any behavior associated with mainstream society. To protect their self-esteem, Black students may develop ineffective coping styles that alienate them from school and are harmful to academic achievement. For instance, in a predominantly White gifted program, Black students may limit or completely avoid contact with their White peers, and they may deliberately exert little effort in school because it is associated with the White culture. Many Black students hide their academic abilities by becoming class clowns, dropping out, and suppressing effort.

Other Black students may have a *diffused identity*, characterized by low self-esteem and alienation from both the Black culture and the mainstream. Their poor academic and social competencies result in educational, socioemotional, and psychological adjustment problems. This identity conflict is most likely to develop when the values, attitudes, and behaviors espoused in the home and at school are incongruent; this incompatibility or dissonance between the home and school can cause considerable stress for Black students, particularly if the schools attempt to assimilate Black youth by eliminating their cultural differences. Unfortunately, although schools require a high degree of mainstream socialization from students, they do not always provide the environments necessary for Black youth to gain mainstream skills while remaining connected to their home and community environments. The result is increased or more intense barriers to gifted Black students' academic success.

Educators must address the attrition of Black students from gifted programs and their determination to camouflage their abilities. Once placed in gifted programs, Black students make numerous social sacrifices and take many risks. They risk, for example, rejection from Black peers, who may perceive gifted Black students as being untrue to their cultural and racial group; they risk isolation and alienation from White peers in the gifted program who do not understand Black students; they risk being under the guidance of teachers who do not understand them. These feelings of isolation and alienation may result in a forced choice between friendships and school. In this emotional tug-of-war, the school and gifted program too often lose.

RECOMMENDATIONS

Reducing prejudice is essential, given the increasing heterogeneity of students and society. Approaches must be learning oriented rather than treatment oriented. Ultimately, we cannot place the responsibility for change directly on the shoulders of students. Educators and other school personnel must seek training in multicultural education that is extensive and ongoing. Black students must feel empowered and have a sense of belonging within and outside school. Teachers and counselors are in an ideal position to empower all students to be culturally sensitive and aware.

Coping Effectively With Feelings

Daily, many students deal with feelings of stress, anxiety, frustration, and anger that interrupt the learning process. For gifted and underachieving Black youth, prejudice may be a daily reality, a persistent reminder of their marginal social and racial status. Consequently, they may come to school angry, enraged, and estranged from schools and educators. When students cannot cope with their angry feelings, the result may be violence, crime, substance abuse, depression, and self-destructive behaviors, including suicide. Further, Black students may choose their teachers and classmates as targets for venting their emotions. Problematic behaviors, however, are not an individual's total personality and behavioral repertoire; they are responses to how students perceive their environment and how they are being treated.

Relaxation training, stress management, and conflict resolution are recommended for helping gifted and underachieving Black students to cope effectively with their feelings. Once they understand stress and how their bodies respond to stress, they will come to see that stress is inevitable and that anxiety and anger can be normal, healthy responses. Helpful exercises include breathing techniques, muscular relaxation, mental imagery, and biofeedback. It is important to provide underachievers and gifted Black students with coping strategies for releasing excessive emotions — walking, singing, writing, or talking, for example. Society expects males to maintain a macho image that negates emotions. It is therefore particularly important that Black males be allowed to *feel* and to *accept* their emotions; that they learn to express their emotions by talking as well as crying. However, schools have not always encouraged the expression of feelings, including the role of feelings in the learning process (Wittmer & Myrick, 1989). Students should be encouraged to ask for time-out, and they need a safe environment where they can vent their frustrations. Other outlets include group counseling, where gifted and underachieving Black students can discuss their concerns and experiences and share effective coping behaviors. For example, Peterson (1990) developed a noon-hour discussion group for gifted students. Topics included stress, personality styles, testing, recognizing strengths and weaknesses, family conflicts, career concerns, and relationships. For Black students, discussions might also focus on coping with social injustices, negative peer pressures and relationships, and poor student–teacher relationships.

Dealing Effectively With Poor Peer Relations

One in six students does not have a friend in whom he or she can confide (Matter & Matter, 1985), and 19% of schoolchildren may be considered social isolates (Byrnes, 1984). Loneliness and isolation are of special concern to educators for various reasons. Specifically, good interpersonal relationships and feelings of relatedness and belonging are considered essential to mental health (Maslow, 1954, 1968; Murray, 1938). Persistent feelings of isolation make students vulnerable to depression, juvenile delinquency, physical illness, and suicide.

The need to belong and to have friends is important for all children; it may be especially important for Black students who participate in racially and culturally homogeneous (predominantly White) gifted programs. The few Black youths in such programs are likely to experience feelings of alienation and isolation, as well as question how they fit into the overall classroom dynamics. Counselors, in collaboration with teachers, can positively influence the classroom dynamics and increase its sense of community so that schools truly become sanctuaries for learning—welcoming rather than alienating places for gifted and underachieving Black students.

Groups have a powerful emotional influence on members, and classrooms represent an important arena for fostering cohesion and belonging. Competition tends to bring out the best in products and the worst in people. Group work and cooperative activities are essential for promoting social contact among minority and White students. Time spent in shared and noncompetitive activities can encourage friendships and decrease students' fears, stereotypes, and feelings of social isolation. Teachers and counselors can help underachievers and gifted Black students discover interests similar to those of other students; they can encourage them to join clubs and organizations, for instance, based on those interests.

Teachers can also work with counselors to create more opportunities for interaction and to build positive and trusting peer relationships. For instance, peer tutoring can be effective in maximizing positive classroom interactions, friendships, and prosocial behaviors, as well as self-esteem and achievement among Black students considered at risk for academic failure. Academic support groups can also improve students' achievement motivation and academic self-concepts.

Cognitive skills training can help gifted Black students explore self-defeating thought processes that contribute to loneliness and inappropriate behaviors (such as attention seeking, becoming the class clown, putting sports before academics). Social skills training includes focusing on conversational skills, asking questions, initiating conversations, giving constructive feedback and comments, and accepting feedback. The best way to prepare students for a satisfying life is to give them a wide repertoire of techniques for lifelong learning.

SUMMARY

Social and environmental factors can hinder the successful identification of gifted Black students and contribute to academic difficulties, including academic burnout. Academic burnout is characterized by emotional exhaustion, depersonalization, and feelings of low personal accomplishment. Low societal expectations, racism, job ceilings, and other forms of discrimination call into question the social justice quotient for Black students. Yet schools can and should be proactive in empowering Black students to deal effectively with social inequities.

Educators must also consider the influence of peer pressure and relationships on students' achievement and effort. Pressure from peers to forgo achievement can undermine the academic success of gifted Black students. The fear associated with losing friends and being isolated from peers because of outstanding achievement can undermine the motivation and effort of gifted Black students. As Tomlinson (1992) observed:

> Peer pressure profoundly influences the academic behavior of students. . . .
> Typically, peer pressure motivates students to stay in school and graduate,
> but even as they frown on failure, peers also restrain high achievement. . . .
> Some student cultures actively reject academic aspirations. In this case, high
> grades can be a source of peer ridicule; and when effort is hostage to peer
> pressure, those high achievers who persist may face strong social sanctions.
> (p. 2)

Because all students need to feel a sense of competence and social belonging, we must direct more attention to their affective or socioemotional needs. And we cannot ignore the extent to which underachievement is shaped by social factors, particularly injustices and inequities.

Chapter 5

Cultural Factors as Correlates
of Underachievement

All social groups face different survival problems and have to adapt to many kinds of environments. There is a great variety of cultures and cultural forms around the world.

—Bullivant, 1993, p. 36

The topic of cultural differences has significantly impacted current research and practice, with data pointing to an ever-increasing cultural gap between teachers and Black students. The term *culture* is often used, misused, and abused. This chapter takes culture to mean those values, beliefs, attitudes, and norms unique to a group bound by race, gender, location, religion, or social class. Shade and Edwards (1987) defined culture as the collective consciousness of a community with its own unique customs, rituals, communication style, coping patterns, social organization, and childbearing attitudes and patterns. Shade and New (1993) defined culture as an aggregation of beliefs, attitudes, habits, values, and practices that form one's view of reality. These patterns function as a filter through which a group or an individual views and responds to environmental demands. Cultural patterns are generally invisible and silent; they are experienced by individuals in terms of acting, feeling, and being (Hall, 1959).

STRANDS OF CULTURAL THEORY

Just as social and psychological factors affect Black students' motivation to achieve and their school performance, so too do cultural forces. When the values of both Black and mainstream cultures mesh, Black students are likely to reach their academic potential. However, when the values are different, antithetical, or even conflicting, underachievement may prevail. In general, three strands of theory attempt to explain the school

83

performance of racial minorities: cultural deficit, cultural difference, and cultural conflict. All these theories carry different implications for the educational outcomes of gifted Black students.

Cultural Deficit Theories

Cultural deficit theories hold that the culture in which Black children are reared is inadequate relative to socialization practices. These theories carry a "blame the victim" orientation, and supporters look upon Blacks and other minority groups as not only culturally but also intellectually inferior.

According to deficit theories or perspectives, "different" is equated with deficient, inferior, and substandard. Educators may cite cultural deficits as a reason for the disproportionately low achievement and intelligence test scores of minority students and, hence, their underrepresentation in gifted programs. According to this view, if Black students test poorly, they must not be gifted. The fault does not rest with biased or irrelevant tests and related identification practices. This point of view ignores teacher biases and historical and contemporary racism. Proponents are strongly against broadening assessment tools and practices, for fear of "contaminating" gifted programs with people who are not truly gifted.

Shade (1978) argued that social science has been able to alleviate any social guilt that might be generated by placing the blame for their academic difficulties on Blacks themselves. Specifically, apologists for our current educational practices ground their conclusions in stigma theory, enabling them to define the problem in terms of bored, unmotivated, and apathetic children influenced by a less than adequate home environment. But if the home environment were not at least initially stimulating, these children would come to preschool and kindergarten bored and apathetic. But they do not. Regardless of their environment, nearly all children initially enter school with a sense of wonder and awe. They are bright-eyed, curious, and ready to learn (Bitting, Cordeiro, & Baptiste, 1992, p. 25).

Cultural Difference Theories

Herskovitz (1958) was a forerunner in identifying values inherent in the Black culture, including funeral practices, religious practices, dances, songs, belief in magic, and the concept of time. His work negated the prevailing belief that Blacks lacked a unique culture. Instead, he argued that Blacks retained much of the African culture after slavery. This cultural competence involves more than learning a conglomeration of superficial aspects such as dance, hairstyle, or other artifacts.

Cultural styles and orientations represent patterns learned at an early age, as one grows up in a given family and community context. As individuals move out of the context of this primary socialization, they respond to new situations with previously learned behaviors and styles. When individuals encounter unfamiliar cultural patterns in these new situations, they may have difficulty making a transition. For Black students, such a new situation may include being placed in a gifted program where teachers and school personnel may not understand their cultural styles and orientations. It is hypothesized that the less congruence there is between home and school, the more difficult the cultural transition and the more negative a student's educational outcome (Vogt, Jordan, & Tharp, 1987). Boykin (1994) examined the cultural styles of Blacks, and although he did not focus specifically on gifted Black youth, it is only reasonable to conclude that they too have adopted cultural styles such as the following:

(1) *Spirituality*: An approach to life that is vitalistic rather than mechanistic, with the conviction that nonmaterial religious forces influence people's everyday lives. It connotes an acceptance of a nonmaterial higher force that pervades all of life's affairs.

(2) *Harmony*: The notion that one's fate is interrelated with other elements in the scheme of things so that humankind and nature are harmonically conjoined. Harmony implies that one's functioning is inextricably linked to nature's order and that one should be synchronized with this order. As such, Black students who are gifted in the visual and performing arts may demonstrate a special sensitivity to harmony.

(3) *Movement*: An emphasis on the interweaving of movement, rhythm, music, and dance, which are considered central to psychological health. It connotes a premium placed on the amalgamation of movement, (poly)rhythm, dance, and percussion embodied in the musical beat; kinesthetic preferences and psychomotor intelligence may be especially evident among these students.

(4) *Verve*: A propensity for relatively high levels of stimulation and for action that is energetic and lively. It connotes a particular receptiveness to relatively high levels of sensate (i.e., intensity and variability of) stimulation; this may be especially evident among students with tactile needs and psychomotor intelligence.

(5) *Affect*: An emphasis on emotions and feelings, together with a special sensitivity to emotional cues and a tendency to be emotionally responsive. This implies the centrality of affective information and emotional expressiveness and the equal and integrated importance of thoughts and feelings; intrapersonal intelligence may be manifested by Black students in this area.

(6) *Communalism*: A commitment to social connectedness that includes an awareness that social bonds and responsibilities transcend individual privileges. This implies a commitment to the fundamental interdependence of people and to the importance of social bonds, relationships, and the transcendence of the group; interpersonal intelligence may be most apparent for Black students in this area.

(7) *Oral tradition*: A preference for oral modes of communication in which both speaking and listening are treated as performances. Oral virtuosity — the ability to use metaphorically colorful, graphic forms of spoken language — is emphasized and cultivated. This connotes the centrality of oral and aural modes of communication for conveying full meaning and the cultivation of speaking as performance. Black students who are gifted in verbal endeavors may show special sensitivity to the oral traditional found among minority cultures.

(8) *Expressive individualism*: The cultivation of a distinctive personality and a proclivity for spontaneity and genuine personal expression. This denotes the uniqueness of personal expression, personal style.

(9) *Social time perspective*: An orientation to time that is treated as passing through a social space in which time is recurring, personal, and phenomenological. This denotes a commitment to a social construction of time as personified by an event orientation.

The frames of reference held by Blacks and Whites are noncommensurable. And although they are not quite polar opposites, there are fundamental incompatibilities between them. When White educators understand the cultural characteristics of Blacks in terms of their integrity and uniqueness, they will have found the missing link in the equitable education of these students. Once their distinctiveness is acknowledged, the cultural capital of Black students will be valued and respected.

Cultural Conflict Theories

Unlike deficit theories, conflict theories acknowledge and respect cultural differences. Conflict theories hold that resistance to assimilation is a form of self-protection. Because the socialization processes of Blacks and Whites may differ significantly, racial minority students have distinct cultural values that may conflict with the dominant culture. This disharmony can negatively affect the education and subsequent achievement of Black students. Thus, unlike White students, Black students must simultaneously manipulate two cultures that may be quite diverse. Students who are unable to make this negotiation confront additional problems in school.

Underachievement increases when the values, beliefs, norms, and attitudes of members of the Black culture are inconsistent with those espoused by the majority culture and most schools. In many instances, academically unsuccessful Black students' skills, knowledge, and learning orientation are in conflict with those of the formal classroom.

CULTURAL FACTORS, SCHOOLING, AND UNDERACHIEVEMENT

When Black students enter the educational arena, they do not shed their cultural backgrounds and orientations. Too many Black students who do poorly in school experience cultural discongruency or discontinuity and social-code incompatibility; they have difficulty shifting their cultural styles to fit school norms and expectations. The result, as described below, is a gap between the contexts of learning and the contexts of performing.

Behavioral Styles

School norms consistently include conformity, passivity, cooperation, quietness, individualized instruction, independence, competition, and teacher-directed instruction. Although teaching styles may reflect the dominant cultural establishment, they do not necessarily reflect what is best and most productive for many students, too many of whom are unwilling and unable to conform to the aforementioned norms.

The model student sits quietly in his seat, asks few questions, works passively and independently, completes assignments in the prescribed manner, and does not challenge the teacher. In general, however, these behaviors may not represent the behaviors that are most comfortable for Black students. For instance, some Black students have difficulty staying in their seats and otherwise being immobile. DellaValle's (1984) study revealed that almost half of Black junior high school students could not sit still for protracted periods of time; 25% could sit when interested, and only 25% engaged in teacher-preferred passivity. Black students also tend to be more socially oriented and extroverted than White students. Boykin's (1986) research, cited earlier, highlights the behavioral verve that is so common among Black students. Many Black students live in environments that condition them to expect a variety of social interactions. Thus, part of the school failure of Black students can be attributed to their inability to master social codes of behavior — codes that they are expected to adopt, but are seldom taught, in school.

Communication Styles

Styles of speaking among Blacks are characterized by expression and affect. Blacks are more persuasive and theatrical; show great emotion; have high levels of energy; and ask more questions, particularly when inconsistencies and injustices are noticed. Similarly, the communication styles of Black students are often (mis)interpreted as confrontational, particularly when verbal communication is accompanied by nonverbal communication (e.g., body language, facial expressions, intonations) that adds strength or momentum to their words.

Racially and culturally diverse students learn early that their communication styles are significantly different from those espoused in school. The most obvious indications of communication differences are bilingualism or fluency in more than one dialect. Schools and standardized tests reward English-only and standard dialect orientations. Students who are unable to code-switch and who are not proficient in standard English often have difficulty achieving and demonstrating their potential in school. For some Black students, frustration and cognitive overload result when they have difficulty translating two languages or dialects.

Learning Styles

As discussed in Chapter 3, a promising area of research in education centers on learning style preferences among students. Because of cultural differences in learning styles, students require an eclectic approach to curriculum and instruction; this approach accommodates individual differences in learning by using multiple approaches, models, and strategies — concrete and abstract, whole-to-part and part-to-whole, visual and auditory, hands-on — that reflect the diverse ways students acquire knowledge.

A MODEL OF SOCIAL AND CULTURAL UNDERACHIEVEMENT: RESISTANCE TO CROSSING CULTURAL BORDERS

One's type of minority status has a significant impact on learning and educational outcomes. According to Ogbu's theory (1983), there are three types of minority statuses, each with different experiences in society and schools: autonomous, immigrant-voluntary, and castelike-involuntary. *Autonomous minorities* are minorities in number only; they include Jewish, Mormon, and Amish groups. Because there are no non-White autonomous minorities in the United States, this section focuses on the remaining two groups. *Voluntary minorities* (e.g., Asian Americans) moved to the United States because of their desire for greater economic and political independence, as well as greater overall opportunities. They came to the United States in search of the American dream. *Involuntary minorities* were brought to the United States against their will.

Both voluntary and involuntary minorities have primary cultural differences that existed prior to immigration, such as communication styles and behaviors, cognitive or learning styles, interaction styles, child-rearing practices, and values. However, involuntary minorities developed secondary cultural differences in reaction to their superior-inferior or dominant-subordinate status. An important feature of secondary cultural differences is cultural inversion — the tendency to regard certain behaviors, events, and symbols as inappropriate for Blacks because they are characteristic of Whites. In other words, in reaction to oppression, Black students may choose to oppose the values espoused in schools. By opposing those values, behaviors, and attitudes associated with White students, Black students develop a stronger social or collective identity.

Unlike secondary cultural differences, primary cultural differences do not develop in response to opposition, nor to protect one's collective identity, self-worth, or feelings of security. Voluntary minorities do not perceive school achievement, for example, as threatening or as giving up one's collective or social identity. Rather, they perceive themselves as "accommodating without assimilating." In effect, they accept biculturality and perceive that "playing the game by the rules" will yield long-term gains — employment, upward mobility, and the realization of the American dream. With these beliefs, voluntary minorities are able to cross cultural boundaries.

The picture is different for involuntary minorities, such as Blacks. Historically, such groups as Blacks, Native Americans, and Hispanic Americans have been denied equitable educational and employment opportunities; they have been relegated to menial social positions that keep them submerged in the underclass and among the educationally disadvantaged. The degree to which gifted Black students support the achievement ideology cannot be overlooked by educators. Individuals who support the achievement ideology increase their chances of succeeding both in school and in life. Such students support the values of middle-class Whites; they believe that one's chances for success and upward mobility increase with effort and hard work. However, such support may not necessarily be found among gifted Black students who underachieve. The achievement ideology represents an important motivator. Essentially, most theories describe achievement motivation using the "expectancy by value" paradigm. Achievement motivation increases when one hopes for and expects success and when one values the task and goal. However, the major shortcoming of motivation theories is their inattention to the social and cultural contexts that affect achievement. All children are born with the motive to achieve; ideally, prior to negative experiences or stimuli, all children are motivated to achieve.

RECOMMENDATIONS

Locke (1989, p. 254) recommended several strategies to enhance social and multicultural competence among professionals:

(1) Be open to the existence of culturally sensitive values and attitudes among students; be honest in relationships with minority students.

(2) Avoid stereotyping racial minority groups (retain the uniqueness of each student); strive to keep a reasonable balance between your views of students as human beings and cultural group members; teach all students how to recognize stereotypes and how to challenge biases and injustices.

(3) Ask questions about culturally and racially diverse students. Encourage gifted Black students to discuss and be open about their concerns, beliefs, and cultural values; talk positively with students about their physical and cultural heritage; make sure that students understand that one's race and ethnicity are never acceptable reasons for being rejected.

(4) Hold high expectations for all students, and encourage others to do likewise.

(5) Participate in the communities of culturally and racially diverse students; learn their customs and values; share this information with students, teachers, and other colleagues.

(6) Encourage school personnel to acknowledge the strengths and recognize the contributions of racial and cultural groups.

(7) Learn about your own culture and cultural values.

With these guidelines, tolerance and acceptance of differences can become commonplace in schools. The initiatives used by teachers and counselors to facilitate intragroup cohesion and support should be multifaceted (eclectic, with varied activities and services); inclusionary (engaging teachers, students, family members, administrators, and other school staff and personnel); developmental (holistic and proactive rather than reactive; prevention and intervention oriented); and continuous and substantive.

Banks and Banks (1993) focused on levels of integration of multicultural content into the curriculum (Figure 5.1). In Level 1, the *contributions approach*, educators focus on heroes, holidays, and discrete elements. This is the most frequently adopted and extensively used approach to multiculturalism in schools. An important characteristic of this approach is that the traditional ethnocentric or monocultural curriculum remains unchanged in its basic structure, goals, and salient characteristics. Students are introduced to racially and culturally diverse heroes such as Crispus Attucks, Martin Luther King Jr., Booker T. Washington, Harriet Tubman, and Benjamin Banneker. These individuals, however, are usually discussed in relation to White heroes such as George Washington and Thomas Jefferson. Further, individuals who challenged the predominant

FIGURE 5.1. Levels of integration of multicultural content into the curriculum (adapted from Banks and Banks, 1993).

Level 4
The Social Action Approach

Students make decisions on important social issues and take actions to help solve them. Students become empowered to make meaningful contributions to the resolution of social issues and problems.

Level 3
The Transformational Approach

The structure of the curriculum is changed to enable students to view concepts, issues, events, and themes from the perspectives of diverse racial and cultural groups. Educators are active and proactive in seeking training and experience with racially and culturally diverse groups.

Level 2
The Additive Approach

Content, concepts, themes, and perspectives are added to the curriculum without changing its structure. Students fail to understand how the predominant culture interacts with and is related to racially and culturally diverse groups.

Level 1
The Contributions Approach

Focuses on heroes, holidays, and discrete cultural elements. Students acquire a superficial understanding of racially and culturally diverse groups.

culture's ideologies, values, and conceptions and who advocated radical social, political, and economic reform are often ignored in this approach. As a result, Martin Luther King Jr. is more likely to be discussed than Malcolm X; Booker T. Washington is more likely to be discussed than W. E. B. Du Bois. The result is that the heroes who are acceptable to White Americans rather than those who are valued by racially and culturally diverse groups are discussed with students.

Another characteristic of this level is that cultural traditions, foods, music, and dance may be discussed, but little (if any) attention is given to their meaning and significance to racially and culturally diverse groups. Also within this level is the "heroes and holidays approach," in which ethnic content is limited primarily to special days, weeks, and months related to racial and cultural groups (e.g., Black History Week or Month, Martin Luther King Jr.'s birthday). Students learn little or nothing about the occasion, group, or individual being "celebrated." The contributions approach is quite superficial; it provides teachers with a quick, nonthreatening way to "integrate" the curriculum, and teachers can adopt this approach without knowing much about racially and culturally diverse groups. It can also reinforce stereotypes and misconceptions about diverse groups and uses safe, nonthreatening heroes who are acceptable to the predominant culture.

In Level 2, the *additive approach*, the content, concepts, themes, and perspectives of racially and culturally diverse groups are added to the curriculum without changing its structure. For instance, teachers may add a book, unit, or course to the curriculum that focuses on diverse groups or topics. Again, although the content changes slightly, there is little restructuring of the curriculum relative to purposes and characteristics. This approach requires little time, effort, training, or rethinking of the curriculum in terms of its nature, purpose, and goals. For instance, Black students learn little of their own history, and White students learn little of the true history and contributions of other racial and cultural groups to American society. Students reading *The Autobiography of Malcolm X*, for example, lack the concepts, content background, and emotional maturity to understand, appreciate, respect, and deal effectively with the issues and problems discussed in the book. The additive approach fails to help all students view society from diverse perspectives and to understand how the histories and cultures of the nation's diverse racial, cultural, ethnic, and religious groups are interconnected (Banks & Banks, 1993, p. 202).

In the third level, the *transformational approach*, the structure of the curriculum is changed to enable students to view concepts, issues, events, and themes from the perspectives of diverse racial and cultural groups. This is a fundamental change from the previous levels; one now sees changes in the basic assumptions, goals, nature, and structure of the curriculum. A primary objective is to help students feel empowered. According to Banks and Banks (1993), the curriculum should not focus on how various racial and cultural groups have contributed to mainstream society and culture; instead, it should focus on how the common U.S. culture and society emerged from a complex synthesis and interaction of diverse cultural elements. This approach requires extensive curriculum revision, teacher training, time, and effort.

In Level 4, the *social action approach*, students make decisions on important social issues and take action to help solve them. Students are not socialized to accept unquestioningly the existing ideologies, institutions, and practices of the predominant group. At this level, students not only feel empowered; they are proactive. They are provided with the knowledge, values, and skills necessary to participate in social change. Student self-examination becomes central in this approach through value analysis, decision making, problem solving, and social action skills. For example, students examine issues surrounding prejudice and discrimination and develop ways to improve race relations. This approach is least likely to be adopted by educators, primarily because teachers often lack training, experience, understanding, and personal knowledge of other minority groups (e.g., histories, values, beliefs, customs). Equally important, few teachers adopt proactive strategies and philosophies themselves, and the majority come from ethnocentrically oriented educational programs. Even at institutions of higher education, curriculum and instruction are at Banks and Banks' (1993) Levels 1 and 2.

Gifted Black learners are hungry for curriculum that reflects diversity, pluralism, equity, and the unacceptability of racism, sexism, and discrimination. Because the infusion of multicultural education into the content is empowering for Black students, multiculturalism must continually permeate the curriculum for gifted students. For instance, a Black History Month each February provides insufficient time to infuse gifted Black students with pride in their racial and cultural heritage and the contributions of their ancestors to American history. All children, regardless of race, benefit from both multiethnic education (which focuses on race and ethnicity) and multicultural education (which focuses on human diversity and individual differences in gender, race, socioeconomic status, and geographic origins). A lack of racial diversity in a school or community, and in a gifted program, cannot be used as a rationale for the absence of multicultural education.

Further, because of cultural differences in learning styles, changes in instruction are essential if Black students are to succeed (Figure 5.2). In Level 1, *assimilation of learning styles*, students are required to assimi-

FIGURE 5.2. Levels of accommodation and assimilation of instruction.

Level 4
Accommodation of Learning and Teaching Styles

Both teachers and students are active participants in students' success. Instruction becomes a partnership between students and teachers. Teachers are aware of and respectful of learning styles; students are aware of and respectful of teaching preferences. Essentially, both students and teachers are proactive and bistylistic.

Level 3
Accommodation of Learning Styles

Students are *taught* how to be bistylistic and socially competent in an academic setting. Students are competent at matching their learning styles to teaching styles and the context. Although teachers may be aware of and sensitive to students' learning style preferences, they may be resistant to certain in-class student accommodations. Thus, students' success is strongly dependent on teacher support.

Level 2
Accomodation of Teaching Styles

Teachers adapt their teaching styles to students' learning styles. Students do not learn to adapt their learning styles to the context. The responsibility for change resides with the teacher rather than students--teachers are active and students are passive recipients. This approach may foster academic incompetence among students.

Level 1
Assimilation of Learning Styles

This approach is most often adopted in schools. Students adapt their learning styles to teaching styles and contexts. For example, visual learners are required but not taught to be auditory learners. Students bear the greatest responsibility for change and for success.

---

late — to give up their learning style preferences in order to succeed in school. For instance, most schools cater to students who prefer lecture-based instruction and are passive, abstract, and auditory learners. Yet Black students tend to prefer didactic learning experiences, and they are often visual, concrete, tactile, and kinesthetic learners. Teachers bear little responsibility for modifying their instruction; students bear responsibility for modifying their learning. This "swim or sink" approach is reminiscent of the melting pot philosophy.

In the second level, *accommodation of teaching styles*, teachers modify the process — how the material is presented and taught. Through either intuition or formal training, teachers attempt to adapt their teaching styles to their students' learning styles. Teachers are the active participants, and students are passive. In this sense, teachers adopt the siphon philosophy, where information is poured into students' heads. This philosophy assumes that teachers possess all knowledge, and that they cannot learn from students. At the individual student level, teachers may modify assignments for students. At the class level, they may use both visual and auditory modes of instruction. With this approach, students can become dependent on teachers who are willing to make modifications in their instruction. When students encounter teachers who adopt the assimilationist approach, they are more likely to experience stylistic conflicts, frustration, and failure. These students become academically incompetent because they lack the skills necessary to achieve with different teaching styles and in different academic settings.

In Level 3, *accommodation of learning styles*, students and teachers are bistylistic. Students depend less on teachers to modify instruction (Level 2), and there is less need for students to bear the sole responsibility for change (Level 1). At this level, students are more academically competent; they can adapt their learning styles to the learning context (e.g., teaching style, instruction, curriculum). For example, visual learners know how to reorganize notes presented in a lecture format to depict models and diagrams; others use tape recorders, borrow notes from classmates, work with classmates to capture themes and concepts, and so forth. Without teacher support, however, in-school modifications or accommodations (e.g., use of tape recorders) may not be possible.

In the fourth level, *accommodation of learning and teaching styles*, both students and teachers are active participants and partners. Teachers are aware of students' learning styles and related needs; similarly, students are aware of and respectful of teachers' instructional preferences. There is mutual understanding, respect, and accommodation of differences and preferences.

Essentially, the model asks three central questions: Are minority students required to assimilate or accommodate their learning styles? To what extent do teachers accommodate their teaching styles to alternative learning styles? To what extent are students taught and do teachers seek to be bistylistic?

SUMMARY

This chapter focused on some of the primary issues facing gifted and underachieving Black students. It emphasized that teachers and counselors have many roles and responsibilities that call for increased attention to cultural factors affecting Black students' achievement and motivation. It also stressed that cultural differences do not have to work to the detriment of these students.

Gifted Black youth are first and foremost human beings in need of understanding, caring, respect, and empathy. Given the nation's changing demographics, educators are experiencing increased contact with Black and other minority students. With an understanding of their needs, educators and school personnel can better serve this student population by celebrating diversity and advocating for the human rights of all students. It is incumbent upon school personnel to help Black students manage and appreciate their gifts, as well as their racial and cultural heritage.

Most educators do not teach minority students how to survive and succeed in school, for example, how to study cross-cultural learning styles, how to adjust communication styles to accommodate school experiences, how to interact appropriately with school administrators and teachers, and how to identify the procedural rules for functioning in different instructional classrooms (G. Gay, 1993). What too many educators fail to remember is that many racially and culturally diverse students live on the margins of the mainstream culture; they have neither a heritage nor a tradition of success in predominantly White schools and gifted programs.

The core cultural ideals of equality, justice, freedom, and democracy carry far-reaching implications for the education of gifted and underachieving Black students. A major function of schools should be the adoption of pluralism, which entails helping all students to acquire the knowledge, skills, and attitudes needed to function effectively within the mainstream culture, within their own cultures, and within and across other cultures.

Chapter 6

Psychological Factors as Correlates of Underachievement

Gifted students are in jeopardy of not reaching their potential in school and in life, particularly if their academic, psychological, and socioemotional needs are not adequately addressed (Manaster & Powell, 1983). Historically, however, those in the education and mental health professions have given little attention to counseling gifted students. Rather, the primary focus has been on educating gifted learners — meeting their academic and vocational needs. Yet, as Silverman (1993) notes, giftedness has both cognitive and emotional components — not only do gifted students *think* differently from their peers, they also *feel* differently (p. 3).

The purpose of this chapter is to help bridge the fields of education and counseling, focusing in particular on the psychological concerns of gifted and underachieving Black students. Whereas Black and White students share many problems and concerns associated with being gifted, Black students also have other issues to contend with as they endeavor to achieve in school and in life. These differences are both quantitative and qualitative. The literature on gifted students frequently ignores these differential needs. This chapter proposes that psychological variables are linked directly to the academic achievement of gifted Black students. Examined are such variables as anxiety, locus of control, self-concept, racial identity, survival conflict, and a paradox of underachievement. Teachers and school counselors must be aware of and sensitive to the unique and individual problems that gifted Black students present to them. As reflected throughout this chapter, counselors and psychologists are in an ideal position to ensure that Black students remain in gifted programs once they are identified and placed; counselors represent an important component of both the recruitment and the retention of Black students in gifted programs.

HISTORICAL OVERVIEW OF THE COUNSELING
MOVEMENT IN GIFTED EDUCATION

The movement in counseling gifted students has been attributed to Lewis Terman (1925) and Leta Hollingworth (1926). Terman's longitudinal study of middle-class White children helped dispel many myths and stereotypes about gifted learners. One myth was that gifted children were inherently well adjusted and, consequently, did not need counseling services. Hollingworth also found that gifted students are not immune from psychological and socioemotional difficulties. Perhaps her greatest contribution was calling attention to the gap between a gifted student's intellectual and emotional development, often described as "old heads on young shoulders."

It was not until the 1950s that increased attention was devoted to counseling gifted students (Colangelo, 1991). Labs and guidance programs were established at several universities. Various scholars highlighted the heretofore ignored issues related to suicide, depression, perfectionism, self-concept, self-esteem, anxiety, and poor peer relations among gifted students.

The history of counseling gifted students regarding their psychological and socioemotional concerns, although not new, remains in its infancy. In particular, few counselors have addressed the affective needs of gifted students, and the term *emotion* is conspicuously absent in the indexes of most books on the gifted and talented, indicating that too little attention has been paid to this important issue (Silverman, 1993). A search of ERIC and PsycLIT abstracts revealed a dismally small number of articles on the counseling of gifted students. Specifically, between 1966 and 1995, 65 articles appeared in ERIC; only 4 appeared in PsycLIT between 1987 and 1994. This paucity of information is even greater relative to gifted Black students. To date, only four articles referenced in the above databases focused exclusively or specifically on counseling gifted Black students from psychological and socioemotional perspectives (see D. Y. Ford & Harris, 1995a, 1995b; D. Y. Ford, Harris, & Schuerger, 1993; D. Y. Ford, Schuerger, & Harris, 1991).

Similarly, there are a limited number of books specifically on counseling gifted students (e.g., Kerr, 1991; Milgrim, 1993; Silverman, 1993) and meeting their social and emotional needs (e.g., Delisle, 1992; Schmitz & Galbraith, 1985; Webb, Meckstroth, & Tolan, 1982). These books contain perfunctory chapters on *special populations*, a term that has become synonymous with minority (most often Black) students. It is unfortunate that the issues confronting gifted minority students are not interwoven throughout the texts, as such an approach would highlight the heterogeneity that exists within the gifted population.

A few studies have explored public school counselors' awareness of issues confronting gifted students, as well as their preparation to work with this student population. Findings indicate that few school counselors and psychologists are formally prepared to work with gifted learners. For example, Klausmeier, Mishra, and Maker (1987) found that most school counselors considered their preparation in recognizing gifted students to be less than average and their training with minorities and low socioeconomic groups to be below average or completely lacking. In their study of state certification endorsement for school counselors in special education, Frantz and Prillaman (1993) found that 11 states required at least one course in special education for certification as a school counselor, 17 were in the process of changing certification requirements for counselors and considering the inclusion of a course in special education, and another 17 states neither required any courses nor were considering changes in certification. D. Y. Ford and Harris (1995b) found, in a national study of university counselors, that only 1 in 10 had training in working with gifted learners. The findings also indicated that the majority of counselors were unaware of or indecisive about the differential issues hindering the achievement of both gifted Black and gifted White students.

Seemingly, counselors have not been an integral part of gifted education, and their roles have been limited primarily to academic counseling and assessment and placement issues. Unfortunately, as Gerler, Kinney, and Anderson (1985) noted, educators and policy makers frequently do not recognize counselors' contributions to students' success in school. Because more children are entering school with serious personal problems, the roles and responsibilities of counselors must change and expand to meet the needs of all students who seek their guidance and assistance (Welch & McCarroll, 1993).

PSYCHOLOGICAL PROBLEMS OF GIFTED YOUTH

Educators and psychologists have associated various psychological problems with gifted students. Dirkes (1985) reported that gifted students tend to have an external locus of control, a low sense of adequacy, and feelings of isolation and self-contempt. Issues related to isolation, locus of control, anxiety, self-esteem, self-concept, and racial identity development are discussed in this chapter, as these factors have a significant impact on students' educational well-being.

Isolation

As discussed in Chapter 4, underachieving and gifted Black students often feel alienated from, unaccepted by, and unconnected to others. They may become introverted as a result of the comparatively small quantity and reduced quality of their socioemotional relationships. The sense of not belonging has also been viewed as the basis of highly gifted students' psychological and socioemotional maladjustments. Issues surrounding isolation are especially important for Black students and other minority students in predominantly White schools and gifted programs. They may have difficulty forming friendships or building social networks in such programs.

Gifted students often face the dilemma of choosing to satisfy their drive for excellence at the risk of sacrificing relationships with peers (Gross, 1989). If friendship is more important, gifted Black students might choose to underachieve to avoid feelings of isolation, which suggests that gifted students who are forced to choose between socioemotional and achievement needs may sacrifice their "gift."

Locus of Control

An external locus of control is more strongly associated with academic underachievement than with achievement. Several studies (J. S. Coleman et al., 1966; Mackler, 1970; Shade, 1978) have found an external locus of control among poorly achieving Black students, particularly those who feel that they have little control over their educational outcomes due to social injustices and other barriers to social mobility and academic success. For example, too many Black students see Black adults in educational and occupational positions who hold little power and prestige. One has only to look at the positions held by Black and White employees in schools — teachers and administrators are most often White; janitors are most often Black. Some of these students have mothers and fathers with college degrees who are unemployed or underemployed. These discrepancies can contribute to an external locus of control among low SES Black students: Why bother with hard work or school? The payoffs are few and limited. Conversely, J. S. Coleman et al. (1966), Mackler (1970), and Shade (1978) reported that achieving and successful Black students perceive themselves as being internally controlled and in command of their academic and social destiny; accordingly, they hold high aspirations and expectations regarding success.

Anxiety

Anxiety comes in many guises — test anxiety, perfectionism, procrastination, and other manifestations of stress. Anxiety is a state marked by heightened self-awareness and perceived helplessness. Anxious individuals are unable to cope with task demands, are unable to understand the situation and related demands, are uncertain about consequences, feel inadequate in coping with demands, have unrealistic self- and other expectations, and are self-preoccupied. All these factors have physiological and behavioral effects, and they interfere with effective and successful task performance. Ineffective performance includes focusing on irrelevant information, misinterpreting test questions and directions, attention blocks or deficits, and self-preoccupation. Maladaptive coping strategies also accompany anxiety. For instance, the individual may cope through avoidance, procrastination, defensiveness, blaming, and anger — common descriptors of underachieving students.

Self-Esteem and Self-Concept

The terms *self-esteem* and *self-concept* are often used interchangeably. However, important and significant distinctions exist between the two. Self-esteem represents the affective component of one's self-perception; it represents the value we place on our worth as a person, a human being. Self-concept represents the cognitive view we hold of ourselves — what we think about our abilities in various areas. One can have low self-esteem but have a high or positive general self-concept; the reverse is also possible.

Self-concept is often referred to as if it were a unidimensional, global construct. However, individuals have self-concepts. The general self-concept, according to Shavelson, Bolus, and Keesling (1980), comprises academic and nonacademic self-concepts. Academic self-concept refers to a student's self-perception in specific subject matters, such as English, math, the sciences, and history. Nonacademic self-concept includes social (e.g., self-perception with peers and significant others), emotional (e.g., feelings and other affective states), and physical (e.g., appearance, strength, health) aspects. One must also examine self-concept domains in specific situations or contexts rather than in isolation from the environment.

Although there are numerous studies of gifted students' self-concepts, few empirical studies have been conducted using gifted Black students as the primary focus. The paucity of research in this area prevents one from drawing definitive conclusions about the roles of self-concept domains in the achievement of gifted Black students. However, by examining the research conducted on the self-concepts of both gifted students and Black students in general, some implications can be drawn.

Cooley, Cornell, and Lee (1991) compared the self-concept domains of gifted Black and White students in grades 5 through 11 and found no significant difference between the measures of academic and social self-concepts of the two groups. Bartley (1980) examined the self-concept scores of Black and White secondary students, including gifted students, and found similarities in the academic self-concepts of the two groups; in fact, Black students had slightly higher general self-concepts than White students. Haynes, Hamilton-Lee, and Comer (1988) compared the self-concept scores of high, normal, and low achieving Black students. They found that high achievers scored highest in the academic, physical appearance, and overall happiness self-concept domains. The authors asserted that a positive relationship exists between academic achievement and self-concept domains in Black students. This assertion is supported by Mackler (1970), who found that achieving Black students have greater self-confidence and self-concepts than poor achieving Black students.

None of the studies just described has examined self-concept among Black students by considering their racial identity. How does racial identity influence the achievement and social relations of gifted Black students?

Racial Identity

An ignored but critically important variable related to the self-concepts of Black students is racial identity. Racial identity plays an important role in their psychological adjustment, academic motivation, and achievement (D. Y. Ford, Harris, & Schuerger, 1993; D. Y. Ford, Harris, Webb, & Jones, 1994). Figure 6.1 presents a model depicting racial identity as an integral component of a Black student's general self-concept. This model expands on the work of Shavelson et al. (1980) by including psychological self-concept as an integral component of nonacademic self-concept. Psychological self-concept includes racial and gender identities.

Black students encounter more barriers to racial identity development than do White students. Moreover, gifted Black students may experience more psychological and socioemotional problems than do Black students who are not identified as gifted. What factors contribute to such difficulties among gifted Black students? Maslow (1954) highlighted the significance of peoplehood and belonging when he suggested that a sense of belonging is essential for mental health. An unhealthy sense of belonging works in opposition to the sense of peoplehood. Peoplehood, which is based on more than just skin color, represents a cultural symbol of collective identity, ethnic consolidation, and mutual interdependence among Blacks. The term peoplehood implies the particular mind-set, or worldview, of those persons who are considered to be Black, and it is used to denote the moral judgment the group makes on its members.

Race creates a common referent of peoplehood, such that individuals

FIGURE 6.1. A multidimensional model of self-concept among Black students.

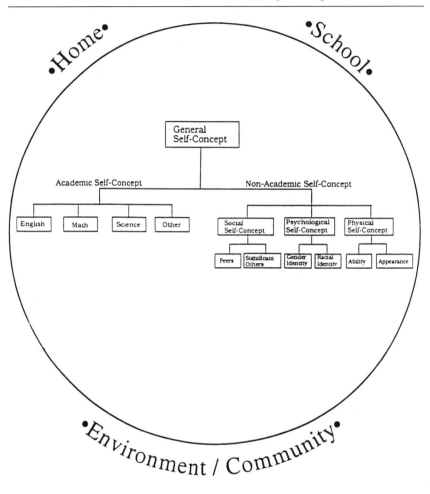

tend to define themselves in terms of membership in a particular group. In other words, the collective identity, in terms of race, represents the sense of ethnic belonging that is psychologically important for people. For Black students, this sense of peoplehood is challenged primarily in school, when school and community compete for the Black student's loyalty. For some Black students, the mere act of attending school is a semiconscious — or even conscious — rejection of the Black culture. School is seen by some

Black students and their families as a symbol of the dominant culture, which communicates both directly and indirectly that, to succeed, Blacks must become "un-Black" (Fordham, 1988, p. 58).

To reinforce the belief that they are still legitimate members of the Black community, gifted Black students may sabotage any chance they have of succeeding outside of it. With this "anti-achievement ethic" (Granat, Hathaway, Saleton, & Sansing, 1986, p. 166), gifted Black students may underachieve, drop out, camouflage their abilities, and otherwise fail to reach their academic potential in school. This underachievement may be especially evident when gifted Black students attend predominantly White schools. They may become confused about which cultural orientations to support. Because of the many factors that can influence the psychological well-being of gifted Black students, an analysis of racial identity development is necessary.

A Model of Racial Identity Development

Racial identity development is a process of coming to terms with one's racial group membership as a salient reference group. Cross (1971) developed a theory entitled the Negro-to-Black conversion to help explain the essence of racial identity for Blacks. The theory is characterized as a five-stage process: pre-encounter, encounter, immersion–emersion, internalization, and internalization–commitment.

Pre-encounter. During this initial stage of identity development, individuals view the world from a White frame of reference such that they think and behave in ways that negate their Blackness. Gifted Black students who are perceived as acting White by virtue of supporting tenets of the American achievement ideology, or by denying the existence of racism and social injustices based on race, might be placed in the pre-encounter stage. Butler (1975) concluded that pre-encounter individuals suffer from poor self-concept, apathy, confusion, self-deprecation, and detachment from the Black community. Cross (1995) reports that Blacks in this stage hold one of three attitudes regarding their social status: low racial salience, social stigma or victimization based on race, or self-hatred. For Black students in this stage, academic self-concept often takes precedence over social self-concept, and there appears to be little attention to one's self as a Black person. In essence, Black students want to be viewed as human beings rather than associated with any particular racial group. They wish to ignore, minimize, or deny their racial minority status and membership.

Encounter. This stage of development takes place when Black students experience an event that is inconsistent with their frame of reference. In the face of conflicting and startling information from such an encounter, Black students reevaluate their self-image, thereby becoming vulnerable and otherwise uncertain about their identity. Gifted Black students in predominantly White schools who are rejected by White peers because of skin color are likely to enter the encounter stage. This rejection can also come from White teachers. The subsequent realization and awareness of their minority status push these Black students to consciously develop a Black identity. Out of a sense of confusion, guilt, anxiety, and betrayal, gifted Black students develop a stronger sense of Blackness. During this stage, a conflict between academic and social self-concepts may ensue.

Immersion–emersion. This stage is the antithesis of the pre-encounter stage. During this stage, Black students adopt a new frame of reference, they struggle to rid themselves of an invisible identity, and they cling to all elements of Blackness. In essence, all that is Black is cherished and glorified. Hence, gifted Black students might wear all-black clothes and support all-Black events to demonstrate to peers and to prove, so to speak, that they are indeed Black. They experience euphoria, rage, effrontery, and high risk taking and may even become destructive. Likewise, they may underachieve to avoid the perception of "selling out" to the White community. These students may become class clowns or athletes to camouflage their abilities to maintain their relations and gain social acceptance. Thus, social self-concept takes precedence over academic self-concept.

Internalization. At this stage of racial identity development, Black students become more bicultural, pluralistic, and nonracist. Tension, emotionality, and defensiveness are replaced by a calm, secure demeanor. Internalized Black students are generally self-accepting and regard themselves positively. Gifted Black students learn to achieve academically without taking on characteristics of the dominant culture — characteristics that appear to threaten the maintenance of the Black community. Achievement is not equated with "acting White" or loss of identity as a Black person. There is greater cohesion between academic and social self-concepts. Students often reach this stage through increased self-understanding and awareness and with the guidance of mentors, role models, and supportive adults.

Internalization–commitment. In this final stage, Black students become more active and proactive (rather than reactive) to bring about change for Blacks and other minority groups. For instance, these students join or develop organizations that promote the academic and social well-being of Black and culturally diverse persons.

Cross's (1971) theory has been criticized for being too simplistic (see

Parham, 1989; Parham & Helms, 1985), yet it helps untangle some of the psychological and socioemotional dilemmas confronting gifted and underachieving Black students. Realizing the usefulness of the theory, several researchers have applied or modified it to understand more fully the psychological needs of gifted Black students. For example, Banks (1979) and Colangelo and Exum (1979) stated that gifted Black students experience cultural conflict relative to supporting the beliefs, values, and norms of the dominant culture as opposed to their parent culture. Consequently, they show ambivalence about their abilities and consider them to be envied by others yet personally undesirable.

D. Y. Ford (1992, 1993b, 1995), Fordham (1988), Mickelson (1984), and others have devoted much attention to the issues that gifted and underachieving Black students confront when assimilating and otherwise adopting characteristics, values, and beliefs of the predominant culture. Findings indicate that racial identity development is affected and determined by social and environmental pressures and circumstances.

Essentially, gifted Black students may confront conflicting values that they must choose from when forming a racial identity. Gifted Black students are especially vulnerable to problems if they feel less accepted by peers, teachers, and parents. Further, due to keen insight and sensitivity, gifted Black students tend to become more sensitive to and preoccupied with racial problems than do other Black youth. Fordham (1988) applied this confusion over racial identity to achieving and underachieving Black students. She argued that high-achieving Black students must often assume a "raceless" persona if they wish to succeed academically. Racelessness is a conscious decision whereby Black students empty themselves of their culture, believing that the door of opportunity will open to them if they stand raceless before it. That is, raceless students deliberately adopt characteristics of the dominant culture (e.g., speaking standard English, straightening their hair, wearing blue or green contact lenses) and subscribe to the White American achievement ideology of hard work, educational attainment, and equality of opportunity. Cross (1971) placed such individuals in the pre-encounter stage of racial identity development. Relative to high-achieving Black students, Fordham (1988) argued:

> Out of their desire to secure jobs and positions that are above the employment ceiling typically placed on Blacks, they have adopted personae that indicate a lack of identification with, or a strong relationship to, the Black community in response to an implicit institutional mandate: Become "un-Black." (p. 58)

Two penalties accompany a rejection of the Black culture: The Black community rejects the successful Black student, and the successful Black student suffers psychologically, emotionally, and socially. Racelessness is perceived as a threat to the survival of the Black community and its culture; it creates suspicion among Blacks about members' loyalty. Hence, the Black community may reject gifted or high-achieving Black students not because they achieve academically but because they appear to be removed and detached from their indigenous community. The Black community may reject high-achieving Black students who identify with the dominant culture, desire to join it, and accept its behaviors as paradigms worth emulating.

Which culture, then, should successful and highly able Black students support when trying to fulfill their potential? Which belief and value system should they incorporate? Black students may vacillate between allegiance to their racial group and allegiance to the dominant group. For some Black students, racelessness is a pragmatic strategy, but for others it represents only a Pyrrhic victory (Fordham, 1988). Thus, gifted and achieving Black students contend not only with concerns of the dominant culture but also with issues associated with being Black and culturally different. The result may be survival conflict and guilt, as well as a paradox of underachievement.

Survival Conflict and Guilt

Relatively unexplored in the achievement literature is the impact of survival conflict or guilt on the poor achievement of gifted or highly able Black students. The concept of survival conflict sheds light on the many psychosocial factors affecting the motivation and achievement of Black students. Academically successful Black students may feel guilt, anxiety, and ambivalence about having survived when others who seem to be equally, if not more, deserving did not.

Survival conflict is a negative reaction to surpassing the accomplishments of family or peers, which is experienced as survival. It manifests itself in one or more emotional responses — guilt, ambivalence, anxiety, depression. These feelings can become debilitating if they are not recognized, resulting in a devaluation of one's academic and social self-concepts, accomplishments, and ambitions. As with fear of success, individuals suffering from survival conflict fear or anticipate negative consequences from competitive strivings.

Individuals who succumb to negative feelings associated with success do so to help maintain loyalty to and a sense of belonging with their family and peers. They seek social and cultural continuity. Academically successful Black students may be especially vulnerable to survival conflict; they experience conflicting feelings about their success and ambivalence about surpassing other Blacks, particularly their peers and family members. Piorkowski (1983) also noted that as individuals move from a lower SES to a higher one, they experience "social class change anxiety." These successful persons find themselves in a quandary, because as achievement increases, so does guilt. To escape survival conflict, students may resort to self-sabotage, procrastination, dropping out, and other behaviors that thwart achievement. Higher SES Blacks may also overcompensate to allay such feelings. For instance, they may overextend themselves to "prove" to other Blacks, particularly lower SES Blacks, that they "have not forgotten who they are." Equally problematic, family members and peers may react negatively to success among Black students. As noted earlier, academically successful Black students may be accused by peers and family members of being raceless or trying to act White.

Personality plays a major role in how students react to success and achievement. For instance, it is contended that low self-esteem and low assertiveness are related to survival conflict and guilt (Piorkowski, 1983). These individuals cannot fend off conflicting messages and statements. Racial identity also plays an important role in survival conflict. That is, students with negative or poor racial identities are less likely to be concerned with racial and cultural affiliations. Piorkowski also maintained that students who have close relationships with their families and peers are more likely to experience survival conflict because of concerns over survival of the individual versus that of the group. Researchers have attributed this concern about group solidarity and survival to cultural factors.

Paradox of Underachievement

Black students, especially adolescents, may have an attitude-achievement paradox, defined as a discrepancy between their beliefs regarding education and their actual achievement or performance in school (Mickelson, 1984). The paradox results from a discrepancy between the positive attitudes Black students have about education and their low achievement in school. It is, according to Mickelson, "the paradoxical faith in education held by Black students who nevertheless fail to perform in school at levels expected of people who believe that education is important" (p. 44).

First, there are abstract or idealistic attitudes characterized by an unrelenting faith in the achievement ideology, the Protestant work ethic, and the promise of schooling, hard work, and effort as vehicles for success and upward mobility. There are also concrete or realistic attitudes that reflect the empirical realities that minority groups experience relative to returns on education from the opportunity structure. These dual belief systems are often in conflict. On the one hand, Black students have been taught by teachers, parents, or both that hard work and effort reap rewards relative to achievement, employment, and upward mobility – that the American dream can become a reality for any person, irrespective of race, gender, or socioeconomic circumstance. On the other hand, for too many Black students, the rewards of education have not proved tangible in terms of good-paying jobs or upward mobility. Instead, they see other Blacks who are underemployed and unemployed. They learn that schooling does not help them reap the rewards promised by the nation's democratic principles, by the achievement ideology. When Black students learn that the rewards and promises of educational attainment do not pay off, it is not long before they realize that acquiring an education carries little guarantee. They conclude that the American dream is a mirage, that Black and other minority students are less likely than White students to achieve in school and in life. The result is a credibility gap between schools and Black students. These conflicting beliefs between the ideal and the real are extremely confusing and can drain the motivation of Black students, especially gifted Black students who are attuned to social injustices and inequities, and Black adolescents dealing with identity and vocational issues.

BARRIERS TO MEETING THE PSYCHOLOGICAL NEEDS OF GIFTED BLACK STUDENTS

The major challenge facing gifted Black students is to integrate their identity as Black individuals and their identity as gifted individuals into their various self-concept domains. This can be an especially difficult task, considering that these two identities often elicit conflicting societal messages. Giftedness and achievement are associated largely with White students; thus, when Black students acknowledge their talents and pursue them in educational settings (especially in gifted programs), their attempts to acknowledge and accept their racial identities may be impeded.

Black students in racially segregated schools (predominantly Black schools) have higher self-concepts than Black students in racially integrated settings. Since many gifted programs consist of disproportionate numbers of White students, Black students can expect to be surrounded not only by students who challenge them academically but also by students who exhibit majority culture values. Separation from culturally similar peers may be extremely detrimental to the social self-concepts of gifted and underachieving Black students. Thus, although any Black student who pursues academic achievement may risk ostracism from peers, those placed in predominantly White gifted programs are likely to experience both social and physical separation from significant others. These concerns are raised not to deter the placement of Black students into racially homogeneous (White) gifted programs but rather to increase the awareness of teachers, program coordinators, counselors, and other school personnel to the special needs of Black students and to encourage them to be proactive in their efforts.

Students in general tend not to seek the assistance of school counselors for personal problems. According to Hutchinson and Reagan (1989), the more personal the problem, the less likely students are to seek out school counselors. In their study, approximately 40% of students said that they would seek assistance with peer conflicts, 46% for assistance in exploring feelings and values, 37% on how to get along in life, and 27% for relieving tension. Yet a 1984 study (Citizens Policy Center for Oakland) found that perhaps the most important component of students' success is fulfilling their psychological need for human contact—finding someone to care about them. Students may require the assistance of counselors to do so.

Just as Blacks are underrepresented in the teaching profession, they are underrepresented in the counseling profession. Compared with White students, Black students may be even less likely to seek guidance and counseling, particularly those who hold negative images of White Americans in general (and, by extension, White counselors). The race of the counselor may be the only factor that causes some Black students to avoid counseling or to prematurely terminate counseling. However, race is often ignored in the helping process because few counselors are aware of how race and ethnicity interfere with the process of growing, achieving, and living fully. Black and other racial minority groups underutilize counseling services and have higher attrition rates from counseling, especially after the first session (Sue & Sue, 1990). In their study of the reasons minority students do not seek counseling, Atkinson, Jennings, and Liongson (1990) found the counselor's race to be a significant factor. The availability of culturally similar and culturally sensitive counselors is an important determinant of counseling service utilization by Black students in gifted education. The issue of race may be particularly important for Blacks in the immersion–emersion stage of racial identity development, where they avoid interaction and any behaviors associated with White students. Another explanation for this underutilization is that Black students may not believe that White counselors have the skills necessary to be culturally sensitive. The expectation is that the counseling experience will be negative or inappropriate because of a lack of understanding, awareness, and empathy, as well as pity, apathy, distrust, and prejudices on the part of White counselors. Hence, Black students may seek psychological and socioemotional support from significant others, such as their families, friends, and religious leaders. The following list represents other variables likely to contribute to the underutilization of counseling services by Black students (see Sue & Sue, 1990):

(1) *Counseling centers often consist of predominantly White staff, even in predominantly Black school settings.* This lack of diversity presents underachieving and gifted Black youth with few mentors and role models and few cultural translators, which makes it difficult for them to seek counseling services.

(2) *The services offered by counseling centers are usually traditional, formal, and individual.* Counseling often occurs in a one-to-one format in the counselor's office. This formal approach may be inappropriate for Black students, who may find the one-to-one format too formal, removed, or alien. A nontraditional, multicultural approach would be to meet Black students in their environment (on their turf) or in a neutral setting, as well as in a group format.

(3) *The primary vehicle for communication in counseling is verbal; one's ability to verbalize is the primary condition for counseling.* A student who is relatively nonverbal, for whom English is a second language, or who uses nonstandard English may be placed at a disadvantage. Counselors (and teachers) want and expect students to be articulate and clear in expressing their feelings and thoughts. When students don't, they may be perceived as inarticulate and unintelligent. Yet Black students prefer to express their ideas in nonverbal ways (with eyes, hands, posture, proximity), and they express ideas and feelings with fewer words than their White counterparts (J. E. Gay, 1978; Hale-Benson, 1986; Sue & Sue, 1990). Thus, counselors must distinguish between verbal students and vocal or self-disclosing students; many capable Black students are unwilling to self-disclose with racially or culturally different counselors.

(4) *Characteristics of counseling can hinder working with gifted Black students.* As indicated below, many of the values and characteristics of both the goals and the processes of counseling are not always shared by Blacks and other minority groups:

(a) *Insight.* Most theories of counseling place a premium on the attainment of insight as the ultimate goal or the medium for "curing" clients. However, insight is not necessarily valued in some minority cultures, and there are SES differences. In other words, insight assumes that one has time to sit back, reflect, and contemplate motivations and behaviors. But this is not a luxury that low SES groups can afford. Their major concerns relate to survival and meeting basic needs: How can I afford to take care of my sick mother, father, brother, or sister? How do I feed my family?

Where do I find a job? This orientation toward insight in the counseling session may, therefore, be counterproductive.

(b) *Affect.* Some cultural groups (e.g., Asian and Hispanic populations) refrain from expressing strong feelings; instead, maturity is seen as the ability to control emotions and feelings. Counselors who are unfamiliar with these cultural values may perceive their clients negatively — as lacking in spontaneity, depressed, and repressed.

(c) *Self-exploration.* Many minority groups believe that thinking too much about something can cause, rather than solve, problems. Focusing on one's own problems is considered selfish and egocentric because one's family should be the center of one's attention.

(d) *Self-disclosure.* Counseling theories often purport that the more one discloses, the healthier one is. Yet going to a counselor is a sign of weakness and a bad reflection on the family for some cultural groups, including Blacks. When students are not open, counselors may erroneously conclude that they are shy, withdrawn, inhibited, repressed, or passive. Counselors must remember that self-disclosure implies that there is a trusting relationship between the counselor and the student. As indicated earlier, Black students may not perceive White counselors as persons of goodwill, which virtually halts self-disclosure.

(e) *Individual orientation.* Counseling is often a one-to-one activity that encourages students to talk about or discuss the most intimate aspect of their lives. This individual orientation is not necessarily valued by Black students, who prefer group settings and situations.

(f) *Monolingual orientation.* Counselors may not be accustomed to the phrases and words used by many Black students (Black English vernacular). Failure to understand imagery, analogies, nuances, and sayings may render the counselor ineffective in establishing relationships with Black students and in gaining some level of awareness about their concerns.

(g) *Long-range goals.* Short-term and immediate needs outweigh long-term goals for some minority groups. Meeting immediate, basic needs may supersede the goals of insight, behavioral change, and increased achievement, for example.

(h) *Cause-effect relationships.* The lives of students in at-risk situations and environments are so complex that cause-effect conclusions are almost impossible. It is more practical and realistic to help students isolate and examine one or two major issues in their overall situation.

(i) *Less attention to nonverbal communication and behaviors.* Minority students, especially Black youth, often master the art of reading nonverbal cues and behaviors, such as recognizing when an individual says one thing but means another. This art or skill is a physical and psychological survival strategy. When gifted Black students note discrepancies, counselors will have difficulty establishing productive counseling relationships.

RECOMMENDATIONS

Counselors, psychologists, and teachers are in an ideal position to serve as catalysts for change; they must seek to integrate and implement change. To the extent possible, counselors can serve as advocates for gifted Black students by training all school personnel to become more culturally competent. Counselors can also work with teachers to involve more Black families in the educational process. Equally important, counselors can help initiate a systematic and comprehensive needs assessment to understand the unique culture of their particular school or district. What are the multicultural needs of students and the school? In what ways do course schedules and grouping practices, for example, contribute to or reinforce gifted Black students' isolation and separation? To what extent do minorities participate in school activities? How positive are interactions or interpersonal relationships among students, as well as between teachers and Black students? In what ways do curriculum, pedagogy, and counseling promote or reinforce biases and stereotypes? How much are Black families involved in the school? Is this participation substantive (e.g., teaching, planning, decision making, site-based management) or superficial (e.g., fund-raising, bake sales)? How comfortable are Black students in the gifted program? How do teachers and classmates feel about racially and culturally diverse students? Is there racial tension in the school and the gifted program?

Counselors can also work collaboratively with teachers to establish human relations opportunities for all students and school personnel. Promoting understanding and awareness among all students requires interactions that are egalitarian, culturally sensitive, systematic, and comprehensive. A human relations group or committee, for instance, could meet to discuss issues and instances of oppression, inclusion, exclusion, and separatism in the gifted program and in the school. Similarly, the group could develop a conflict resolution program in which problems are discussed and resolved by a supervised and neutral peer board that has received substantive training in conflict resolution and culturally sensitive conciliation skills.

Counselors and educators must adopt many roles – advocate, mentor, role model, teacher, and collaborator with teachers and families — to meet the academic and nonacademic needs of gifted Black students. Few counselors would disagree with Rogers's (1951, 1961) sage advice that the first step toward helping students is to build a trusting relationship. Erikson (1968) viewed trust versus mistrust as a critical issue of the first developmental stage. Maslow (1954, 1968) maintained that children who do not feel safe cannot trust. They are stuck at the level of trying to keep safe; energy is directed toward trying to maintain security, which results in self-doubt rather than self-certainty. A student who develops a stance of trust has developed a base for reaching out to the world and making contact (Eisenberg & O'Dell, 1988). Thus, the underlying principle of many counseling theories and orientations is that healthy development cannot occur when safety and trust are absent.

Care and empathy from a school counselor or teacher can help restore a sense of safety and trust in gifted and underachieving Black students, particularly those who feel disenfranchised from the educational system and school personnel. Hence, when working with Black students, counselors must draw upon Rogers's (1951) notion of unconditional positive regard, in which students are looked upon as individuals with unique concerns — irrespective of the color of their skin, socioeconomic status, and gender. Stated differently, acceptance and approval are of the utmost importance in the individual's developmental sequence; yet feelings and emotions are seldom recognized in the classroom (Wittmer & Myrick, 1989).

Ultimately, to work effectively with Black students, counselors must enhance their own cultural knowledge, awareness, sensitivity, and skills. This introspection broadens our perspectives of personal values, increases our ability to learn new skills, and enables us to work more effectively with students of color. Gaining a deep awareness of diverse cultures empowers counselors with more appropriate counseling skills and an increased respect for individual and group differences. The challenge before counselors is to become sensitive to cultural pluralism, to become aware of how their values can hinder the counseling relationship. This introspection requires courage and time, especially when one risks looking inward at how one's own behavior can be unhealthy. Once knowledge, skills, and awareness are enhanced, counseling issues can be addressed and intervention can begin. As an African proverb says, "before healing others, heal thyself."

As discussed in Chapter 7, an eclectic and developmental approach to counseling is recommended in which counselors consider the uniqueness and individuality of gifted and underachieving Black students relative to their particular needs and concerns. Counselors must be willing to redefine the counseling situation so that communication, change, and growth are possible. Regardless of one's counseling orientation, counselors must be ever mindful of the worth and dignity of Black students and their right to be respected; their capacity for and right to self-direction; their ability to learn responsibility; their capacity for growth, for dealing with feelings, thoughts, and behaviors; their potential for change and personal development; and their individuality relative to values, lifestyles, and aspirations.

SUMMARY

Few studies have examined the psychological and socioemotional needs of gifted students in general, and gifted Black students in particular. This chapter focused on some of the primary issues facing gifted, achieving, and underachieving Black students — specifically, self-perception, racial identity, and conflict issues. Counselors have many roles and responsibilities that call for increased attention to barriers to gifted Black students' achievement and motivation. They must recognize both individual and group differences among *all* students.

Clearly, race and ethnicity affect our psychological health. The issue of race may be more salient for Blacks than for any other minority group. Essentially, White youth are less likely to experience the chronic stress and problems associated with racial identity because the color of their skin is not a barrier. Skin color is often a liability because of attendant racism and discrimination.

The most promising strategies for helping Black students succeed in gifted programs focus on racial identity (or identity that includes being both gifted and Black), peer pressures and relations, feelings of isolation from both classmates and teachers, sensitivity about feeling different, and coping effectively with success. Ultimately, we must teach gifted Black students how to be bicultural — how to cope with cultural conflicts and differences, and how to live and learn in two cultures that may be dissimilar.

The central idea of this chapter is that gifted Black students are first and foremost human beings in need of understanding, caring, respect, and empathy. With this basic awareness and appreciation, teachers and counselors can begin the process of effective education and counseling. It is incumbent upon school personnel to help gifted Black students manage and appreciate their gifts. With an understanding of their needs, teachers and counselors can better serve this student population by celebrating diversity and advocating for the human rights of all students.

Counseling programs should be based on the premise of valuing cultural diversity and should guard against teaching gifted Black students that they are "different" from their cultural group, thereby encouraging them to abandon the values of that group. Instead, Black students should be helped to understand their abilities and the compassion needed by gifted people. They should be free to be themselves and to develop and appreciate their gifts. There are no easy solutions to the many problems facing gifted and underachieving Black students. Certainly, however, with teachers and counselors as advocates and mentors, gifted Black students will be better prepared to achieve in school and in life.

Chapter 7

Gender Issues in Underachievement and Educational Attainment

Students' identity and school experiences are shaped by their memberships in sociodemographic groups. Educators concerned with equity in education frequently direct their efforts toward issues of race and SES, often ignoring how gender affects and is affected by school experiences. Because females constitute 51% of the U.S. population, they do not fit traditional notions or definitions of minority status. Yet the attributes traditionally associated with minority group status are often applicable to females (e.g., low teacher expectations, discrimination, underrepresentation in positions of power, underemployment, unemployment). Gender is virtually ignored as an equity issue in schooling. It is not considered a relevant category in the analysis of school excellence; that is, the goal of excellence does not have the female student in mind.

Researchers, educators, and reformers frequently examine, in isolation, the effects of race, gender, and SES on students' educational and vocational outcomes. This tendency ignores the reality that every student comes to school as an endangered person due to his or her membership in a particular racial and social class group (Bennett deMarrais & LeCompte, 1995). Thus, when one speaks of equality of educational opportunity, it is in reference to providing all students the same educational opportunities, support, and expectations, irrespective of gender, race, and SES.

This chapter presents an overview of gender issues in gifted education. Unlike most publications in the field, which focus almost exclusively on underachievement among females, this chapter focuses on males and females in gifted education. It also diverges from the norm by focusing on the combined effects of race and gender on achievement and educational outcomes. The rationales for this chapter are numerous. Several shortcomings are evident in the research and literature on gender issues in gifted education. First, the majority of research on gender issues among gifted students focuses on White females, thereby ignoring gifted males and minority males and females. Second, researchers frequently write as if all females are the same. But we are acutely aware that Hispanic American females in Texas differ from Native American females in New Mexico, who differ from Asian American females in California. These differences carry important implications for their educational achievement and attainment. Third and similarly, gender differences in achievement and educational attainment are equally apparent across SES levels. Low SES females and males have different experiences than their higher SES counterparts. Fourth, conclusions based on predominantly White females and White males cannot be generalized to females and males of color. This is because research and literature are seldom disaggregated by race and gender, or by SES and gender. In 1992, the Wellesley College Center for Research on Women conducted an extensive review of the literature on the education of females. The center found that researchers seldom break down data by gender and race. Similarly, interactions between the two variables are rarely studied.

Several premises guide this chapter. One premise is that gifted males and gifted females face differential issues as they endeavor to achieve in school and in life. A second premise is that Black males and Black females have different academic and socioemotional needs. These two premises lead to the third premise: Issues facing gifted students cannot be examined without considering the confounding effects of gender and race. More specifically, researchers in gifted education cannot sufficiently describe the issues facing males and females without also focusing on the impact of race. Research and assumptions gathered from studies must examine the specific issues of gifted White males, gifted Black males, gifted White females, and gifted Black females. As emphasized throughout this book, neither gifted nor minority students are a homogeneous group. Studies and discussions of gender and race in education must reflect the heterogeneity of gifted students.

This chapter begins with an overview of the research on gifted females in general, which is followed by a discussion of the triple quandary that gifted Black females may find themselves in by virtue of being Black, female, and gifted. Also discussed are the various needs of gifted males in general and Black males in particular. A brief discussion of gender bias in tests, curriculum, and instruction is also presented. Finally, recommendations are offered for educators and professionals who are interested in the broader nature of gender issues in gifted education, particularly issues confronting Black females and Black males.

GIFTED FEMALES

The surge of research on gifted females has been attributed to Leta Hollingworth. Silverman (1989), for example, considers Hollingworth not only one of the founders of gifted education but also "the first champion of the cause of gifted girls and women" (p. 86). Research by Reis (1987, 1991), Hollinger and Fleming (1992), Callahan (1991), Noble (1987, 1989), Reis and Callahan (1989), and other scholars has raised the alarm that gifted females represent a population in need of special intervention to thwart failure or reverse underachievement in school and adulthood. The National Association for Gifted Children even has a special focus group on gifted females.

As Hollingworth (1926) observed, because the number of males and females is approximately equal at birth, the same proportion of females as males should be recognized for their achievements. Historically, however, significantly fewer women have become eminent than their male counterparts (Read, 1991). They are underrepresented in such fields as science, government, industry, and business (Rensberger, 1984). Fox and Zimmerman (cited in Read, 1991) reported that high school girls refuse to enroll in advanced mathematics, computer, or physics classes and choose not to pursue graduate-level work. Kaufmann (1981), in her follow-up studies of presidential scholars, found that women were overrepresented among the unemployed and in clerical positions. Eccles (1985) concluded:

> Gifted females do not achieve as highly as do gifted males either educationally or vocationally. They are less likely to seek advanced educational training, and even when they do, they do not enter the same fields as do their male peers. They are over-represented in the fields of education and literature, and under-represented in science, math, and engineering. Most importantly, they are, in fact, under-represented in all advanced educational programs and in the vast majority of high-status occupations. (p. 261)

In a longitudinal study of high school valedictorians and salutatorians, Arnold (1993) found that the self-reported intelligence of females declined in the sophomore year of college. Females also chose less demanding careers than did males, even though female valedictorians had outperformed males in college. Similarly, Benbow and Arjmand (1990) reported that of the mathematically precocious youth they sampled, the aspirations of females decreased significantly, and fewer majored in the sciences. Further, during adolescence, girls tend to find the label gifted to be unacceptable; thus, they deny their gifts and talents and insist on being called normal (Kerr, 1991).

Less than 2% of American patentees are female, and 36% of the 1987 National Merit semifinalists were female (Banks & Banks, 1993; Ordovensky, 1988). Read (1991) studied the achievement and career choices of both gifted males and gifted females in 142 school districts nationally. Under investigation was the extent to which males and females were enrolled in gifted programs, the ratio of boys to girls by grade level in gifted programs, the ratio of differences by school district, and the self-identified factors that discourage students' participation in gifted programs. Results indicated that proportionately more girls than boys were in gifted programs — at the elementary level there were more girls, but at the high school level this trend reversed itself (in grades 10 through 12, males outnumbered females).

Underachievement among females is often measured by enrollment in mathematics and science classes when they are students and by income and occupational or vocational positions when they are adults. Course enrollment alone, however, does not provide clear evidence that females have gained access to challenging course work. It is one thing to get equal access to a course, but another thing to get equal access once placed in the class. Ironically, females attain higher GPAs at all grade levels than do males, yet females achieve less in terms of money, power, and status than males as adults (Arnold, 1993; Feingold, 1988).

Research suggests that females are at greater risk for underachievement than are males for numerous reasons. First, they have less confidence in their own intellectual abilities, particularly in mathematics and the sciences. Second, they are likely to have higher social service than intellectual values. Third, they are more likely to be concerned with peer or social acceptance than with intellectual development. Fourth, they experience more conflict and confusion than do gifted boys with respect to their life goals. Numerous social, environmental, and cultural influences can be attributed to underachievement by gifted females. Barriers include rejection by family, teachers, and peer groups when gifted females achieve at high levels; an underestimation of abilities by family members, teachers, vocational counselors, and others; less encouragement and fewer incentives than males to reach their potential as adults; and reduced opportunities for females to develop their abilities because of their tendency to repudiate the label of gifted for themselves. For instance, Reis (1987) stated that some gifted females are unwilling to prepare for the future because they believe that someone else will take care of them, and they have unrealistic expectations about the future. Because many females fear success, Clance and Imes (1978) introduced the idea of the imposter phenomenon, whereby gifted females deny or hide their intelligence. For the most part, it seems reasonable to conclude that many gifted females are unaware of, ambivalent about, or frightened by their potential.

The avoidance syndrome — that is, the motive to avoid success — among females appears to be influenced by socialization practices. Parents teach females to be yielding, selfless, accepting, and nurturing, whereas boys are taught to be assertive, self-reliant, and defensive of their masculine beliefs (Sadker & Sadker, 1982). Females are also taught to abandon risk taking and independence. Consequently, a femininity–giftedness conflict develops. Differential socialization patterns lead to differences in the goals of schooling for males and females. Males and females are expected to play different roles and are trained to fulfill these roles. By age 6 or 7, children have a clear idea about gender roles; they prefer to play segregated by gender and strive to conform to stereotypic gender roles (Bennett deMarrais & LeCompte, 1995). These perceptions continue into adolescence and adulthood. Kahle (1986) found that females and males hold different and stereotypical sex-role notions about science-related and social science fields. Engineering, physics, geology, chemistry, mathematics, and biochemistry are highly represented by males and considered masculine fields. Conversely, females have high enrollment in the liberal arts, social science, and nursing, all of which are perceived as feminine occupations (or occupations with feminine characteristics). These various perceptions are a function of sociocultural influences that work to marginalize women in the scientific enterprise (Kahle & Meece, 1994).

Many variables influence the academic choices students make. According to Eccles (1989), students' decisions to persist and to excel at a particular course of study are related to their expectations for success and the subjective value of the achievement area. These perceptions are shaped by their experiences with related activities, cultural norms, encouragement from others, and the opportunity structures that exist in society. The model is based on expectancy-value theories of achievement motivation.

Essentially, although gifted (White) females do not necessarily underachieve in school, they do experience underemployment, lower salaries, and poor representation in math and science-related fields as adults. Thus, equal ability and achievement in school do not necessarily guarantee equal opportunity to achieve success and career satisfaction. Notwithstanding the legitimate problems facing gifted females in general, educators must also examine issues associated with being a member of a racial minority group. Underachievement among gifted females is indeed a valid area of concern, but there are other compelling reasons to address the specific concerns of gifted Black females. As discussed below, when racial background is considered in relation to gender, gifted Black females are at greater risk for underachievement, dropping out, and school failure than are White females.

GIFTED BLACK FEMALES

Gifted Black females find themselves in a triple quandary by virtue of being gifted, Black, and female. That is, by virtue of being Black, they face racial discrimination, are underrepresented in programs for the gifted, are overrepresented in special education classes, are more likely to confront social barriers to achievement, and are more likely to experience cultural conflicts than are White females. They also face gender discrimination, including that associated with tests, schooling, and employment opportunities. Specifically, Black females struggle with numerous social, cultural, and psychological barriers to achievement and success, despite legislative and legal efforts to provide quality and equity in education. Problems related to race, gender, and class remain in today's schools and in society at large.

Despite the aforementioned differences between Black and White gifted females, the two groups are treated as one in the literature. A review of articles referenced in ERIC since 1982 revealed that 131 focused on gifted females. Similarly, 43 articles on this topic were referenced in PsycLIT since 1987. Noteworthy, however, is that none of the articles in the two database systems specifically addressed the issues of gifted Black or other minority females.

Irvine's (1991) research illustrates the powerful effect of teacher expectations on Black females. Along with numerous others, Irvine found that, compared with White females, Black females are often subject to low teacher expectations at all educational levels. In general, they receive less positive feedback and response opportunities from teachers, are often asked by teachers to take on caregiver roles with other students, are often ignored by teachers, and are more likely to be rebuffed by teachers when they seek attention. These researchers also found that Black females are often expected by both Black and White males to adopt service roles, they tend to be left out of friendship networks, and they rarely attempt to interact with teachers (i.e., Black females choose to become invisible). It is little wonder that Black females have such high dropout rates. In the High School and Beyond Study of sophomores in 1980, the dropout rate for Black females was 14%, even though they represented 6% of the public school population. Along with other minority students, Black females most often cited a dislike of school (34%) and poor grades (30%) as important push-out variables (Whalen, 1984). Gender inequities toward females in education and society cannot be denied or disregarded. The following sections focus specifically on problems in curriculum, instruction, and testing.

Bias in Curriculum and Instruction

The formal school curriculum serves as the core for the daily activities of teachers and students. A hidden curriculum, discussed in Chapter 8, also operates in schools relative to gender. Hitchcock and Tompkins (1987) evaluated six recent editions of popular basal reading texts to determine the gender of the main characters, and the range and frequency of occupations for female characters. Of the 1,121 stories reviewed, females were portrayed in 37 occupations (compared with 5 occupations in 1961–1963 readers and 23 occupations in 1969–1971 readers). The authors found that 18% of main characters were male and 17% were female. Most often, the main characters were neutral (e.g., talking trees or animals). Rather than accepting the changes as proactive efforts, Hitchcock and Tompkins maintained that textbook publishers were avoiding issues of sexism by creating neutral characters. Further, Applebee's (1989) national study of book-length works used in high school English courses found only one female author and no minority authors in the 10 most frequently assigned books. Applebee argued that little progress had been made in reading lists from 1907 and 1963; required books continue to be dominated by White male authors. In their work on gender equity and females, Sadker, Sadker, and Long (1993) identified at least six forms of bias:

(1) *Linguistic bias*: One of the most common forms of bias in education is the use of masculine terms and pronouns in curricular materials.

(2) *Stereotyping*: Many curricular materials contain stereotypes relative to gender and race. For example, White females are often portrayed in passive, docile, and dependent roles, whereas White males are characterized as ingenious, independent, athletic, and assertive. When one examines both racial and gender stereotypes, data indicate that White males tend to be portrayed as doctors, soldiers, and police officers; Black males are portrayed as workers, farmers, warriors, and hunters; White females are commonly depicted as mothers, teachers, authors, and princesses; and Black females are depicted primarily as mothers and teachers, followed by slaves, workers, porters, and artists (Britton & Lumpkin, 1983).

(3) *Invisibility or omission*: Few curricular materials highlight the contributions that females and minority groups have made to the development of the United States. In many subject areas (such as history, science, math, and language arts), minorities and females are underrepre-

sented. Given that females represent a little more than half of the U.S. population, students are deprived of information about a significant number of women.

(4) *Imbalance*: Too often, curricular materials present one interpretation or perspective. For instance, the perspectives of both females and minority groups are often given limited attention or completely ignored.

(5) *Unreality*: The United States is often portrayed in an unrealistic and idealistic manner — as dominant, superior, victorious, and powerful. Americans are portrayed as humane, compassionate, and equitable. Curricular materials also ignore or minimize controversial issues such as prejudice, sexism, and other forms of discrimination.

(6) *Fragmentation*: Curricular materials discuss the contributions of females and minority groups in a piecemeal, isolated fashion. This fragmentation is evident in the cursory book chapters (or sections of chapters) on females and minority students. There is little, if any, integration of gender and racial issues throughout the materials.

Tests and Gender Bias

Gender bias in tests and testing practices contributes to underachievement among gifted females. Yet increased social conscience has led to movements in psychometrics and gender issues that parallel movements in psychometrics for students of color. Thus, educational and psychological tests have been examined for possible bias against females. In 1989, a federal court judge in New York ordered that colleges stop awarding scholarships based on SAT scores because of their unfairness to females. It was found that the SAT scores of females were significantly lower than the scores of males, even though females had higher GPAs (Worthen, Borg, & White, 1993). Generally, females perform as well as or better than males on educational tests. A major exception is that females tend to score lower than males on mathematics tests (Plake, Ansorge, Parker, & Lowry, 1982; Waetjen, 1977). Tittle (1978) and Tittle and Zytowski (1978) concluded that various standardized and nonstandardized tests are biased against females for several reasons:

(1) Achievement tests are selectively biased against females in language usage (as evidenced by an imbalanced ratio of male to female noun and pronoun referents).
(2) Achievement tests are selectively biased against females in content (e.g., male characters are mentioned more often).
(3) Achievement tests contain and reinforce numerous gender-role stereotypes (e.g., female characters are portrayed in more passive roles, whereas males are represented in more active roles).

(4) Vocational and career interest inventories often restrict individual choices for females because they have separate norms for males and females that result in differential and gender-specific counseling about career options.
(5) Aptitude tests are often written and interpreted according to gender-role stereotypes.

Despite the reality of gender bias in instruments, curriculum, and instruction, the nature-nurture controversy often rears its ugly head in discussions of gender differences in math and science achievement. Innate differences, cultural attitudes, and societal expectations and stereotypes continue to be advanced as explanations for test score and achievement outcomes relative to gender. Figure 7.1 presents questions for monitoring curricular materials for gender and racial biases.

GIFTED MALES

A special issue of *Roeper Review* (1991) focused on the socioemotional and academic needs of gifted males. The authors noted that gifted males contend with issues of bonding, emotionality, and maintaining a macho image (Alvino, 1991; Hebert, 1991; Kline & Short, 1991; Wolfle, 1991) often by channeling their efforts into sports rather than academics. The authors also noted that gifted males are more likely than females to be labeled hyperactive, and they are less likely to be recommended for acceleration, early school entrance, and grade skipping. More recently, Colangelo, Kerr, Christensen, and Maxey (1993) found that 90% of the underachievers in their large national study were White males. One shortcoming of the special issue, however, is that "gifted males" were addressed as if they were a monolithic group; little attention was devoted to issues confronting gifted Black males. As discussed below, although gifted Black and White males may share similar issues and barriers to achievement, gifted Black males have additional, distinct problems that can undermine their achievement and success.

GIFTED BLACK MALES

National statistics help explain what many refer to as the "endangered Black male" (Kunjufu, 1993). In 1984 and 1985, the *Carnegie Quarterly* and the College Board revealed the dismal educational status of Blacks in this nation: Black males are three times as likely as White males to be in a class for the educable mentally retarded but only half as likely to be placed

FIGURE 7.1. Recommendations for analyzing curricular materials for sexism and racism.

What evidence is there of ethnocentricism?

How will the materials affect students' self-image and self-esteem?

Check illustrations for stereotypes and tokenism (e.g., minority families have many children; the father is noticeably absent; the family is poor; only one minority person appears in the entire book or material; females are depicted as nurses and teachers, whereas males are doctors and administrators).

Check story lines for standards of success and resolution of problems.

Check lifestyle portrayals for inaccuracies and inappropriate depictions. How are families depicted?

Examine the relations depicted between people. Who has power? Who solves the problems? How are problems resolved?

Who are the heroes? Are they people of color? Are they males and females?

What are the qualifications of the authors, illustrators, and other personnel?

Are there loaded and offensive words?

What is the copyright date?

How might a student interpret the nonverbal messages in the material?

What is the quality of the illustrations? Do females and minority groups have stereotypical features; exaggerated features; poor clothing, housing, and cleanliness?

in a class for the gifted. The U.S. Department of Education (1990) and Shapiro, Loeb, and Bowermaster (1993) reported that Black males continue to be referred to and placed disproportionately in special education—more than any other ethnic or racial group of adolescents. Such disproportionate placement in special education results in separate and unequal circumstances. This mislabeling of students as behavior disordered or seriously emotionally impaired increases their probability of school failure.

Although Black males constitute 6% of the total U.S. population, they are overrepresented among high school dropouts, school suspendees, prisoners, and special education classes students; they are underrepresented in gifted programs (see Figure 7.2). Equally disturbing, Black males score lower than any other group on standardized tests (Governors' Commission on Socially Disadvantaged Black Males, 1989). Although these data do not focus specifically on gifted Black males, one can reason by analogy that bright and highly capable Black males are represented in these alarming figures.

Black females outnumber Black males in gifted programs by a ratio of 2 to 1. Gallagher and Gallagher (1994) attributed this finding less to test performance and more to teacher perceptions; teachers were more willing to accept Black females as gifted due to their greater tendency toward conformity and greater responsibility for learning. In terms of teacher expectations, Irvine (1991) found that Black males at all educational levels are most likely to receive qualifying praise and controlling statements. Black males are most likely to be labeled deviant and described negatively, to receive nonverbal criticism, to be reprimanded and sent to the principal's office, and to be judged inaccurately and negatively by teachers. They are least likely to receive positive teacher feedback and to interact with teachers. Relative to student relations and interactions, Black males

FIGURE 7.2. Educational and social indices of the status of Black males (U.S. Bureau of the Census, 1990; Kunjufu, 1993).

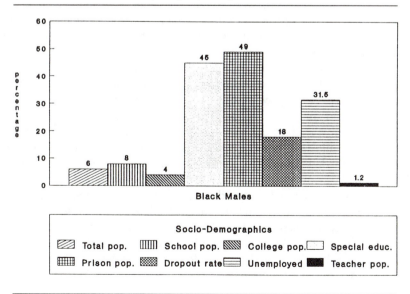

are most likely to interact with other Black males and to be socially isolated from White students; when interactions occur, they are not likely to be academic. Other distinctions by race and gender are illustrated in Figure 7.3.

D. Y. Ford (1993c) examined gender differences in underachievement among early adolescent gifted Black males and females. Black males were more likely than females to be underachievers; they exerted considerably less effort in school and held more negative attitudes about school than females. They found school less relevant and personally meaningful than did their female counterparts. Further, Black males were more pessimistic about social factors than were Black females. For example, several of the early adolescent Black males spoke with anger and disappointment about the injustices Blacks must wrestle with. These young Black males held abstract rather than concrete beliefs about the American dream or achievement ideology. The findings suggested that the Black males needed and desired more positive information about their racial heritage, more exposure to male and Black role models, increased affective educational experiences to feel connected to teachers, an increased sense of ownership of their schooling, and counseling experiences to cope more effectively with their anger and disappointment regarding social injustices.

Hebert (1993) focused exclusively on gifted Black males in an ethnographic study. He utilized participant observations, ethnography, interviews, and document reviews to enter the lives of 12 inner-city minority adolescents, half of whom were underachieving. A primary goal of the study was to explore resiliency among these males, to examine why males in similar family and educational situations take alternative paths to achievement and success.

Several factors distinguished resilient and achieving gifted Black males from nonresilient and underachieving gifted Black males. Achievers had a strong sense of self; they were sensitive and compassionate; and they had aspirations and an inner will to achieve. Further, successful minority males were nurtured by one or more adults, which often included a teacher or family member. Their families were spiritual and optimistic, and they provided opportunities for their sons to develop and maintain their abilities. Conversely, underachieving males vacillated in their journeys; they often became filled with despair and confusion and eventually lost sight of their goals. These students had negative curricular and counseling experiences. According to Hebert, they *learned* to dislike school and teachers who ignored their individual learning styles. Underachievers also faced social difficulties, such as problematic, complex family situations and negative peer environments.

FIGURE 7.3. Differential social and educational outcomes relative to gender and race.

	Male	**Female**
White	Probability of facing racial discrimination (1)	Probability of facing racial discrimination (1)
	Probability of facing gender discrimination (1)	Probability of facing gender discrimination (3)
	Unemployment and underemployment rates (1)	Unemployment and underemployment rates (2)
	Suspension rates (3)	Suspension rates (1)
	Dropout rates (2)	Dropout rates (1)
	Standardized test scores (4)	Standardized test scores (3, 4)
	(particularly in math and science and spatial ability tests and subscales)	(particularly on reading, vocabulary, and comprehension tests and subscales)
	Teacher expectations (4)	Teacher expectations (3)
	Representation in gifted programs (3, 4)	Representation in gifted programs (3, 4)
	(varies, depending on grade level)	(varies, depending on grade level)
Black	Probability of facing racial discrimination (4)	Probability of facing racial discrimination (3)[*]
	Probability of facing gender discrimination (2)	Probability of facing gender discrimination (4)
	Unemployment and underemployment rates (3)	Unemployment and underemployment rates (3)
	Suspension rates (4)	Suspension rates (2)
	Dropout rates (4)	Dropout rates (2)
	Standardized test scores (1)	Standardized test scores (2)
	Teacher expectations (1)	Teacher expectations (2)
	Representation in gifted programs (1)	Representation in gifted programs (2)

Note: Ratings are on a 4-point scale. 1 = least likely or lowest probability; 4 = most likely or highest probability.

[*] Black and other minority females are the only group among the four to face both racial and sexual discrimination.

RECOMMENDATIONS

As this chapter indicates, educators and researchers must consider seriously the combined effects of race and gender on underachievement and other educational outcomes. The following recommendations focus on gender equity for both males and females. Due to the nature of the topic, some of the suggestions overlap with recommendations for racial equity.

Gender Equity and Females

Educators must confront biases in curricular materials. Rather than ignore biases, teachers should take the proactive stance of discussing them with students. Educators must fill voids and omissions in curricular materials with supplementary materials. It is also important to examine the classroom environment for segregation. By examining seating arrangements and sociograms, teachers can see if students are forming self-selected social networks relative to race, gender, or both. Peer tutoring and cooperative learning can help increase positive social interactions among males and females.

The American Association of University Women (1992) proposed that gender-fair curriculum should adhere to the following characteristics:

(1) it must acknowledge and affirm diversity within and between groups of people;
(2) it must be representative, having a balance of multiple and alternative perspectives;
(3) it must be inclusive so that all students can identify positive messages about themselves;
(4) it must be accurate, presenting verifiable and data-based information;
(5) it must ensure that the experiences, interests, and needs of all students are integrated; and
(6) it must be affirmative by valuing the worth of individuals and groups.

Because school environments foster and nurture gender inequity, they must be explored. For instance, to what extent are all students encouraged to take leadership roles in school? Are all students exposed to a variety of professional and successful role models in school? Are special guidance and counseling groups available for issues facing males and females and minority students? Are all students encouraged to pursue traditionally male- and female-dominated careers, academic majors, and courses? Are school personnel (e.g., teachers, vocational guidance counselors) trained to recognize and eliminate covert and overt biases relative to race, SES, and gender?

Self-understanding and knowledge must be examined when working with minority students. For example, teachers must confront their own biases in instruction (e.g., questioning patterns, feedback, reinforcement, and expectations) and choice of curricular materials (e.g., monocultural books, sexist books, and noncontroversial topics). Males and females must be presented in a positive, yet realistic manner. This self-examination must focus on teachers' beliefs, stereotypes, fears, and behaviors, not just toward males and females in general but toward minority males and minority females as well. Educators must explore their gender and racial stereotypes before they can work effectively with these students regarding their expectations and aspirations, sense of competence, achievement behaviors, and so forth.

Gender Equity and Males

Several educational recommendations were suggested by Hebert's (1993) research on gifted minority males in urban environments, the majority of which were directed at reforming schools. First, it was urged that high schools be reorganized into smaller schools that are better structured to attend to students' socioemotional needs and better able to match curriculum to learning styles. Second, schools should employ talent development specialists to facilitate appropriate educational programs for gifted and potentially gifted Black males. Two responsibilities of talent specialists would be working with school personnel in program planning and implementation and working with teachers to identify and reverse underachievement.

Extensive staff development on underachievement for counselors and faculty was a third suggestion. The fourth and fifth recommendations involved restructuring students' time to provide for substantive and meaningful extracurricular experiences (e.g., summer enrichment programs, Upward Bound, tutoring), and replacing study halls with more productive options (e.g., tutoring, independent study, guest lectures, enrichment minicourses and workshops). Exposing minority males to role models who have successfully balanced academics and athletics and who encourage academics was also strongly recommended. Finally, Hebert advocated for stronger family–school partnerships in behalf of underachieving, gifted, and potentially gifted minority males.

A developmental and holistic approach to helping gifted and underachieving Black students is necessary for them to reach their potential in school and in life (Figure 7.4). The model assumes that the needs of gifted elementary, middle, and high school students are quantitatively and qualitatively different. These issues can be categorized as affective, psychological, and academic, and they represent the primary means for prevention and intervention. Further, some issues are most germane to adolescent males but are irrelevant and inappropriate for younger children and females. Similarly, some issues may be more important or critical for females. However, if all the issues are addressed at an early age (during preschool and elementary years), many of them may not be present in later years. Proactive efforts, therefore, seek prevention over intervention, and they are holistic because they address affective, psychological, and academic needs. The focus on prevention and affective development is important for all students, particularly males.

In general, Black and underachieving students need and seek greater self-awareness, self-understanding, and appreciation; they seek stronger and more positive social relations; they need opportunities to express their emotions and feelings in positive and productive ways. This includes dealing effectively with stress and anxiety and understanding the use of defense and cognitive mechanisms.

Suggested strategies for prevention and intervention include exposing Black males and females to role models and mentors at an early age and throughout their lives; using counseling (peer, small group, individual) for affective development; using cinematherapy and bibliotherapy for increased understanding; employing relaxation training (e.g., journal writing, breathing, walking, exercising) as an emotional outlet; increasing their problem-solving skills; and helping students examine their defense and coping mechanisms.

SUMMARY

Every student enters the classroom with differential characteristics and needs. These needs are a function of their memberships in various groups. Research that focuses on gender and race in isolation provides insufficient data for educational practice. For example, the finding that females are underrepresented in math and science-related classes and professions obscures the reality that Black males are also underrepresented in these areas. On this same note, when we find that males are overrepresented in math and the sciences, we must carefully interpret the findings, because Black males are underrepresented in these disciplines. Educators and researchers must use caution in generalizing findings from studies that focus exclusively on gender differences.

FIGURE 7.4. A developmental intervention model for Black males a/

Affective Development (Social and Emotional)

Goals:

To increase intrapersonal skills and competencies (e.g., self-understanding, self-awareness, self-respect, and confidence), particularly healthy self-concepts and self-esteem [Eb, Mb, Hb]

To improve interpersonal skills (e.g., social relations with peers, parents, teachers, and authority figures) [Eb, Mm, Hm]

To appreciate similarities and differences between self and others [Eb, Mb, Hb]

To understand and handle physical [Mb, Hb] and socioemotional [Eb, Mb, Hb] development associated with adolescence

To accept self as an emotional being; to view compassion and empathy as humane rather than feminine [Em, Hb, Mb]

To clarify values, set priorities, and resolve inner conflicts, particularly regarding school, achievement, and social relationships [Em, Mb, Hb]

To promote biculturalism and enhance social competence [Em, Mb, Hb]

To use abilities proactively and prosocially [Mm, Hm]

To understand and cope effectively with frustration and anger, especially feelings of injustice regarding racial discrimination [Em, Mb, Hb] and sexual discrimination [Mf, Hf]

Psychological Development

Goals:

To increase understanding of racial identity and its relationship to academic achievement, self-concept, and racism [Eb, Mb, Hb]

To explore fears, anxieties, and stressors associated with success and achievement [Eb, Mb, Hb]

To increase internal locus of control and self-efficacy [Mb, Hb]

Academic Development

Goals:

To develop positive attitudes toward school and achievement [Mb, Hb]

To improve academic and test performance [Eb, Mb, Hb]

To improve basic skills, including testing-taking and study skills [Eb, Mb, Hb]

To strengthen critical thinking and problem-solving skills [Eb, Mb, Hb]

To understand academic strengths and shortcomings, including learning style preferences and strategies for accommodating teaching styles [Eb, Mb, Hb]

To explore options and experiences that nurture one's abilities [Eb, Mb, Hb]

To set realistic and appropriate goals [Eb, Mb, Hb]

To select challenging academic courses [Eb, Mb, Hb]

To understand and resolve problems that inhibit school performance (e.g., perfectionism, procrastination, fear of failure or success, test anxiety, poor motivation, negative peer pressures) [Eb, Mb, Hb]

FIGURE 7.4. Continued.

Vocational or Career Development

Goals:

To explore aspirations and expectations [Eb, Mb, Hb]

To develop an understanding of vocational options based on personal strengths and shortcoming [Mb, Hb]

To explore (extensively) careers relative to educational requirements, salary, job requirements and future demand or need [Eb, Mb, Hb]

To visit postsecondary institutions and programs related to current career interests [Eb, Mb, Hb]

Note: The suggestions are specific to students at various school levels. E = elementary students; M = middle school or junior high school students; H = high school students; m = males; f = females; b = both males and females. The model does not assume that the issues listed are equally important for males and females or for students at the three school levels. The model is a guideline but is best used on an individual basis.

Black students are a heterogeneous population. Black males and females have differential needs and concerns. For instance, Black males tend to have lower test scores, higher dropout rates, and higher unemployment and underemployment rates than Black females, despite the fact that Black females (and other minority females) deal with both racial and gender inequities. Black males and females do not have the same chances for equal educational and employment opportunities; similarly, their opportunities differ considerably from those of White males and females. It cannot be denied that the United States is a male-dominated society; more accurately, however, it is a White male-dominated society. Black males and females do not share the cultural capital of White males and females.

The literature is scarce regarding the interrelationship of race and gender among gifted students. As the preceding chapters indicate, gifted Black students, regardless of their gender, face psychological, social, and cultural barriers to achievement. These factors must be explored relative to the combined influence of race and gender on students' academic well-being. This neglect, this inattention to individual differences, must be rectified in future research and literature on gender and equity in academic achievement and educational attainment.

Chapter 8

School Influences on Underachievement

There is no such thing as a neutral educational process.

—Shaull, 1993, p. 16

On a daily basis, educators, researchers, and social scientists expound on the problems of schools, and numerous reform reports highlight the concerns of educators and parents. More often than not, these reports and critiques examine pedagogy, curriculum, and quantity issues (such as more course work, longer school days and years, increased graduation requirements, and so forth) rather than the environments in which students learn. Yet learning environments have a significant impact on students' achievement, motivation, and attitudes toward school and teachers. School and classroom environments — their culture, climate, atmosphere, ethos, or ambience — set the psychological and affective milieu for students' learning.

Critical features of learning environments in schools, classrooms, and, by extension, gifted programs go beyond the physical facilities and classroom sizes. Their climates include the prevailing norms and values, the sense of community and cohesion, student–teacher and peer relations, and student and teacher morale. School and classroom climates are also influenced by demographic variables, teachers' expectations of students, their attention to individual student needs, and curriculum and instruction. In their metareview of research and literature, Wang, Haertel, and Walberg (1993/94) identified 28 variables that help or inhibit students' learning. Those variables having a direct impact on students' learning were students' cognitive ability, motivation, and behaviors; the quantity and quality of instruction; parent encouragement and support for learning at home; and classroom climate. Lewin (1936) noted that students' behaviors (B) are a function (f) of their personality characteristics (P) and the learning environment (E): $[B = f(P,E)]$.

This chapter focuses on literature and research addressing learning

135

environments and Black students' achievement. Why study learning environments? The most obvious answer is that students spend a significant amount of time in schools. Csikszentmihalyi and McCormack (1986) went so far as to state that the time students spend with teachers is the single most important opportunity for them to learn from adults in our culture. Second, the quality of schools varies considerably, as does their impact on students' achievement. Students in low SES schools, for example, often have different and fewer learning opportunities than those in high SES schools; similarly, teacher resources, training, and morale can vary considerably in schools with different SES levels. Third, school climates vary considerably from teacher to teacher; some classrooms are warm, nurturing, and supportive, and others are hostile and unfriendly. In the latter instance, low teacher morale, low expectations, and poor relationships with students can frustrate and inhibit students' achievement and motivation to achieve.

THE LEARNING ENVIRONMENT

The school environment is often as palpable as the weather. Some schools have a warm, friendly ambience, whereas others have a cold, unnurturing environment. In numerous studies of urban and Black high school dropouts, a common theme is that school was not only boring and unchallenging but also a hostile place (Fine, 1986; Rumberger, 1987). This lack of warmth can be debilitating to students' morale and attitudes toward learning. For instance, Schlosser (1992) reported that the ultimate act of disengagement — dropping out — is influenced significantly by low teacher expectations, lack of teacher understanding, teacher distance and impersonalized classroom environment, teacher-directed and lecture-based instruction, poor achievement, isolation from classmates, cultural dissonance and conflict, little opportunity for success, irrelevant curriculum, and an inability to identify with school.

Fantini and Weinstein (1968) interviewed urban students to identify their perceptions of school-related problems and needs. Most problems were related to identity, connectedness, and powerlessness. Fantini and Weinstein found that schools reinforce disconnectedness by depriving students of meaningful discourse with their peers at the affective or socioemotional level; disconnectedness is also reinforced by the formal businesslike relationships between teachers and students.

The primary purpose of school is to educate students, to provide them with the knowledge and skills deemed necessary for national and international survival. Thus, it is essential to explore how the learning environment of schools and classrooms impedes or facilitates this goal. Schools are social organizations that, like individuals, have their own personalities and psychosocial characteristics. Thus, measures of learning environments are like measures of motivation and achievement (Fraser, 1994). Perceptions are the primary means for measuring the quality of learning environments. Such perceptions vary from student to student and between teachers and students. Learning environments also vary from one classroom to another, or from one teacher to another. For example, Fraser and Fisher (1982) found that teachers tend to perceive the classroom or learning environment more positively than do students; further, students would often prefer a more positive climate than is actually present.

Learning environments can be described by their climate and culture. School climate is the relatively enduring quality of the learning environment that is explained by participants' affect and behavior; it is based on their collective behaviors and perceptions (Hoy & Tarter, 1992). According to Taguiri and Litwin (1968), organizational climates are defined by their ecology—the physical environment in which groups interact; milieu—the social characteristics of individual and group participants in the organization; social system—the patterned relationships of persons and groups; and culture—the collectively accepted beliefs, attitudes, values, customs, and meanings of the group. It is the cultural component that gives schools and classrooms their distinctive identity.

Edmonds (1979, 1986) described characteristics of effective urban schools that distinguish them from their less effective counterparts. Edmonds's measures of effectiveness included more than just high test scores. At the very least, effective schools generate higher achievement among students; they hold high expectations for students; they strive for excellence; they have high student and teacher morale; they have effective leadership; they respect individual differences; and they show warmth, concern, and appreciation for students. Equally important, such schools are safe and orderly, with well-functioning methods to monitor school inputs and student outputs.

Lightfoot's (1983) ethnographic research suggests that high-achieving secondary schools have staff who are concerned about the well-being of students and the integrity of the curriculum and are committed to academic pursuits. High teacher expectations lower students' sense of futility and communicate that teachers care and students can succeed. When teachers have low expectations for students, they are more critical, offer fewer rewards and less feedback, desert students during failure situations, call on them less often to answer questions, pay less attention to students, and demand less work and effort (Brophy, 1988; Rosenthal & Jacobson, 1968). Although different expectations of students are inevitable, problems arise when students receive or perceive differential treatment. When Black students notice such differential treatment — particularly rejection — they may reject teachers.

A positive school climate for gifted and underachieving Black students is characterized by high staff expectations for students and the instructional program; strong demands for academic performance; denial of the cultural-deprivation argument and the stereotypes that support it; high staff morale, including strong internal support, job satisfaction, a sense of personal efficacy, a sense that the system works, and a sense of ownership by teachers and students; and the belief that resources are best expended on people rather than on educational software and hardware (Carter & Chatfield, 1986).

Teachers' satisfaction with their work is positively related to learning environments and students' achievement. Teachers with high morale are more supportive of students; students who perceive that their teachers are satisfied with their jobs are likelier to have high levels of attendance and achievement, high morale about their school and learning environment, and stronger academic self-efficacy and confidence (Edmonds, 1979, 1986; D. Y. Ford, 1995). Stated differently, high teacher morale maximizes students' chances of developing and nurturing positive attitudes about their own abilities, which promotes achievement and motivation. When teacher and student morale is high, a circle of causation (Stockard & Mayberry, 1992) is established in classrooms — high student achievement affects teacher morale, efficacy, and expectations, which, in turn, influence students' achievement, motivation, and attitudes toward school.

Key Variables Affecting the Learning Environment

As described below, numerous variables influence the learning environments of schools and classrooms, including teacher demographics, teacher training in gifted education, teacher training in multicultural education, teachers' attitudes and beliefs, and an ethnocentric and monocultural curriculum.

Teacher demographics. The majority of teachers are White females (76%). The number of minority teachers is dismally small — approximately 12% for all minority groups combined, and only 6% for Black teachers (including 1.2% for Black males) (American Association of Colleges for Teacher Education [AACTE], 1990; King, 1993). Although having a disproportionate number of minority teachers is commonplace, even in urban areas, no studies have reported the percentage of Black and minority teachers in gifted education programs (D. Y. Ford, 1994c; D. Y. Ford

& Harris, 1994, in press). It seems reasonable to assume that, just as they are underrepresented in regular education, so too are Black teachers (especially males) underrepresented in gifted education.

Serwatka, Deering, and Stoddard (1989) found the percentage of Black teachers to be a significant predictor of the underrepresentation of Black students in gifted classes: As the percentage of Black teachers increases, the placement of Black students in gifted programs should also increase. Accordingly, more Black teachers may increase the aspirations, expectations, motivation, and, ultimately, achievement of gifted Black students.

Teacher training in gifted education. Many states lack certification laws for teachers of the gifted. Specifically, 61% of the teachers surveyed by Archambault et al. (1993) had no staff development in gifted education. Similarly, Karnes and Whorton (1991) found that half of the states require no certification or endorsement in gifted education. Three states make this training optional. Only 5 states have statements of competencies, only 14 require practicum experience, and only 8 require teaching experience in the regular classroom prior to working with gifted students. Similarly, as described in Chapter 6, counselors and psychologists frequently lack training in gifted education.

Teacher training in multicultural education. Few teachers are trained in multicultural and/or urban education. Misconceptions, naive thinking, and prejudices are more apparent when teachers lack urban and multicultural education preparation. It is inconceivable, given the nation's changing demography, that educators of the gifted would not be required to take course work and practicums in multicultural education. Several states (e.g., California, Pennsylvania, North Carolina, Minnesota, and New York) require multicultural training for the recertification of school personnel. Minnesota was one of the first states to require training in human relations to develop intercultural skills. According to Filla and Clark (1973), teachers were trained to understand the contributions and lifestyles of various racial, cultural, and economic groups; create learning environments that contribute to the self-esteem of all persons and to positive interpersonal relations; recognize and deal with dehumanizing biases, discrimination, and prejudices; and respect human diversity and personal rights.

An important factor in improving underachieving and gifted Black students' achievement is improving teachers' behaviors and attitudes; multicultural preparation promises to increase teachers' effectiveness in this regard. With this training, teachers are less likely to hold negative expectations of Black students, abuse identification practices, and abuse tracking. As long as educators perceive the causes of poor achievement as resting entirely with Black students and their parents, however, they are not likely to examine their own behaviors and attitudes toward minority students. Meaningful multicultural education begins with teacher self-awareness.

As described below, a lack of training and inadequate experience in working with urban and minority students contribute to negative teacher attitudes and stereotypes about minority students (particularly low teacher expectations and unwillingness to recognize giftedness and potential among minority students), ethnocentric curriculum, and ethnocentric instruction.

Teacher attitudes and beliefs. Education is not a neutral profession. Teachers are human beings; as such, they are not immune to racial and cultural biases. Teaching is influenced by the status of race relations in the larger society. It is unrealistic and fruitless to assume that teaching occurs in isolation from societal illnesses — social and political forces influence both our personal and our professional lives.

Negative attitudes and expectations of educators who do not believe that racial minority students are capable of high levels of intelligence and giftedness persist. Academicians have created a cult of failure whose doctrine holds that variations in school resources have limited effects on learning, that schools themselves have little to do with who learns what and how much they learn, that children's backgrounds have the greatest influence on educational outcomes, and that reform is meaningless for such students (Bitting, Cordeiro, & Baptiste, 1992). Proponents of this perspective believe that Black students are intellectually inferior, that race itself explains their intellectual inferiority, and that this deficiency is, therefore, biologically determined or inherited (Burt, 1972; Goddard, 1912; Jensen, 1969, 1979; Spearman, 1927).

Burstein and Cabello (1989) found that 38% of student teachers believed that poor academic achievement and performance among minority students were due to cultural deficits. Teacher expectations for minority students are a function of their attitudes and beliefs. Teacher expectancy theory (Rosenthal & Jacobson, 1968) holds that teachers communicate their expectations of students through both subtle and overt behavioral cues (see Figure 8.1). For instance, a teacher who believes that Black students are not as competent as White students might communicate this belief by assigning easy tasks to Black students and assigning more difficult and challenging tasks to White students. The teacher's behavior communicates that Black students are incapable of mastering challenging work and

FIGURE 8.1. Factors affecting teacher expectations of students.

Factor	Teacher Expectations
Gender	Lower expectations for elementary boys and for older girls; expectations are often related to subject areas and vocational choices.
SES	Lower expectations for lower SES students (including parents' level of education, types of jobs, place of residence).
Race	Lower expectations for racially and culturally diverse students.
Test scores; permanent records	Belief in "fixed ability" keeps one from recognizing progress, especially small successes.
Negative comments about student	Lounge talk, other teachers' or principal's evaluation results in lower teacher expectations.
Type of school	Lower expectations for rural and inner-city (urban) students; higher for suburban.
Oral language patterns	Lower expectations for anyone who speaks nonstandard English or English as a second language.
Neatness; appearance	Lower expectations associated with general disorganization—poor handwriting, dress and so forth.
Halo effect	Tendency to label a child's overall ability based on one characteristic (e.g., teacher lets child's giftedness, rather than effort, motivation, and actual performance, play a major role in evaluations).
Teacher training institutions	Perpetuation of myths and ideologies of limitations of certain groups.

that White students are more competent. Other messages come from giving Black students fewer opportunities to speak in class, seating them at the back of the class, ignoring their questions or raised hands, and offering less praise to them.

Beliefs, attitudes, and stereotypes also influence tracking decisions and placement. Tracking contributes to the poor educational outcomes of many capable Black students. Although tracking is commonplace in many American school systems, it is one of the most controversial school practices. Proponents argue that tracking helps teachers better target individual needs and that, subsequently, students learn more. Opponents argue that tracking stereotypes students by labeling them as "unable" or "less able." The latter concern carries significant implications for minority, poor, and urban students who are found disproportionately in the lower ability groups.

In general, the majority of the literature, research, court decisions, and reform proposals suggest that tracking has few positive effects because lower-track students, the majority of whom are economically disadvantaged and Black, achieve less than their high-track counterparts (Oakes, 1988). Placing students into groups based on academic ability or teachers' perceptions of students' abilities and potential negatively affects lower-track students. They typically have lower self-concepts than higher-track students. Lower-track placement contributes to decreased levels of motivation to achieve, and lower-track students have higher dropout rates, more school misconduct, and greater delinquency than students in higher tracks. In other words, tracking contributes to stereotyped and stratified roles that inhibit the social development of lower-track students. This inhibition is characterized by poor relationships with peers, parents, and teachers — key variables in student achievement.

Tracking also affects teachers' level of encouragement and their assumptions regarding lower-track students' abilities or potential. The underlying belief is that these students can accomplish very little academically; low placement is equated with low potential. This is quite disconcerting, considering that standardized testing is the primary method of deciding group placement. Because of the high representation of Black students in lower tracks, Irvine (1991) called tracking "educational ghettos" for Black students.

Ethnocentric and monocultural curriculum. Students learn more in school than is included in their formal curriculum. The hidden curriculum contains the implicit messages that convey "appropriate" values, behaviors, and beliefs to students. These messages are transmitted to students through the underlying rules that guide the routines and social relations in schools and classrooms. The hidden curriculum exacerbates achievement problems among Black students because it conveys different messages to students of different SES, gender, and racial groups. That is, schools magnify or reinforce racial, gender, and SES differences (Bowles & Gintis, 1976; Giroux, 1983).

Monocultural curriculum and instruction in both general and gifted education predestine too many Black students to diminished self-concepts, feelings of inferiority, and, subsequently, underachievement. Segregation of the curriculum and instructional inequities exist in a wide array of schools (and, by inference, gifted programs), where students are denied equal access to high-status knowledge and learning opportunities because of biases about their gender, race, nationality, cultural background, or SES:

> "Curriculum segregation" occurs when different course assignments, instructional styles, and teaching materials are routinely employed for different groups of students; it constitutes a form of discrimination that mirrors the prejudices and inequities in the larger educational system and in society. In the books and content that are regularly taught, the role models that are commonly presented, the way students are treated in classroom interactions, and the assignment of certain students to instructional programs all convey subtle — but powerful — messages about just how separate and unequal education is. (G. Gay, 1990, p. 56)

The curriculum consists of implicit and explicit messages to students about differential power and social structures — students learn what kinds of knowledge are valued and devalued, and how students are valued and devalued. These messages are learned informally and sometimes unintentionally as a result of formal structure and curriculum. That is, students learn through acts of omission and commission; they learn from what is present in and left out of the curriculum.

Much of the focus on multicultural education has centered on curriculum rather than instruction. Yet instruction has a major impact on students' achievement. Ladson-Billings (1990a, 1990b, 1994) distinguishes between teachers who hold assimilationist as opposed to pluralistic conceptions of teaching relative to themselves as teachers, their social relationships with Black students, and their views about knowledge (Figure 8.2). Assimilationist teachers see themselves in isolation from the school community; they are strangers to Black students because they are detached and neutral. They also accept failure, which is considered inevitable for some students. Assimilationists perceive the student-teacher relationship as hierarchical, and knowledge is viewed as static. Moreover, they encourage competitive and individualistic learning environments. Although competitive environments can be motivating and invigorating for some students, they are uncomfortable for others. Through competition, students are encouraged not to cooperate, not to help or show compassion, and not to trust. The sense of community that is so important for learning and students' socioemotional well-being is disrupted. Conversely, teachers who hold pluralistic perspectives see teaching as an art; they believe that all students have the potential to learn, and they seek a sense of community in the classroom. Further, social relations between students and teachers are humanely equitable and not confined to the four walls of the classroom.

Kitano (1991) wrote one of only a few articles specifically on promot-

FIGURE 8.2. Assimilationist versus pluralistic philosophies of teaching (adapted from Ladson-Billings, 1990a; 1990b).

Assimilationist	Pluralistic
Conceptions of Self and Other	
Teacher sees self as technician; teaching is a technical task	Teacher sees self as artist; teaching is an art
Teacher does not see self as part of the community; encourages achievement as a means of students' escaping the community	Teacher sees self as part of a community and teaching is giving back to the community; teacher encourages students to do the same
Teacher believes that failure is inevitable for some students	Teacher believes that all students can achieve
Teacher homogenizes students into one "American" identity	Teacher helps students make connections among their community, racial, ethnic, and national origins
Teacher sees teaching as putting in knowledge—like banking	Teacher sees teaching as pulling out knowledge—like mining
Social Relations	
Teacher–student relationship is fixed, hierarchical, and limited to formal classroom roles	Teacher–student relationship is fluid, humanely equitable, and extends to interaction beyond the classroom into the community
Teacher has a weak, superficial, and/or idiosyncratic relationship with individual students	Teacher demonstrates a connectedness with all students (oneness)
Teacher encourages competition; individual achievement is a priority	Teacher strives to have a community of learners; cooperation is valued and encouraged
Teacher encourages students to learn individually, in isolation	Teacher encourages students to learn collaboratively; students are expected to teach and be responsible for one another
Conceptions of Knowledge	
Knowledge is static, passed in one direction—from teacher to student	Knowledge is dynamic—continuously recreated, recycled, and shared by teachers and students; it is not static or unchanging; students revise old ideas based on new information
Student performance relies heavily on innate ability	Student performance relies heavily on environment, teaching, and nurturance
Knowledge (content) is infallible	Knowledge (content) is viewed critically
Teacher is detached, neutral about content	Teacher is passionate about content
Teacher expects students to demonstrate prerequisite knowledge and skills (students build their own bridges)	Teacher helps students develop prerequisite knowledge and skills (build bridges or scaffolding)
Teacher sees excellence as a postulate that exists independent of student diversity or individual differences	Teacher sees excellence as a complex but achievable standard that may involve some postulates but takes student diversity and individual differences into consideration

ing pluralism and multicultural education in gifted programs. Kitano argued that gifted programs continue to espouse assimilation rather than employ pluralistic approaches to cultural diversity. Assimilationists favor the relinquishment of a diverse student's original culture (Figure 8.3). These students are expected to adapt to the values, attitudes, and behaviors of the predominant culture. Educators who favor assimilation are likely to blame Black students for their poor achievement, whereas pluralists acknowledge the role of the educational and social systems in promoting poor achievement. Consequently, pluralists in gifted education seek to empower Black and underachieving students. Pluralists retain and maintain a student's original culture. When accommodation of schooling to the diverse gifted student's experiences occurs, the school bears the responsibility for changing. In short, when the culture of the student is valued, educators are more likely to witness fundamental and essential changes in that student's achievement, motivation, attitudes, and behavior. Collaboration and cohesion among all students are goals of pluralistic teachers.

MULTICULTURAL EDUCATION:
PHILOSOPHIES AND RATIONALE

Although all of us are racial and cultural beings, belonging to a particular group does not automatically endow a person with multicultural competence or with the skills necessary to be a culturally competent and responsive educator. As Sue, Arrendondo, and McDavis (1992) stated, being born and raised in a family does not mean that one will be a competent family educator.

What is multicultural education? Multicultural education is education that values cultural pluralism. It rejects the perspective that schools should dissolve cultural differences and opposes the view that schools should merely "tolerate" cultural pluralism. It affirms that educational institutions should strive to preserve and enhance cultural pluralism. To endorse cultural pluralism is to endorse the principle that there is no one model American (AACTE Commission on Multicultural Education, 1973, p. 264).

Effective implementation of multicultural education has four major objectives: to teach values that support cultural diversity and individual uniqueness, to encourage the qualitative expansion of diverse cultures and their incorporation into the mainstream of American socioeconomic and political life, to explore alternative and emerging lifestyles, and to encourage multiculturalism (AACTE Commission, 1973). Banks and Banks (1993) defined multicultural education as:

FIGURE 8.3. Assimilationist versus pluralistic perspectives of minority students (adapted from Banks, 1988; and Kitano, 1991).

	Assimilationist	**Pluralist**
Source of underachievement	Cultural deficit perspective—underachievement is the result of an inadequate, inferior culture as well as childhood and family experiences; intervention efforts are directed at deficits	Social deficit—underachievement is influenced by negative interactions between the system and the child; seeks to empower children and to change the system
Purpose of schooling	Assimilation—Transmission of mainstream values for the maintenance of the predominant culture; melting pot philosophy	Accommodation—Understanding many cultural perspectives to create a pluralistic society that values diversity; salad bowl philosophy
Identification	Culture of identification—standardized practices, instruments, and procedures are relied on extensively or exclusively; unidimensional instruments prevail	Culture of assessment—dynamic, authentic, multidimensional, and comprehensive; culturally sensitive
Instructional practices	Focus on individual achievement and competition; ignore or negate individual and group (between and within) differences in teaching and learning	Focus on democratic principles and cooperation; cultural differences in teaching and learning styles are acknowledged
Curriculum	Academically responsive—Problem solving and critical thinking based on mainstream culture and history; monocultural or ethnocentric orientation; materials and teaching styles promote a common culture in which cultural differences are ignored or deemed unworthy of attention; idealized and noncontroversial ideologies are espoused; concepts of racism, classism, and other forms of discrimination are given little (if any) attention; concepts about diverse groups are appended to the regular or core curriculum; deficient or pathological perspectives of minority groups are overtly or covertly advanced	Socially and academically responsive—problem solving and critical thinking apply to the culture and history of diverse groups; builds skills to transform society; multicultural education is practiced; curriculum focuses on students' strengths, helps students learn to function effectively within the predominant culture, their own culture, and other cultures; curriculum reflects a pluralistic perspective or ideology; content about minority groups is integrated as a regular, integral part of the curriculum
Teacher training and experience	Teachers refuse or oppose training in working with minority students; teachers are unfamiliar with minority child development theories, principles, and perspectives.	Teachers are active and proactive in seeking professional development to work effectively with minority students; teachers are familiar with minority child development theories, principles, and perspectives.

an educational reform movement designed to change the total educational environment so that students from diverse racial and ethnic groups, both gender groups, exceptional students, and students from each social-class group will experience equal educational opportunities in schools, colleges and universities. (p. 359)

Attention to multicultural issues and concerns has increased as the nation becomes more racially and culturally diverse. Multicultural education gained momentum in the 1980s, with the past and current works of Banks (1994), Bennett (1990), Gollnick and Chinn (1994), Heid (1988), Locke (1992), Sleeter and Grant (1993), and others. These authors addressed several needs: (1) to develop multicultural curriculum and instruction; (2) for multiculturalism to permeate educational practices and programs; (3) for commitment by educators, policy makers, and decision makers to the cause; (4) for a more racially and culturally diverse teaching force; (5) to view multicultural education as a legitimate enterprise; and (6) to study the quality of multicultural education so as to ensure that it is substantive and integral rather than superficial and ancillary. Their collective works indicate that most teachers, the majority of whom are White females, have little (if any) formal training in multicultural education; similarly, they have little daily or practical experience with minority students because most teachers do not live in the same neighborhoods in which they teach (Darling-Hammond, 1994; King, 1993). To be culturally competent in working with these students, educators must take a proactive stance in incorporating standards and practices that reflect the diversity of the United States and its well over 16,000 school districts.

RECOMMENDATIONS

If students have emotional, social, or environmental blocks that have tied their freedom to develop and destroyed their motivation to achieve, then schools have a responsibility to help them become free from those handicapping conditions. (Whitmore, 1980, p. 167)

Schools are ill-designed to accommodate today's minority students. Although almost every aspect of U.S. society has entered into the technological age, the U.S. school system remains in the industrial age. The programs, curricula, and buildings are essentially the same as they were 100 years ago. Probably the only thing that has changed is the learner (Baptiste, 1992, p. 13). But as Korman (1974) stated, professionals have an ethical responsibility to seek training and preparation in working with racially and culturally diverse persons:

The provision of professional services to persons of culturally diverse backgrounds by persons not competent in understanding and providing professional services to such groups shall be considered unethical. (p. 105)

Although speaking specifically to the counseling profession, Korman's statement is equally appropriate for the education profession. The practice of professionals without training or competence working with racially and culturally diverse persons is unethical and potentially harmful, which borders on a violation of human rights (Sue et al., 1992, p. 480). If teachers are willing to receive training and experience in working with minority and urban students, if they are willing to avail themselves of such an opportunity, there is no reason that they cannot attain an adequate knowledge of their minority students.

Teacher preparation programs must emphasize diversity and demonstrate that it is integral to their faculty, staff, and curriculum. Teacher education curriculum in gifted education should require future teachers to gain classroom experience with Black and/or gifted Black students and require teachers to study the worldviews, histories, and cultures of other groups (including myths, values, music, child-rearing practices, communication styles, interpersonal styles, and language). Teachers need opportunities to understand and cope with their apprehension, fear, and reactions to Black students (especially males). Teachers must be reflective practitioners and develop the observational skills that are essential for evaluation and assessment. Ultimately, teachers need training to become bicultural or culturally competent. The more teachers know about the Black students they teach, the more proficient they become at guiding and facilitating their students' learning.

Multicultural education is one means of proactively addressing issues of diversity. The lack of multicultural education in schools contributes to poor educational outcomes for minority students (see, e.g., Au & Kawakami, 1994; Banks, 1993; Gollnick & Chinn, 1994). In gifted education, similar issues have been raised (Baldwin, 1989, 1994; D. Y. Ford, 1994c; D. Y. Ford & Webb, 1994; Frasier, 1989; Kitano, 1991). How is the underrepresentation of minority students in gifted education a function of monocultural and ethnocentric education and related practices?

B. A. Ford (1992) proposed a multicultural framework entailing six essential components:

(1) engaging teachers in self-awareness activities to explore their attitudes and perceptions concerning cultural groups and beliefs and the influence of their attitudes on students' achievement and educational opportunities;

(2) exposing teachers to accurate information about various cultural and ethnic groups, including their historical and contemporary contributions, lifestyles, interpersonal communication patterns, and parental attitudes about education;

(3) helping educators explore the diversity that exists within and between cultural and ethnic groups;

(4) showing teachers how to apply and incorporate multicultural perspectives into the teaching–learning process to maximize the academic, cognitive, personal, and social development of learners;

(5) demonstrating effective interactions among teachers, students, and families; and

(6) providing opportunities for teachers to manifest an appropriate application of cultural information to create a healthy learning climate. (p. 108)

Additional suggestions relate to teachers becoming culturally competent and responsible.

Characteristics of Culturally Competent Educators

This section presents an overview of characteristics of culturally competent educators. I have adopted and adapted the model proposed by Sue and Sue (1990) and Sue et al. (1992),[1] which holds that culturally competent professionals have the following core characteristics:

(1) *Self-awareness and self-understanding.* Culturally competent educators seek greater self-awareness and self-understanding regarding their biases, assumptions, and stereotypes. This self-awareness is reflected in their worldviews and an understanding of how they are products of their cultural conditioning. They recognize that assumptions and biases influence their teaching and their relationships with racially and culturally diverse students.

(2) *Cultural awareness and understanding.* Culturally competent educators seek to understand the worldviews of racially and culturally diverse students without making negative judgments. They do not have to adopt these views, but they respect them as legitimate rather than inferior or otherwise substandard.

(3) *Social responsiveness and responsibility.* Culturally competent educators seek to increase multicultural awareness and understanding among *all* students. Thus, educators practice multiculturalism even in homogeneous settings where there is little racial and cultural diversity. The shortage or absence of Black and other minority students in a gifted program,

school, community, or state is not used as an excuse for lack of attention to multiculturalism and related educational practices.

(4) *Appropriate techniques and strategies.* Culturally competent educators seek to deliver more effective education to racially and culturally diverse students. Education is relevant, appropriate, and sensitive to students' diverse needs, including attention to teaching and learning styles. In general, such educators seek to adopt principles of learning that are necessary to meet the academic, psychological, and affective needs of minority students.

Dimensions of Cultural Competence

Sue and Sue (1990) and Sue et al. (1992) also proposed that cultural competence falls into at least three areas:

(1) *Attitudes and beliefs.* This dimension refers to the need to check biases and stereotypes, to develop positive orientations toward multiculturalism, and to understand the ways in which beliefs and attitudes interrupt the educational process as well as the academic, affective, and psychological development of Black students.

(2) *Knowledge.* Educators understand their own worldviews as well as those of other racial and cultural groups. Moreover, they understand social and political influences on educational practices and student outcomes.

(3) *Skills.* Culturally competent educators acquire skills and strategies to work more effectively with minority students. These competencies include social, communication, affective, and educational skills and strategies.

Figure 8.4 presents a more in-depth description of the relationship between the four characteristics and the three dimensions that promise to increase the cultural competence and responsiveness of educators and other school personnel.

SUMMARY

It is the role of the educator to change conditions until opportunities for action and reflection are created that promote student learning. (Dewey, 1963, p. 58)

Schools often permit a significant degree of marginality — that is, disconnection between students and the conditions designed for learning. In

FIGURE 8.4. Characteristics and dimensions of culturally competent educators.

DIMENSIONS

CHARACTERISTICS	Attitudes and Beliefs	Knowledge	Skills
Self-Awareness	Aware of themselves as cultural beings; seek to understand their own cultural heritage Aware of their own biases, attitudes, and values and how they influence the educational process Recognize limits of their competence and experience Comfortable with differences between themselves and students relative to race, ethnicity, and culture	Knowledgeable about their own cultural heritage and how it affects them both personally and professionally Understand the social and cultural privileges of being White (i.e., how racism, prejudice, and discrimination and subsequent oppression also affect them personally and professionally)	Seek educational training experiences to enrich their understanding of and effectiveness in teaching and working with minority students Seek consultation to enhance their effectiveness Seek to understand themselves as racial and cultural beings and actively work for a nonracist identity
Cultural Awareness	Aware of their negative reactions toward minority students; seek to be nonjudgmental Aware of stereotypes and preconceived notions about minority students Familiar with research and latest findings regarding education and minority students (e.g., understand that traditional identification and assessment practices tend to be ineffective in identifying gifted characteristics among minority students)	Understand how cultural differences influence and may conflict with their teaching and with students' learning (including learning styles, communication, and behaviors) Aware of culturally sensitive identification and assessment practices, including appropriate tests and other instruments	Seek to redress in equities in education relative to curriculum, instruction, identification, and assessment (e.g., inform colleagues and others of pitfalls and promises in these areas) Advocate for minority students; confront injustices at all levels—classroom, school, community, social—on their behalf Actively involved with minority students outside of school setting (e.g., family and community events, social and political functions, celebrations); their relationship with minority students is more than an academic exercise Work with families to enhance the educational process for minority students (including extended family members)

151

FIGURE 8.4. Continued.

CHARACTERISTICS	DIMENSIONS		
Social Responsiveness	Seek to increase racial harmony within classrooms—seek to decrease negative beliefs and attitudes of White students toward minority students through awareness and understanding of human diversity and individual differences Address issues of social injustices in both heterogeneous and homogeneous classrooms; the lack of cultural diversity is not used as an excuse for ignoring social and cultural problems	Aware of problems associated with monocultural and ethnocentric educational practices relative to White students Seek to acquire facilitative skills to understand and meet students' affective and cognitive needs	Practice multiculturalism and substantive multicultural education on a consistent basis Able to address inequities as they arise in the classroom and school Seek to empower all students to be proactive, culturally aware, and respectful of individual differences
Appropriate Techniques and Strategies	Have a clear and explicit knowledge and understanding of the generic characteristics of teaching and learning and how they may conflict with cultural values of minority students	Aware of social and institutional barriers that prevent minority students from truly having equitable and equal education Interpret test results and school performance in a culturally sensitive manner	Able to engage in a variety of helping responses; eclectic in teaching; willing to adapt teaching styles to learning styles and teach students how to be bistylistic in learning Recognize when students' problems stem from racial injustices Take responsibility for modifying curriculum and instruction so that they are culturally sensitive Take some of the responsibility for teaching minority students to be bicultural, to understand their educational rights, and to have realistic and high expectations and aspirations

other words, schools allow individuals or subgroups to develop and sustain faulty, incomplete relationships with other school members and programs. Most schools tolerate the existence of a fringe population that is not fully involved in the mainstream school life. These marginal students learn and contribute only a fraction of what they can and thus use only a portion of their potential at school (Sinclair & Ghory, 1987, 1992).

Far too many Black students have difficulty relating and connecting to school settings. This is not to say that schoolwork is difficult for these students or that it is beyond their ability. Rather, the point is that the quality of the relationships between Black students and teachers, for example, is less than adequate. Such poor relationships and lack of mutual understanding make it difficult for Black students to appreciate school tasks and objectives.

Many school practices contribute to underachievement among gifted Black students. Schools that consistently are unsuccessful with Black students tend to be mired in a slough of attitudes and counterproductive practices that defy efforts by underachieving students, parents, and educators to break the cycle of failure (Sinclair & Ghory, 1992). The primary issue of underachievement in school is the irresponsiveness of schools to diversity among students. Part of Black students' poor motivation and achievement can be attributed to culturally assaultive classrooms. L. Clark, DeWolf, and Clark (1992) noted that such an environment exists when teachers do not focus on the essence of a people's belief and way of life, focus more on differences than on similarities, treat social injustices as if they existed only in the past, teach (perpetuate) incorrect or stereotypical versions of how people live and give token representations of a group, ignore individuals *within* the group, and do not integrate the curriculum with a pluralistic philosophy. In contrast, in effective and affective classrooms, attitudes of diversity saturate the classroom; teachers seek to inoculate students against racism and help students experience enrichment from diversity — not fear, apprehension, anxiety, and low self-esteem.

Too little research exists on how gifted Black students perceive the process of schooling. Some Black students question the merits of formal education, even though an education promises social improvement. They *learn* to become distrustful of the educational process, viewing it less as an opportunity for social advancement and more as an instrument of the dominant culture designed to rob them of their unique cultural values, beliefs, attitudes, and norms. Unidimensional instruction and monocultural curriculum contribute to and may exacerbate stereotypes about racially and culturally diverse groups. All students, including White students, are miseducated when schools and programs adopt curricular and instructional practices that are devoid of diversity. All students benefit from education that is pluralistic.

When gifted Black students underachieve, it is important to understand how schools may force a disconnection between learning and achievement. Educators and professionals have a moral responsibility to teach the *whole* child. A crucial priority of educators is not only to find meaningful ways to identify and serve gifted Black students but also to get in touch with their interests and values. This is particularly important for gifted underachieving Black students, who may not find sufficient reasons or means for being successful in school. Genuine concern for these students promises to produce constructive changes in their lives and school performance. When students enter schools, teachers have 6 hours each day to use their creativity and determination to help resolve educational problems facing Black students.

The school doors and teachers' arms must be open to Black students. Schools are social institutions, but they are also communities. Schools without a sense of community contribute to underachievement or poor student motivation. Schools should provide a supportive and nurturing environment for all students. This requires embracing Black students as individuals and helping them to feel connected to the school. It is liberating and empowering to Black students to know that teachers care and have their best interests at heart. Learning outcomes appear to be related, at least in part, to the ability of teachers and school personnel to balance the affective dimensions of schools and classrooms. Teaching is an art; it requires great sensitivity to the needs of all students. There is no magic or teacher-proof curriculum (Brophy, 1988) patented to benefit all students. Thus, teachers' skills play a significant role in optimizing Black students' achievement. Students learn best in an environment designed to mitigate against social isolation and to establish a sense of self-efficacy and identity. Black students (gifted, potentially gifted, underachieving) cannot learn in a culturally assaultive classroom.

The preparation of school personnel to work with Black students is never ending. School personnel must be trained or retrained to work more effectively with the gifted student population. A significant portion of this preparation should also be in multicultural counseling and education. Gifted Black students need a place to turn emotionally in order to express their concerns. This support is especially meaningful and effective if imparted by a professional (e.g., teacher or school counselor) who is trained to work with both gifted and racially diverse students.

A philosophy of multiculturalism must be infused throughout the educational curriculum, including courses in gifted education. Comprehensive preparation should (re)educate teachers and other school personnel so that inaccurate perceptions and uninformed beliefs do not restrict Black students' learning. Too many minority students fail in school because the culture of the school ignores or degrades their families, communities, and cultural backgrounds. Teachers who reflect ethnocentric values may single out for criticism the values and behaviors of Black and culturally different students. They can crush the socioemotional well-being of gifted Black students and neglect the strengths that these students bring to the educational workplace. Schools must work diligently to narrow cultural gaps among students, teachers, and other school personnel.

NOTE

1. The work of Sue and colleagues is aimed specifically at counseling professionals. In this chapter, their recommendations have been adapted for educators; a fourth characteristic of culturally competent educators (social responsibility) has been added.

Chapter 9

Families and Gifted Black Students

Family issues have received much attention in gifted education. The foci of this literature and research have varied, but common issues include family dynamics, sibling rivalry and relations, parenting styles, labeling, and parental concerns regarding how best to understand, cope with, and meet a gifted child's academic and affective needs. A resounding finding is that the presence of a gifted child in a family can be a stressful event, one that changes, in many ways, the dynamics of the family (as is the case with other children with special needs).

Much of this work has limited external validity to families of gifted Black children. The limited generalizability of the literature on families of gifted children exists for at least three reasons: differential family structures between Black and White families, differential child-rearing practices between the two groups, and life experiences that have quantitatively and qualitatively different implications for gifted Black students and their families. Given the paucity of empirical and theoretical work on Black families with gifted children, this chapter draws implications from gifted education and urban education to highlight concerns of Black families with gifted children. Finally, recommendations for educators and researchers are offered.

FAMILIES AND GIFTED CHILDREN

J. S. Coleman (1987) noted that mass formal schooling has a short history, in that it hardly existed until the twentieth century. Until that time, children grew up in the context of the household and the community. All the activities and training of children were confined to on-the-job training, which was closely linked to household activities. For many children, then, the family and community constituted their school, as continues to be the case in many Third World countries. With this in mind, it is little wonder that families, both then and now, represent a significant factor in the educational and affective well-being of their children. In essence, parents provide the initial and basic climate for learning in the home and at school.

Families are critical variables in the translation of talent, ability, and promise into achievement. They provide the context for the transmission of values through direct and indirect behaviors and modeling, including the importance of hard work, success, effort, independence, and self-sufficiency. Parents also play a major role in talent development by selecting and providing opportunities for children; by monitoring, organizing, and prioritizing children's time; and by setting, communicating, and reinforcing standards for performance and achievement.

Bloom (1985) emphasized that parents who set high achievement standards for their gifted children pressure them to achieve by stressing a strong and positive work ethic and by valuing intellectual endeavors, success, ambition, and diligence. It goes without saying that parents play a powerful role in the development of children. For better or worse, the capacities and proclivities of children reflect the influence of parents.

Parental Concerns

The concerns of parents of gifted children are numerous. General concerns include feelings of personal inadequacy, frustration, and helplessness in meeting the various needs of their children (e.g., lack of financial resources and support, lack of understanding and experience); feeling threatened by their children's abilities; feeling guilty when their children experience socioemotional problems or are not readily accepted by their peers; being fearful of what giftedness means and its long-term implications; and holding unrealistic expectations for their children. These various issues have one common denominator — preventing underachievement among their gifted children. The main issues of parental concern are discussed below.

Labeling. Parents generally feel ambivalent about labeling their children as gifted. Contrary to general beliefs, most parents do not pray to have gifted children (Silverman, 1993). Parents' feelings and reactions may vacillate from denial to rejection to overidentification. In the latter situation, parents may live vicariously through their gifted child, seeing giftedness as a status symbol or even exploiting the child's ability. The child's giftedness becomes the family's principal concern; family members forget that the gifted child is a "child with gifted abilities." This narcissism or overinvestment can have a debilitating influence on students' achievement and identity, resulting in perfectionism and underachievement, for example.

Giftedness is a family affair (Silverman, 1993), thus, having a gifted child can negatively affect marital relations, particularly when parents hold opposite perceptions of giftedness (e.g., one parent perceives the child's giftedness as a burden and the other sees it as an asset). Further, when only one child in a family is identified as gifted, nongifted siblings may feel neglected or have lowered self-esteem; when the nongifted child is older than the gifted child, he or she may feel resentful; when two or more children are gifted, competition, resentment, and anxiety may occur (Keirouz, 1990). Having a child identified as gifted also impacts family adaptability and cohesion (West, Hosie, & Mathews, 1989). Adaptability, which ranges from rigid to chaotic, represents the family's ability to be flexible as its power structure, role relationships, and family rules change in response to the context or situation. Cohesion, which ranges from disengaged to enmeshed, represents the degree to which members of the family are separated from or connected to one another. It is generally assumed that balanced families are more effective at nurturing and sustaining their children's achievement. Findings by West et al. (1989) indicate that most (86%) of the parents of gifted children sampled were balanced (in the midrange of the variables) in terms of family functioning. The findings are generalizable, however, only to intact families — the focus of the study by West et al. (1989). The extent to which such studies have external validity to minority families is questionable, since demographic data were not reported.

Educational needs. Colangelo (1988) identified common questions and concerns of parents of gifted students. Many of these concerns related to meeting students' educational needs, understanding and addressing gifted children's socioemotional adjustment, determining appropriate placement (e.g., the benefits of gifted education versus regular education), working effectively with school personnel, and providing appropriate stimulation at home.

Kaufmann and Sexton (1983) surveyed parents of gifted students regarding their primary concerns. The responses of parents with students at three school levels were summarized: preschoolers, 1st through 6th graders, and 7th through 12th graders. Noteworthy is that one-third of parents with children at all three levels expressed dissatisfaction regarding the school's ability to meet their children's needs. In terms of specific academic needs, parents of children in formal schooling (grades 1–6 and 7–12) expressed the following concerns:

(1) 61% of parents of elementary students and 39.9% of parents of children in junior high and high school did not believe that their children were challenged intellectually in school.

(2) 46.4% (parents of elementary students) and 27.4% (parents of junior and high school students) did not believe that their children's social needs were being met.

(3) 51% and 33.1%, respectively, did not believe that material was covered in depth.

(4) 48.3% and 31.2%, respectively, did not consider learning opportunities to be adequate.

(5) 52.1% and 34.2%, respectively, were not satisfied with enrichment experiences.

(6) 58.1% and 36.5%, respectively, did not believe that their children's higher-level needs were being met in school.

The concerns of parents with preschool children were distributed somewhat evenly across the items just mentioned.

Underachievement. Green, Fine, and Tollefson (1988) studied the families of 45 underachieving gifted males. The gifted males were identified as those scoring in the top 2% on the WISC-R or Stanford-Binet; underachievers were identified using one of three criteria: earning a C or below in one or more major academic subjects, having at least a 1-year difference between expected and actual performance on a standardized achievement test, or failing to complete work or submitting incomplete work at least 25% of the time as indicated by teacher records. They concluded that family relations and other adjustment issues played a central role in underachievement. Specifically, family stress and conflict, poor communication, overemphasis on dependence, and low parent achievement orientations were identified by gifted underachieving males as major adjustment issues. Thus, the majority of the families were considered dysfunctional, as perceived by their underachieving gifted male children. The findings of Green and colleagues, however, lack generalizability because of the homogeneous nature of the sample — participants included only male students in nuclear and upper SES families. Further, the definition of giftedness was exclusive and narrow (based on a unidimensional definition and one criterion).

Most studies have found that male underachievers considerably outnumber female underachievers (Bloom, 1985; Gallagher & Gallagher, 1994; Colangelo, Kerr, Maxey, & Christensen, 1992). Rimm and Lowe (1988) reported that underachieving gifted students often had families characterized by inconsistent expectations, organization, and structure. Parent relations were oppositional, sibling rivalry was extreme, and parent–child relationships were negative. The children viewed their parents as inconsistent, weak, and manipulatable. Further, although parents of underachievers showed concern about their children's achievement, they did not promote intrinsic and independent learning; nor did they model positive commitment to their careers to the same extent as parents of achieving gifted students. Other barriers to achievement included parents' direct opposition to teachers and school policies. Qualitative differences in enrichment activities were also noted, with underachievers having a plethora of activities and lessons that were so time-consuming as to leave little room for independent projects and intrinsic learning.

Family Structure. As Figure 9.1 indicates, families are more diverse in structure than ever before. All families, whether or not they have gifted children, are experiencing major changes in structure due to divorce, widowhood, separation, and teen pregnancy. There is limited research on gifted children in single-parent families, even though almost 25% of children under the age of 18 live with only one parent (U.S. Bureau of the Census, 1990). Projections indicate that 50% of all children will live in a

FIGURE 9.1. Changing structure of U.S. families, 1970–1990 (U.S. Bureau of the Census, 1970; 1990).

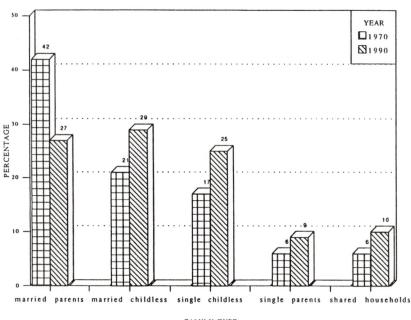

single-parent family for at least part of their childhood (Demo & Acock, 1988).

It is a common assumption that children in nuclear and middle to upper SES families are more academically successful than children from demographically different families. For example, the U.S. Department of Education (1993) reported that higher SES students represent 44% of those in gifted programs nationally, compared with 25% for lower SES students. Some studies reveal even lower percentages. For instance, VanTassel-Baska and Willis (1988) reported that only 15% of gifted students in their study were low SES; in a different study, VanTassel-Baska (1989) reported a figure of 20%. The underrepresentation of low SES students is significant, given that at least 50% of students live in poverty, especially minority students.

DeVaul and Davis (1988) also reported that children in single-parent families are less likely than students in nuclear families to be identified as gifted. One explanation is that single-parent status and poverty often go hand in hand; the terms are almost synonymous. Students in either or both situations are often discriminated against by educators in terms of lower teacher expectations, neglect, and humiliation (Zill, 1983).

Despite the inevitable differences in family structure, only one article (Gelbrich & Hare, 1989) specifically focused on gifted students in single-parent families. Thus, research on the family structures of gifted students has not kept pace with the times — the increase in diverse family structures has not been accompanied by an increase in research on these families. Our knowledge base about gifted children living in single-parent families, whether a function of choice, divorce, widowhood, separation, or some other reason, is virtually nonexistent.

Researchers have taken a piecemeal approach to studying gifted children and their families. They have focused almost exclusively on issues (e.g., concerns, fears) in isolation from processes (e.g., child-rearing practices, achievement orientations, socialization), on parents rather than families, and on homogeneous families rather than heterogeneous families relative to composition and structure, race, and SES.

Zuccone and Amerikaner's (1986) review of the literature concluded that the level of family functioning may be more relevant to the treatment of underachieving behaviors than are SES, family size, ethnicity, and other characteristics. That is, the difficulties of gifted underachievers may be understood best as part of the larger family context, for this is the context within which the most significant transactions occur. However, only with a comprehensive study of family processes and functioning, as well as demographic variables, can we gain a thorough understanding of gifted students and their families.

Conspicuously absent from the literature on families of gifted children is attention to Black families. Although gender differences were discussed in some of the studies, none of those cited above addressed the concerns of Black families and their gifted children. The following section addresses these shortcomings. It is contended that Black families are quantitatively and qualitatively different from White families. These differences are evident in not only their experiences but also their family structure and composition, child-rearing practices, educational involvement, achievement orientations, and demographic variables.

BLACK FAMILIES: A REVIEW OF RESEARCH AND THEORY

The Black family is like any other family institution in that it wants the best that life has to offer educationally, financially, spiritually, politically and socially for its members. Simultaneously, it is unlike any other family due to its unique status imposed by the deep structure (warp and woof of racism) of the American social system. . . . Black families have not been entirely free to manipulate the essential components of life to the same degree as have their White counterparts. (Jenkins, 1989, p. 139)

The culprit of underachievement among Black students has frequently been attributed to their families and communities. Given the high rates of school failure, underachievement, illiteracy, and dropping out of school, social and behavioral scientists have begun to explore more diligently the role that families play in students' school success or failure. One goal of this work has been to demythicize (mis)perceptions of Black families, some of which are that:

(1) Black families are homogeneous.
(2) Black parents have little interest in their children's education.
(3) Parents who do not become involved in the schools are not interested in their children's educational well-being.
(4) Grandparents and other extended family members provide economic rather than educational or academic support.
(5) The matriarchical structure of Black families is dysfunctional.

The initial research on the "pathology" of Black families appeared in the 1960s. These studies compared Black families with White families using data gathered on the latter group. Holding the nuclear family as the norm, the researchers proceeded to label extended families as pathological. Not surprisingly, a cultural deficit perspective emerged from this era.

Low SES, large, extended, and/or matriarchical families were equated with low achievement orientations rather than viewed as strengths and sources of support for members. Black families became both the victims of and accountable for the circumstances of their children. For example, the famous but controversial Moynihan (1965) report blamed the pathology of the Black family on the inability of fathers to find steady employment and to achieve at higher levels academically. The report, however, failed to probe the many factors associated with chronic unemployment and underemployment; it failed to examine the social circumstances of life for Blacks in the United States: racism, discrimination, and prejudice. In issuing a general indictment of Black families, Moynihan indicted Blacks; the family replaced the IQ in determining Black children's learning potential (Slaughter & Epps, 1987, p. 11). This indictment invited a general denial of the heterogeneity of the Black culture, and it encouraged a disregard for individual and within-group differences among Blacks.

The nuclear family—traditionally comprising mother, father, and children—has represented the "ideal" or "typical" family pattern in the United States and several other countries until quite recently (Wilson, 1989). That is, the general notion of "family" has been associated most frequently with two parents and their dependent children. This is not necessarily the typical model today. The nuclear family structure has been treated historically as the norm, the perspective from which other family structures are compared. This trend continues. D. Y. Ford (1994a) surveyed almost 500 college students majoring in education or family studies regarding their definitions and perceptions of diverse family structures (e.g., nuclear, extended, single-parent). Results indicated that the vast majority of the students, most of whom were White females, held traditional notions of families that included a husband, wife, and offspring. Students were less likely to perceive extended families, cohabiting individuals, and single parents as families.

Many cultures eschew the nuclear family as the family arrangement to be emulated, imitated, or idealized. Among Blacks, extended families are quite common. Anderson and Allen (1984) reported that Blacks are twice as likely as Whites to have grandmothers in residence. Statistics indicate that in 1984, 31% of Black single parents lived in extended families, compared with 19.8% of married Blacks (U.S. Bureau of the Census, 1985a, 1985b). In their study of the Woodlawn community in Chicago, Pearson, Hunter, Ensminger and Kellam (1990) found that 28% of 1,392 households consisted of extended families of various compositions.

Many Black students place a priority on their family relations. Extended families in particular represent an important and consistent element in these students' lives, providing financial independence, emotional support, and educational encouragement. As such, extended families help blunt social and economic injustices and hardships; in the process, they promote self-efficacy, self-esteem, and self-reliance (D. Y. Ford, 1993a; D. Y. Ford, Harris, Turner, & Sandidge, 1991).

Until recently, the importance of the extended family in influencing child development has been largely ignored because the normative nuclear definition of family necessarily implied that the extended family was not a legitimate form of American family life. In the next decade, society can expect to see even greater numbers of diverse families. The major demographic shifts under way suggest that, as a society, we should question our notions of the "ideal" family when such a family is on its way toward extinction. For minority cultures especially, the nuclear family tends to offer an inadequate survival or pragmatic nurturing strategy. Rather, diverse families increase the chances for improving Black students' situations.

R. Clark (1983) studied low SES Black students' achievement and underachievement in the context of their families. Achieving Black children had parents who

(1) were assertive in their involvement efforts;
(2) kept abreast of their children's school progress;
(3) were optimistic and tended to perceive themselves as having effective coping mechanisms and strategies;
(4) set high and realistic expectations for their children;
(5) held positive achievement orientations and supported tenets of the achievement ideology;
(6) set clear, explicit, achievement-oriented norms;
(7) established clear, specific role boundaries;
(8) deliberately engaged in experiences and behaviors designed to promote achievement; and
(9) had positive parent–child relations characterized by nurturance, support, respect, trust, and open communication.

Conversely, underachieving Black children had parents who

(1) were less optimistic and expressed feelings of helplessness and hopelessness;
(2) were less assertive and involved in their children's education;
(3) set unrealistic and unclear expectations for their children; and
(4) were less confident in terms of their parenting skills.

Lee's (1984) research with rural Black adolescents and their families also revealed psychosocial variables that contributed to students' academic success:

(1) close family relations and structure;
(2) high degree of parental control;
(3) moderate to high degree of family openness;
(4) strong family values;
(5) high level of educational encouragement and achievement orientation;
(6) good relations with siblings;
(7) extended family networks; and
(8) a sense of responsibility fostered through required chores.

Similarly, MacLeod's (1987) research on low SES Black males indicated that achievement-oriented students had parents who set clear, high, and realistic expectations for their sons. Parents encouraged their sons to achieve and to support the achievement ideology of hard work and effort.

In essence, although all parents, regardless of SES, want to provide stimulating, directive, supportive, and rewarding environments for their children, higher SES parents have the fiscal and social means to provide such opportunities. More specifically, Black parents have always viewed schools as the common denominator of the American dream. Unfortunately, too many Black families may be more survival oriented than child centered due to economic and social hardships. The need to survive may mitigate against an education-centered approach to child rearing and to educational involvement; yet children are the most precious resources of Black families (Slaughter & Kuehne, 1988). In essence, too often we see Black parents as being good or not so good without fully considering the circumstances of their lives:

> Black children have always borne a disproportionate share of the burden of poverty and economic decline in America and they are at substantially higher risk than White children for experiencing an array of social-emotional problems. (McLoyd, 1990, p. 311)

R. Clark (1983) concluded that the form and substance of family psychosocial patterns are the most significant components for understanding the educational effects of high achievers' families and low achievers' families, not their race or social class background per se. That is, family processes and culture rather than structural and demographic variables determine the achievement orientation of Black children. Quality of life is not always determined by family composition, marital status, income, and the educational level of parents. Neither are educational outcomes necessarily determined by these demographic variables.

Black parents continue to experience crises regarding their children's education; there is a crisis of confidence in the schools and in children's ability to benefit from them (Slaughter & Kuehne, 1988). Although Black families favor schooling as a means for achieving upward mobility and success, they worry about the efficacy of schools in meeting the affective and academic needs of their children.

BLACK FAMILIES AND GIFTED CHILDREN

VanTassel-Baska (1989), Marion (1980, 1981), D. Y. Ford (1993a), Exum (1983), and Prom-Jackson, Johnson, and Wallace (1987) have provided the only work specifically on gifted Black students and their families. Exum (1983) identified key issues among families of gifted Black children, and although the article was written for counselors, the concerns raised have important implications for educators as well. Exum cautioned counselors against attempting to understand gifted Black children in isolation from their family context and encouraged counselors to work with extended family members. Four major parental-familial concerns were described: (1) loss of authority and control of the gifted child, (2) the child's loss of respect for the family, (3) the child's loss of respect for the community and/or culture, and (4) the child's emotional stability and ability to interact with other people. More specifically, issues surrounding elitism and assimilation may prevail among Black parents, which makes placing their children in gifted programs a dilemma. Black parents may be concerned (and rightfully so) that school curricula will be monocultural and ethnocentric—devoid of culturally relevant material needed to promote self-esteem, identity, and pride in their children. On a similar note, Black parents may be concerned about the schools promoting individual rather than group affiliation and otherwise contradicting the values traditionally espoused by Black families. Marion (1980, 1981) noted that Black parents of gifted children may cling to the belief that children are gifted to the extent that they embody the values and beliefs highly prized by their culture. Gardner (1983) and Sternberg and Davidson (1986) also recognized the significance of cultural and contextual definitions of giftedness.

Exum (1983) described a cycle in which Black parents may become more authoritarian in their child-rearing practices in order to prevent assimilation by their children; children react by underachieving and attempting to disprove their giftedness in an effort to return the family to homeostasis. However, because the family knows that the child is gifted, it applies even more pressure to promote achievement. Ultimately, the gifted Black child may seek refuge in his or her peer group, all of which results in frustration, disappointment, and puzzlement by both the gifted child and his or her family.

VanTassel-Baska (1989) focused on the role of families in the lives of 15 economically disadvantaged gifted students, eight of whom were Black, and many of whom lived in single-parent families. Her findings revealed that low SES Black families had high expectations, aspirations, and standards for their children, as well as positive achievement orientations. Along with extended family members, the Black parents sought to promote self-competence and independence in their children. Parents were described as watchful of their children, hyperaware of children's accomplishments, and actively involved in developing their abilities. The Black students most often attributed their accomplishments to maternal figures, namely mothers and grandmothers, who represented sources of socioemotional support. These maternal figures also instilled positive achievement orientations, the work ethic, independence, and self-sufficiency in children. VanTassel-Baska's findings underscore the reality that children in economically disadvantaged families have parents whose values are more similar to than different from the values of economically advantaged parents; that the high and positive achievement orientations of Black and low SES parents can and do promote academic, social, and psychological resilience in children; and that family structure may play a secondary rather than primary role in gifted Black students' achievement behaviors and motivation to achieve. Strong Black families do exist and are quite adept at fostering resilience in their children.

Educators and researchers must systematically study home environmental variables and their effect on gifted Black students' achievement, a line of research that promises to explain why some Black children do well academically and others do not (D. Y. Ford, 1994b). Prom-Jackson et al. (1987) argued for less research on family structure and configuration (e.g., single versus nuclear family) and more research on Black parents' values and beliefs. They conducted a study of 767 minority graduates of A Better Chance, Inc. (ABC), a nonprofit educational organization that identifies academically gifted low SES minority students as possible candidates for college preparatory secondary schools. Twenty-eight percent lived with their mothers only, and 13% lived in extended families. The ABC graduates were surveyed regarding their school experiences, academic performance, career choice and progress, perceived academic ability, leadership and athletic skills, and personality and attitudes. Information was also gathered on parents' educational level, occupational status, self-aspirations, family size and structure, expectations for their children, attitudes toward achievement, and encouragement for education.

Prom-Jackson et al. (1987) concluded that low SES gifted minority students had parents of all educational levels. Parental educational level was not a good predictor of minority students' academic performance. Further, living in single-parent families did not negate the development of academic excellence and success; contrary to what might be expected based on previous research, the ABC students in single-parent families had slightly higher achievement scores than students in two-parent families. Mothers in both single- and two-parent families had the greatest impact on gifted Black students' educational achievement and self-identity. In summary, the evidence about parental beliefs and values suggests that in spite of social hardships and barriers, which often limit achievement and social advancement, this group of parents had high aspirations for and high expectations of their children and encouraged them to pursue high levels of education and challenging careers. This finding is consistent with the research of R. Clark (1983), D. Y. Ford (1993a), Lee (1984), and VanTassel-Baska (1989).

Research on gifted Black students and their families, although limited, suggests the need to consider student achievement in the total context in which beliefs, aspirations, and expectations are developed. Children's self-esteem and self-perceptions are formed initially under the auspices of the family and primary caregivers. The influence of Black parents and families on the socioemotional and academic status of their children carries equally important implications for their identification and assessment.

Families and the Identification of Gifted Black Students

In addition to transmitting roles, rules, and values, families can assist gifted program personnel in understanding the abilities and potential of Black children. Parents know their children, especially young children, better than anyone else. There are more parents who have gifted children but don't know it than there are parents who don't have gifted children but think they do.

Because testing can cause friction between schools and Black families, parents can help examine instruments (tests, checklists, and nomination forms) for bias relative to language, topics, questions, and illustrations. Information on assessing noncognitive variables can also be gathered from interviews with parents and extended family members.

Black parents should be encouraged to visit the gifted program prior to a placement decision. Parental questions regarding the classroom climate and demographics, for example, can be addressed more fully once they have met teachers and other students. How might Black parents define a "good education" for their gifted children? Certainly, a good education consists of high academic standards and students' exposure to a great deal of enriching, challenging, and relevant content. However, parents of Black students may define quality education from an affective, child-centered perspective. Thus, a good education recognizes, first and foremost, the worth of Black children as individuals and human beings. This means that schools affirm Black children.

When deciding whether to place their children in gifted programs, racial composition is an important consideration for Black parents. Is diversity celebrated in the school and in the gifted program? Determining the answer to this question requires that parents visit the school and the gifted program and talk with staff, administrators, and other school personnel. Beyond such discussions, visits to the gifted program allow parents to "see" whether school personnel are racially and culturally diverse and to observe how school personnel interact with students. Are students racially and culturally diverse? Where are they seated? Do Black students appear comfortable or inhibited? Are they interacting with other students? Do students segregate themselves racially? Do they socialize outside of the school? Are there social and educational activities that focus positively and proactively on the Black experience? Similarly, in what ways do curriculum and instruction respect and reflect diversity? To what extent are Black parents and families involved in school organizations? What efforts have been made to seek their involvement?

Black parents visiting gifted programs also have the opportunity to "listen" for diversity. What do school personnel say about diversity, or does a color-blind philosophy permeate the school ("I don't see differences . . . children are children whether they are black, white, red, yellow, brown, or polka-dot")? Do school personnel have high and realistic expectations for students of color? Do they welcome parent and family involvement? Do school personnel feel comfortable with questions regarding the lack of diversity in the gifted program? What efforts have been initiated to increase the representation of minority students in the program? How diverse are teachers of gifted students, and what are their experiences in working with gifted Black students?

Well-informed parents can be intellectual consumers of information. There should be a consensus among parents and teachers that the education and welfare of children are paramount (Marion, 1980). All families can benefit from information on understanding and nurturing giftedness, understanding children's specific areas of giftedness, recognizing underachievement and how it can be prevented or reversed, learning how to meet children's socioemotional needs, understanding developmental issues specific to gifted students, and learning how to set realistic and appropriate expectations relative to strengths. Figure 9.2 presents an outline of parent and family education for empowerment — for understanding and working effectively with children.

RECOMMENDATIONS

Many data point to the extended family as a problem-solving and coping system that adapts to and focuses the family resources on both normal and nonnormal transitional situations and crises. In addition and more generally, it helps family members beat the odds in a nation that is still plagued by injustice. Franklin (1988) persuasively states:

> The strong family tradition among Blacks thus survived the slave system, then legal segregation, discrimination, and enforced poverty, and finally, they had to contend with racially hostile governmental and societal practices, policies, and attitudes. (p. 25)

The time is long overdue for studying more thoroughly the importance of grandparents, especially grandmothers, as socialization agents in the extended family design. Educators and counselors must pay closer attention to cultural family patterns and to the reality that grandparents and other relatives often represent persons of significance to gifted Black students. Subsequently, researchers should begin to study more carefully the influence that grandparents exert on the achievement of children. Along with researchers, school personnel must expand their definition of the family to include those persons of significance typically found in extended families. Figure 9.3 presents some guidelines for working effectively with Black parents and families.

More specifically, researchers should study the impact of the more or less continual presence of grandparents, stepparents, cohabiting adults, and same-gender relationships on gifted and underachieving Black students' developmental outcomes. This broadened perspective highlights the dynamic nature of families (Figure 9.4) and the contextual nature of achievement.

Parents — a child's first teachers — play an integral role in Black students' orientation toward achievement, not simply because they have the "right" to, but because they do, in their priorities, expectancies, and behaviors, influence the course of a child's achievement development (Slaughter & Epps, 1987). The significance of parents in nurturing the abilities and potential of their children is well established. The role of

FIGURE 9.2. Family education for empowerment: A model for Black families with gifted children.

I. What is giftedness?
   A. Overview of local, federal, and contemporary definitions of giftedness
   B. Overview of contemporary theories of giftedness

II. Programming options and characteristics
   A. Purposes, types, pros and cons of each
   B. How gifted education differs from regular education, teacher training, and experiences

III. Identification and assessment of giftedness
   A. Local criteria and instruments, along with their implications for gifted Black students

IV. General characteristics of racially and culturally diverse gifted students

V. Information on specific areas and characteristics of giftedness for their children

VI. Developmental issues of gifted minority students
   A. Academic needs (including curriculum and instruction)
   B. Social and emotional needs (including peer relations, teacher relations)
   C. Psychological needs (racial identity, self-esteem, self-concept)

VII. Underachievement
   A. Definitions, types, contributing factors, strategies for prevention and reversal

VIII. Concerns of family members
   A. Parents
   B. Siblings
   C. Extended family members

IX. How to be an advocate for gifted minority children
   A. Parent and family involvement
   B. School and community organizations
   C. Professional associations and organizations

Note: The specific topics and their order should be generated based on a family or parent needs assessment survey; various professionals should provide training, which should be ongoing; racially diverse professionals should be an integral part of the process.

FIGURE 9.3. Suggestions for working with Black parents and families.

Remember that parents have the ultimate authority over their children for decisions. Work with rather than against parents to meet students' needs. Avoid too liberal an interpretation of *loco parentis*, which does not justify teachers having absolute control over students.

Be receptive to the diversity of family structures. Seek substantive and active parent and family involvement.

Recognize that not all parents have the natural ability to parent (just as not all teachers have the natural ability to teach).

Establish a good rapport; try to put family members at east using kindness, friendliness, humor, and informality (if appropriate). Communicate with parents when feedback is positive (as opposed to constant negative feedback). If working with underachieving students, contact parents even when progress is small or slow.

Use clear language and avoid jargon. Avoid being overly complicated; only when both parties understand each other can ideas be exchanged.

Be genuine and sincere. A genuine interest in Black families and their children will increase their trust and self-disclosure about feelings, fears, and concerns.

Try to empathize and avoid sympathy. Try to put yourself, to the extent possible, in the place of the family members.

Understand and be aware of all means of communication, particularly your own verbal and nonverbal messages; seek consistency between the two. Nonverbal communication (e.g., facial expressions, gestures, distance, body posture, intonation) can be more of a barrier to establishing a healthy relationship with minority parents than verbal messages.

Gather as much information on the child's family as possible before talking with members. Collect data regarding demographics, educational status, occupation, etc., to better understand the family's circumstances. Do not use this information to stereotype or categorize, but rather to set a tentative framework for understanding.

Be familiar with minority child development principles; be aware of the numerous factors affecting minority children's behaviors and achievement.

Identify community leaders and how they can work with families on behalf of Black children.

Identify resources to help families meet students' needs (e.g., mentors, educational organizations, journals and publications).

Avoid being judgmental; try not to show surprise or disapproval of what parents say. Due to potential cultural differences, teachers and parents may have differential (and perhaps oppositional) values, beliefs, and behaviors. Make compromises with families that result in win–win situations for children.

Be proactive and optimistic—operate from the assumption that Black parents have their children's best interest at heart.

Remember that the ultimate goal of family involvement is to enhance the academic and socio-emotional well-being of students.

FIGURE 9.4. Dynamic nature of families: A contextual perspective.

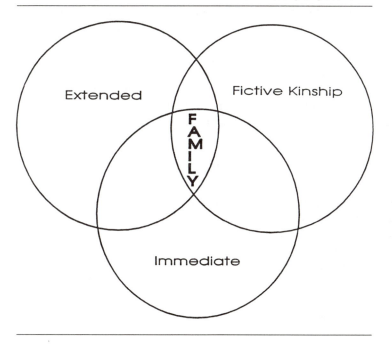

parents in this respect does not cease when children enter formal school; thus, parents must become partners with teachers in the educational process. This partnership begins with empowering parents and families, asking parents and other family members for their guidance and knowledge, and then using that information to ensure the successful recruitment and retention of Black students in gifted education. Without this partnership, identification, placement, and programming for gifted Black students cannot be optimal.

Respect, understanding, and effective communication are key factors to active and proactive Black family involvement. Harry (1992) recommended that substantive Black family involvement be manifested in several roles: (1) parents who join official assessment teams can alter or even eradicate the assumption that educators have a monopoly on knowledge; (2) parents can form policy as members of advisory committees and local educational agencies, as members of site-based school management teams, and as teachers' aides; and (3) parents can serve as advocates and peer supports, whereby they offer advice and input in the assessment and placement of their children. These recommendations are also appropriate for other family members — grandparents, aunts and uncles, cousins, and significant others in students' lives and homes. Families make a difference in the lives of their children, but only when their role in schooling is meaningful, empowered, and sustained (Langdon, 1991). Empowered families of gifted Black students are aware of the nature and needs of their children; definitions and theories of giftedness and underachievement; resources for meeting their children's specific needs; how to recognize, prevent, or reverse underachievement (see Figure 9.5).

SUMMARY

The primary premise of this chapter is that our notions about traditional nuclear families and parental involvement must be broadened. This broadened notion of families includes greater attention to working with grandparents, aunts, and uncles, for example; it includes increasing family involvement in the educational process.

FIGURE 9.5. Staff development outline for involving Black families in the educational process.

I. Social awareness and knowledge
    A. Information on changing social and familial demographics

II. Self-awareness
    A. Knowledge, attitudes, and misperceptions regarding diverse families and family involvement

III. Communication and social skills
    A. Modes of communication (e.g., nonverbal and verbal), including one's own style
    B. Effective interpersonal communication strategies and skills
    C. Power issues; compromising and resolving conflicts

IV. Parents' rights in the educational process

V. Improving family–teacher relations

VI. Types of family involvement
    A. Personal perceptions about the types

VII. Strategies for increasing family involvement

Note: Training should be consistent, ongoing, and based on a needs assessment. Training should be conducted by various professionals who are racially and culturally diverse: family specialists, educators, counselors, psychologists.

There is almost unanimous agreement that parents make a significant contribution to the identification of gifted children (Colangelo & Dettman, 1983). Parents and significant others also play an essential role in the development and nurturance of children's abilities. Unfortunately, the research and writings on Black families and gifted students can be counted on one hand. There is a critical need to conduct more research on gifted children in diverse family structures, to conduct more research on gifted minority students, and to focus on the strengths of Black families. It is an unfortunate reality that educators working with gifted Black and underachieving students have little by way of theory and research to guide their practice. Parents from all racial groups bring to schools valuable insights and unique perspectives from which to enhance home-school relations and student achievement.

Society's long-standing belief in the ubiquity of the nuclear family is inconsistent with the experiences of those millions who do not live in households or families made up of mother, father, and children. The increasing number of single and never-married mothers, teenage parents, and divorcees; the persistence of poverty among Blacks; and the vicious circle of racism and discrimination against Blacks and other racial minorities guarantee the proliferation of extended families. Given these conditions, educators can ill afford to ignore the contributions that extended families make to the educational and socioemotional well-being of Black students. In fact, extended Black families deserve credit for helping children escape the more debilitating repercussions of poverty and racism. Consequently, we need additional research on the significance of extended Black families in children's socioemotional lives. In such family structures, it may be the grandmother who serves as the person of influence. No longer, then, can we speak of the singular influence of mother, father, or both on Black students' achievement. As in the past, the concept of parental involvement is passé. Family involvement is more realistic and educationally sound.

Chapter 10

Promising Practices, Paradigms, and Programs

When addressing the issue of underachievement, educators and reformers often call for changes in curriculum and instruction. Yet the cycle of underachievement among Black youth remains unbroken in spite of commitments made by school districts and gifted programs to curriculum and instruction.

In 1988, Congress passed legislation to promote the interests of gifted students in U.S. public schools. The Jacob K. Javits Gifted and Talented Students Education Program was authorized under Title IV, Part B of the Hawkins-Stafford Elementary and Secondary Amendments of 1988. The legislation calls for the U.S. Department of Education to carry out three major activities that, collectively, are designed to provide national leadership in gifted education. The first type of activity provides funding via grants to assist state and local educational agencies in meeting the various needs of gifted students. The second activity is the creation of a national research center on gifted and talented students (hereafter referred to as NRC G/T). The center is the first comprehensive research effort on gifted education in the United States. The third activity responds to the legislative mandate that the Javits Program serve as a national focal point in gifted education. Thus, it calls additional and much needed attention to the needs and concerns of gifted students. This chapter focuses primarily on the first and second activities (Javits programs and projects and NRC G/T research studies) as they relate specifically to gifted and potentially gifted Black students.

JAVITS PROJECTS RELATED TO GIFTED AND POTENTIALLY GIFTED BLACK STUDENTS

Legislation requires that at least half of the Javits projects include activities to serve economically disadvantaged students.[1] Moreover, priority is given to projects directed at students who are disabled, have limited English skills, or are at risk of being unrecognized and underserved in gifted education. Over a 5-year period (1989 to 1994), the Javits Program funded 75 grants nationally, most for up to 3 years. These grants often had the expressed goals of:

(1) Improving identification and assessment instruments and practices;
(2) Developing challenging and appropriate curricula;
(3) Individualizing instruction;
(4) Sponsoring summer institutes;
(5) Designing and implementing technical applications of knowledge;
(6) Expanding educational opportunities for gifted students through collaborations and partnerships with businesses, industry, and other organizations;
(7) Offering technical assistance and disseminating information to the public about services available for gifted students; and
(8) Involving parents and families in the educational process (USDE, 1994).

In sum, many of the projects seek comprehensiveness in meeting the various needs of gifted and potentially gifted students, many of whom are economically disadvantaged. Several projects focus on teacher education and training, parent education and involvement, and community involvement. Many also address the academic, social, and emotional needs of targeted gifted and potentially gifted students, particularly those at risk for underachievement and underidentification. Further, nontraditional and state-of-the-art practices have been sought relative to identification and assessment. These practices represent a call to move beyond arrogant assumptions about standardized tests and the tendency to ordain IQ scores. For expedience and due to space limitations, only those projects funded in 1992–1993 targeted specifically at gifted and potentially gifted minority students are described. Twenty-three projects at various educational levels are briefly described, the majority targeted at the elementary school level.

Elementary School Level Projects

Project First Step is a San Diego city schools project for Black, Hispanic, and limited-English-proficient Hispanic students in preschool through grade two. The project's primary goal is to identify and to ensure the increased participation of minority students in the district's Gifted and

Talented Education (GATE) program by preparing students for GATE certification as second graders. Strategies include training teachers to integrate higher-level-thinking instructional strategies into the curriculum, training teachers to recognize potential among students who do not score high on intelligence tests or do not achieve high grades in school, and encouraging parents to identify and nurture giftedness.

The *Full Potential SEED* (Supporting Early Education and Development) program in the Atlanta public schools targets Black students in preschool and kindergarten. The project collaborates with the Atlanta University Center (the nation's largest consortium of historically Black colleges and universities). The project's underlying premise is that educators must take proactive and preventive steps to identify and meet the various needs of young gifted Black students. The program is a developmentally and culturally based program that nurtures students at home and in school. To meet objectives, personnel restructure the educational environments of students so that learning is active, cooperative, and engaging. Language development is emphasized, using the whole language philosophy to integrate other subject areas (e.g., science, mathematics, social science and geography, foreign languages), and students are taught critical thinking and creativity skills through the use of literature. Family involvement and education are also addressed. This component provides family members (parents, older siblings, and others) with information about general and cultural expressions of giftedness. Children and their families also have access to books and videos for family enrichment; they are encouraged to read and review materials cooperatively; and family members are trained to work more effectively with the educational material.

Another project at the early childhood level is located at Western Kentucky University. *Restructuring Primary Gifted Education* is a response to Kentucky's Education Reform Act of 1990. The act mandated that an ungraded primary program (K–3) be developed to meet the needs of all children in multiage and multiability classrooms using a developmentally appropriate curriculum. In collaboration with the Kentucky Department of Education, the project addresses issues that inhibit young gifted children from being identified and served. Issues addressed by the project to meet the needs of young, economically disadvantaged, and disabled gifted children are teacher understanding of the nature and needs of these children, nontraditional identification methods and instruments, collaboration among professionals, and teacher training in developing and implementing curricula that meet the varied learning needs of young children. The project's six major objectives are to establish a group of parents and educators to serve the needs of targeted children, examine various staff development models for implementing a state-mandated program, connect the primary program and reform components (e.g., school-based decision making, curriculum frameworks, classroom technology, performance assessment, and family resource centers), generate a variety of exemplary curricula and appropriate practices for developing the abilities and interests of students, develop and pilot identification procedures based on the Kentucky performance-based assessment system, and design teacher preparation experiences that enable future teachers to develop the potential of targeted students.

The *Pittsburgh K–3 Gifted Project* seeks to develop a model that effectively screens, identifies, and serves young low SES and minority students. The project focuses on both the cognitive and the affective development of targeted students. Important components include assessment, teacher training, and parent services and support. To facilitate the preparation of preservice teachers, counselors, and psychologists, there is a school district–university collaborative initiative. Staff development is aimed at administrators, regular classroom teachers, preservice teachers, and teachers of gifted students and focuses on screening, identification, programming, and current research in gifted education. Educational services and support for parents include a resource room, monthly parent–student seminars, and a help line to address parents' concerns. Another component consisting of school–business–community partnerships is aimed at identifying and training mentors for students through sponsor scholarships, academies (Saturday and summer), and cultural experiences. Finally, the project has an evaluation component to assess the effectiveness of each project objective.

Project Discovery, located in LaGrange, Kentucky, is targeted at rural and economically disadvantaged students in kindergarten through grade three. Its overriding goal is to nurture giftedness in young children by increasing teachers' sensitivity to creative and productive giftedness. Teachers are trained to involve students in making independent investigations and creating new knowledge and products through original research. By choosing research topics of interest, students acquire increased problem-solving, creative, and critical thinking skills. Students also have the opportunity to share their products with an authentic audience.

In-service training helps teachers become "talent scouts" in discovering gifted and potentially gifted young children in the regular classroom. Project Discovery seeks to increase the percentage of economically disadvantaged students identified as gifted at the grade of formal entry into each district's gifted program; improve the attitudes, knowledge, behavior, and skills of teachers relative to recognizing and nurturing these young gifted students; increase and sustain students' self-esteem, creative thinking, critical thinking, and productive problem-solving skills; and increase parents' knowledge of giftedness and their confidence in nurturing the abilities of their children.

Wright State University in Ohio received funding for *A Project to Enhance Teacher and Parent Interaction Related to the Teaching of Minority and Disadvantaged Gifted Students.* The targeted population is prekindergartners through third graders. A major goal is to increase the role of parents in identifying and meeting the needs of their gifted children through a parent–school intervention model. Parents participate in group experiences that cover such topics as identification, motivation, discipline, stress management, and peer relations. The training promotes parental empowerment through increased knowledge and skills. Professional development is also aimed at teachers, who are surveyed about their knowledge of targeted gifted children and their attitudes toward minority and low SES parents. Teachers receive information about targeted students, including family information and strategies to enhance parent–school relationships.

The South Carolina Department of Education received funding for *Project SEARCH* (Selection, Enrichment, and Acceleration of Rural Children), which targets low SES rural minority students. Its primary goal is to increase the representation of targeted students in state-funded gifted and talented programs. Project SEARCH hopes to develop a screening system that utilizes nontraditional methods to identify potentially gifted students, to develop a model program that nurtures students' potential, and to disseminate best practices from the project. Initiatives are developmentally appropriate and focus on language development through literature, drama, tactile experiences, and student-centered teaching in the sciences and mathematics. Field studies and open-ended projects are used to enrich students' experiences. Teachers participate in continual staff development activities to enhance their teaching skills and effectiveness, to equip them with strategies and materials that provide challenge and stimulate students' learning, and to improve their identification skills.

Project ARTS (Art for Rural Teachers and Students) at Indiana University works with rural third through fifth graders who are disadvantaged and racially and culturally diverse (Hispanic American, Native American, Black). The consortium implements visual and performing arts programs for gifted students. Community members and local artists are also involved in the project. Key objectives are multifaceted:

(1) to modify and develop instruments and procedures for identifying the targeted population;

(2) to modify and develop promising curriculum in visual and performing arts at the elementary school level;

(3) to modify and develop in-service and preservice training procedures and materials;

(4) to modify and develop instruments and procedures for evaluating the progress and achievement of identified students;

(5) to modify and further develop a prototypic manual for identifying, programming, and evaluating;

(6) to implement new technologies and encourage the exchange of locally developed curriculum materials; and

(7) to involve parents and local community members in all phases of the project.

Multiple Intelligences: A Framework for Student and Teacher Change is located in the Montgomery County public schools in Rockville, Maryland. Prekindergarten through fifth-grade students are identified using Gardner's theory of multiple intelligences. The program allows children to reveal gifts that are masked by economic deprivation, limited English proficiency, or learning disabilities. It attempts to remove the "verbal veil" that prevents teachers from recognizing these youngsters' nonverbal multiple intelligences (U.S. Department of Education, 1994, p. 25). The primary goals are to confirm the validity and value of using Gardner's theory to identify targeted students and to develop a curriculum based on Gardner's theory. Parental involvement, in-service teacher training, and research are also significant aspects of the project.

The *Javits 7+ Program*, located at Community School District 18 in Brooklyn, New York, also utilizes Gardner's theory. Low SES, limited-English-proficient, and disabled kindergartners through fifth graders are targeted for participation. The project meets both the academic and the noncognitive needs of students by focusing on self-esteem enhancement and by identifying the individual strengths of potentially gifted students in the regular classroom. Through staff development, teachers are trained to provide more effective and individualized instruction to targeted populations. Parent education occurs in workshops on nurturing their children's multiple intelligences. Another objective is to develop a full curriculum — an interdisciplinary, theme-based, multiple intelligences curriculum — that integrates the visual and performing arts with traditional school subjects for early childhood students.

The University of Medicine and Dentistry of New Jersey's project on *Early Identification and Education of Gifted Minority Students* serves students in kindergarten through second grade. The project is designed to develop a multiple-entry screening and assessment procedure to identify targeted economically disadvantaged students. Teachers are trained to provide enrichment activities within the regular classroom through workshops, teacher conferences, materials, and a teacher hot line with information on students' needs and classroom activities.

Project CUE (Creating Urban Excellence) is located in Community School District 9 in Bronx, New York. Low SES Hispanic and Black students in kindergarten through grade three are introduced to basic mathematics and science content, as well as scientific inquiry. Targeted students are enrolled in both regular and special education classes. The collaborative project employs an instructional approach that is in direct contrast to the "deficit model" commonly used in urban areas (U.S. Department of Education, 1994, p. 37). Stated differently, rather than focusing on students' weaknesses, the project targets enrichment activities in the sciences and mathematics for students who have learning patterns that may make them candidates for special education classification.

Three levels of developmentally appropriate learning environments provide students with opportunities to develop mathematics and science skills. Students receive enriched instruction in their regular classrooms and with cluster teachers. Students demonstrating exceptional science and mathematics abilities receive enrichment in special school-based seminars and extracurricular activities. Project CUE is designing performance-based assessment for identification purposes. Ongoing staff development is an additional component of the project.

The ArtsConnection, Inc., developed the *New Horizons* project for economically disadvantaged minority, bilingual, and handicapped students in grades three through six. The program has a major affective component: It attempts to increase the motivation of targeted students to attend school and program activities, to develop strong work and study habits, and to improve their personal and social skills. These objectives are accomplished through dance, music, and theater training. During summer institutes, teachers are trained in talent identification through various art forms and dimensions of artistic talent. They are also sensitized to recognize the positive values of nurturing and reinforcing talents through creative pedagogy rather than through remediation.

Project Synergy: Outreach is located at Teachers College (Columbia University) in New York. The project is developing, field-testing, and validating nontraditional methods of identifying potentially gifted children (grades K–3) from urban, economically disadvantaged backgrounds. The project combines prevention with intervention through transitional services, parent and teacher training, and mentorships that nurture the potential of targeted students. Teachers are encouraged to participate in the project with teacher-as-researcher minigrants. Finally, school reform and restructuring methods are addressed relative to authentic assessment, site-based management, private–public school partnerships, upgraded teacher professionalism, family involvement and choice, and integrated services. A quasi-experimental research design is employed to assess the efficacy of the project intervention.

Project START: Support to Affirm Rising Talents is a project of the Charlotte-Mecklenburg Board of Education in North Carolina for culturally diverse and economically disadvantaged students in kindergarten through grade three. The project seeks to enhance students' academic performance in the regular classroom. The family outreach component recruits and trains parents in gifted characteristics, child advocacy, nurturing talents, working with teachers, and volunteerism. Curriculum modifications include training teachers to develop students' language fluency, to provide performance-oriented environments, and to affirm multicultural values. A mentoring component consists of community volunteers who work with students semimonthly in academic tutoring and enrichment experiences. A research component, in collaboration with the NRC G/T at the University of Virginia, addresses various questions, particularly the degree to which teacher attitudes toward students change as a result of training and which intervention strategies are most effective at increasing targeted students' academic performance.

Low SES and minority students (K–5) are also the focus of the *Center for Arts and Sciences*, located at the University of Tulsa. The project works directly with teachers through summer workshops in the performing arts. Experts in art, drama, and writing work with teachers to develop techniques that foster the active construction of knowledge in their classrooms. Teachers develop and implement challenging curricula that integrate various disciplines. Children also participate in workshops in the arts and sciences, problem solving, and developing creative and original products.

Elementary and Middle School Level Projects

Project Spring II (Special Populations Rural Information Center for the Gifted) is a three-state rural consortium. Students in grades three through eight who are economically disadvantaged and from Appalachian, Black, Hispanic, and Native American backgrounds are targeted for participation. Its primary purpose is to identify and educate the aforementioned gifted students by developing teacher training procedures, identifying appropriate science programs and teaching strategies, providing rural teachers and students access to information and opportunities for interacting with professionals and peers, and involving parents in the identification and educational process. A series of training manuals are under development, along with nontraditional and multiple criteria and material to better identify and assess targeted students.

A second project at this educational level (K–8) is *Project Mustard Seed*, located at Baylor University in Texas. It is a cooperative effort designed to identify minority and low SES students and to select mentor teachers, cohort teachers, administrators, and community representatives. A trainer-of-trainers model helps practicing teachers become exemplars of instructional excellence. Teachers are trained to develop interdisciplinary curricula appropriate for gifted students and those at other ability levels in the regular classroom. Curricular efforts also focus on individualized curriculum and instruction that integrates the sciences, mathematics, fine arts, humanities, and social sciences.

Middle or Junior High School Level Projects

The *Urban Scholars* program at the University of Massachusetts seeks to increase urban disadvantaged and minority students' access to mathematics and the sciences at the middle school level. Major goals are to develop an extensive mathematics and science program for targeted students and to design staff development activities that enhance teachers' capacity to develop students' potentials through education and guidance.

High School Level Projects

Project Urban Consortium for the Talented and Gifted (PUC-TAG) is a collaborative effort among four Chicago high schools and three universities. The consortium is designed to identify gifted ninth graders and serve them until they enter postsecondary education institutions. These students are minority (primarily Black), are economically disadvantaged, and have limited English proficiency. This intervention-oriented program attempts to reconcile academic, cognitive, and social skills deficiencies. Noncognitive factors are also addressed, including self-esteem, values clarification, and career awareness. Students are accelerated through placement in classes for juniors and seniors and are taught critical thinking and creative problem-solving skills. Staff development and parent education and involvement are deemed critical to the success of the project. In-service and university training is provided for teachers. Parents receive assistance in understanding and guiding their children at home; they also learn how to work more effectively with schools.

Learning Unlimited, a project of Chelsea public schools in Massachusetts, is aimed at high school students who are economically disadvantaged and have limited English proficiency. Its primary goal is to identify potentially gifted students — defined as students who do not fit the standard pattern or profile of academic achievement. In-service training is provided to teachers to develop the potential of students at risk of not being identified as gifted. Students take elective classes to develop independent work projects, and an additional trimester of courses in mathematics, the sciences, and English is taken by potentially gifted students.

Kindergarten Through High School Level Projects

The University of Arizona received funding for *DISCOVER III* (Discovering Intellectual Skills and Capabilities While Providing Opportunities for Varied Ethnic Responses). The program, targeted at Native American, Hispanic, and Black students in grades K–12, has three major objectives. First, it is designed to implement and validate innovative procedures for identifying the aforementioned gifted minority students; second, it collaborates with participating communities and local education agencies (LEAs) to develop curricula and provide staff development. To enhance the abilities of minority students, attention is given to problem solving with a cultural context and to Gardner's theory of multiple intelligences as a framework. Third, *DISCOVER III* disseminates information designed to communicate expectations of higher achievement by economically disadvantaged and minority students.

To meet objectives, project personnel sought the assistance of LEAs in identifying the strengths and abilities of minority students at all grade levels. Developmental and longitudinal profiles of students' strengths were maintained; seminars were provided for high school students and teachers; workshops were held for educators, parents, and interested individuals based on needs and interests; and collaborative relations were developed among teachers, administrators, counselors, educators, and community members.

The *LEGACY* Project (Linking Educators and the Gifted With Attorneys for Civic: Yes!) is located at the Wake Forest University Law School in North Carolina. Public school students who are economically disadvantaged, have limited English proficiency, or are disabled are targeted for participation. The project's primary purpose is to develop and disseminate improved civic education curriculum materials for teachers of gifted students, particularly those at risk for poor educational outcomes. Nationally, teachers participate in a training institute to develop such materials. LEGACY also addresses the critical need for mentoring and for technical assistance in curriculum preparation. Teacher training is in the form of teacher-mentor relationships, and a volunteer attorney-partner helps develop, test, and demonstrate the curriculum.

PROGRAM AND PROJECT THEMES RELATIVE TO IDENTIFICATION AND ASSESSMENT

Several themes regarding identification and assessment of economically disadvantaged, gifted, and potentially gifted Black students permeate the projects:

(1) *Increased acceptance that giftedness is multidimensional.* For example, several projects adopted Gardner's (1983) theory of multiple intelligences.

(2) *Greater recognition that giftedness has numerous manifestations.* This necessitates nurturing more than only academic and intellectual giftedness.

(3) *Giftedness is contextually and culturally sensitive.* What is gifted in one situation or culture may not be so in another.

(4) *A culture of assessment rather than identification.* Numerous programs adopted authentic assessment tools and strategies for profiling students' strengths and shortcomings.

(5) *Emphasis on continuous and long-term assessment* as a more effective means of examining students' performance and development. The programs also used additional sources of information (e.g., out-of-school activities, families) for decision making.

(6) *A philosophy of inclusiveness.* This is particularly relative to talent development and potential. Thus, students who are traditionally underrepresented in gifted education have more opportunities to be identified and served.

(7) *A prescriptive philosophy.* There is a solid connection among identification, assessment, and instruction. Information is used for student programming and teacher training.

(8) *Collaborative partnerships* among public schools, postsecondary institutions, businesses, communities, and families are deemed integral to the success of students and the projects.

(9) *Staff development and parent and family education* are considered critical to the success of the programs and students.

(10) *A commitment to reform in gifted education.* This is reflected by the use of performance assessments and portfolios, the focus on talent development, and the need to serve gifted students in regular classroom settings.

NATIONAL RESEARCH CENTER PROJECTS AND RESEARCH

Some of the most contemporary research on gifted, potentially gifted, and underachieving Black students is being conducted by the National Research Centers on the Gifted and Talented at the University of Virginia, the University of Connecticut, the University of Georgia, and Yale University. The NRC G/Ts' mission is to conduct and plan theory-driven research that is quantitative, qualitative, problem based, practice relevant, and consumer oriented. The mission includes broad-based dissemination and the formation of a national cooperative composed of research practitioners, policy makers, and others concerned about the educational and socioemotional well-being of gifted and potentially gifted students.

Numerous studies conducted at the NRC G/Ts are targeted specifically at minority students. Because space does not permit an in-depth review of all studies, and because many studies are in progress, only a few are described in this chapter. Hebert's (1993) research on gifted urban males was described in Chapter 7. Additional ethnographic studies of gifted and potentially gifted minority males and females are also under way. These collective works investigate resiliency among students in inner-city schools to help explain why some low SES minority males and females are able to overcome numerous obstacles to achievement. The application of resilience to the educational setting is relatively new. This concept has its origin in medicine, where it provides one explanation of why some individuals, but not others, adapt and react positively to stress and adversity (Rutter, 1990). Despite its important contributions, however, the concept has seldom been applied to gifted students, perhaps because of the misperception that gifted students experience few barriers to academic achievement and the myth that they have few socioemotional concerns. Similarly, although studies have examined resilience among minority youth, they have not focused on gifted minority youth. Research at the NRC G/Ts seeks to fill this void.

Another line of research focuses on learning outcomes of students after placement in gifted education. In the Learning Outcomes Study, more than 1,000 second through fourth graders in geographically diverse communities (urban, suburban, and rural) and five different programs (no program, pullout programs, within-class programs, special classes, and special schools) were surveyed over a 2-year period regarding their achievement, attitudes toward learning, and general interests. Parents and teachers were also interviewed regarding students' learning characteristics, interests, motivation, behaviors, and socioemotional adjustment. Further, measures of self-concept and achievement (group tests) were given. The study focuses on students' affective and academic development and needs. Results of the qualitative and quantitative study are expected to answer the following questions: How do achievement and attitudes change over time? How does placement influence students' self-concepts and behavioral adjustment? How are minority students affected by different types of programs? What factors characterize an exemplary program for each of the four kinds of programs? Each program's curriculum, teaching methods, goals, and teacher training are also analyzed.

Another component addresses motivation and underachievement in urban and suburban preadolescents. Factors that create the discrepancy between potential and performance are being studied among gifted and nongifted students using qualitative, observational methodologies. Variables under investigation include the effectiveness of differentiated programs for students in terms of self-efficacy and underachievement, for example. Do urban and suburban gifted preadolescents have different motivational processes? Are motivational patterns of identified students quantitatively and qualitatively different from those of nongifted students? How does being labeled gifted affect motivation and related behaviors? How can task commitment and learning goals be fostered among the various groups of students?

D. Y. Ford (1995) recently completed research with more than 150 Black students in grades six through nine. The students attended five school districts in Virginia that were demographically diverse relative to racial composition, geographic locale, and SES. Forty-three of the students had been identified by their districts as gifted. Students were surveyed regarding their attitudes toward school and school subjects; perceptions of the classroom and learning environment; test anxiety; learning style preferences; racial identity; and perceptions of social, cultural, and psychological factors that affect their school performance. These variables are being analyzed relative to gender, program (gifted, nongifted), grade level, geographic locale, and SES differences. Equally important, factors distinguishing achievers from underachievers are being investigated. The results are expected to provide important information to educators regarding how best to prevent or reverse underachievement among capable Black students. (Preliminary findings have been presented in previous chapters.)

SUMMARY

The Jacob K. Javits Gifted and Talented Students Act of 1988 marks the culmination of the efforts of gifted education proponents and seeks to ensure equity for minority and economically disadvantaged students. This chapter highlighted recent efforts in gifted education under the auspices of the Javits Act to ensure equity for underachieving, low SES, and minority students who are gifted or potentially gifted. Many of these efforts are prevention and intervention oriented. They focus on parent and teacher education, more effective identification and assessment instruments and practices, and curriculum and instruction modifications, and they address the affective needs and development of gifted and potentially gifted minority students.

Common themes among the projects and studies are talent development, equity, and comprehensiveness. Also evident is the need to change teacher attitudes and behaviors toward targeted students and to empower parents. School partnerships with postsecondary education institutions, community organizations, and business and industry have also been developed. Ultimately, the recruitment and retention of gifted and potentially gifted minority students are the overarching goals of the projects and studies.

NOTE

1. The information described in this section is referenced in the *Javits Projects Abstracts*, published by the USDE (1994). The USDE pamphlet and this chapter describe funded projects in 1992–1993, the most recent period that funds were awarded.

Chapter 11

Summary and Directions for the Future

Gifted children are highly inquisitive beings who normally should become "high achievers" as a result of their curiosity, experimentation, discoveries, assimilation-organization-use of information, perceptions, relationships, and memory. Gifted children are made into underachievers as a result of specific handicaps—a dull, meager curriculum that destroys the motivation to achieve in school, inappropriate learning styles, or a lack of adult assistance to the child in need of learning how to handle socio-emotional conflict, to gain self-control, and to set realistic expectations.

—Whitmore, 1980, p. 132

Underachievement is a symptom with a variety of causes and factors, and its etiology is open to interpretation. Living with one or more risk factors can contribute to or worsen underachievement for gifted and potentially gifted Black students. School practices (e.g., the instruments used for the identification of giftedness and underachievement, as well as an ethnocentric curriculum) play important roles in underidentification and underachievement among these students. The hidden curriculum promotes assimilation, to which many Black students may object. The combination of academic frustration and the desire not to conform creates problems for some gifted Black students, particularly Black students who are radical and spirited in disagreement, uninhibited in expressing their opinions, and concerned about social injustices.

For gifted Black students, particularly those who perform poorly on standardized tests, underachievement is a ubiquitous concept. Such students, by virtue of taking tests normed on middle-class White students, tend to perform poorly and may, therefore, not be identified as gifted, underachievers, or both. The heavy and sometimes exclusive reliance on test scores to predict ability and potential, as well as the faith placed in tests, has been educationally harmful for many underachieving, gifted, and potentially gifted Black students. This reliance fails to consider the effects of gender, race, SES, practice and experience, quality of education, physical development and maturity, learning style preferences, test anxiety, language differences, noncognitive variables (e.g., motivation, interest, task commitment), and test-taking conditions on test outcomes.

THE SIGNIFICANCE OF GIFTED BLACK UNDERACHIEVERS

Gifted programs are among the most segregated programs in public schools. They are disproportionately White and middle class, and they serve primarily intellectually and academically gifted students. The underrepresentation of Black students in programs for the gifted has been well documented, and the many barriers have been identified. Findings reveal that two of the most neglected populations in gifted education are individuals whose talents may not be actualized because they are culturally different from the mainstream and socially and culturally disadvantaged individuals. The following list sets forth several reasons for studying this population and increasing recruitment and retention efforts on their behalf:

(1) *Changing demographics of the nation and its schools.* One the most noticeable trends in American education has been the increase in the racial and cultural diversity of the nation's schools. In 1986, one-sixth of the approximately 12 million students were either Black, Hispanic, or Asian-Pacific. By 2020, racial minorities are expected to constitute 48% of all school-age children from age 5 to 17 (Hodgkinson, 1988). The increasing number of minority students demands that educators and researchers delve beneath the surface of what may easily be referred to as the abysmal state of education in America.

(2) *Traditional tests are inadequate for assessing giftedness among Black and underachieving students.* Educators and decision makers insist upon relying on standardized tests as the ultimate arbiter of educational success and ability. Too often, the well-documented biases of these tests in predicting academic success among minority and low SES students have had little effect on educational policy and decision making. Many educators rely indiscriminately on intelligence tests and other unidimensional instruments to assess giftedness. Seemingly, Binet and Simon's (1905) warning that his IQ test was primarily a measure of school-related proficiency and should not be used otherwise was not heeded.

A multitude of instruments and strategies should be used when judging intelligence, giftedness, underachievement, and potential. Therefore, educators who rely solely on standardized tests to identify giftedness among Black students ignore that tests can and do misinterpret ability and potential.

Black students have always been a puzzle to educators because of their unresponsiveness to standard measures of ability — yet educators know that they have substantial talent. We all know of at least one person who passed standardized tests yet "flunked" life, and one person who failed tests but succeeded in life. In essence, students' performance on standardized tests do not measure innate aptitudes. To interpret IQ scores and test results in this manner is a dangerous method of social and educational oppression.

(3) *Traditional definitions and theories of giftedness are inappropriate for use with Black students.* Each culture defines giftedness in its own image, and giftedness in one culture may not be considered gifted in another culture. Thus, traditional theories of giftedness, which focus exclusively on intellectual and academic ability, may not be useful for some racial and cultural groups. Giftedness is also dependent on the times, for what is deemed gifted and valuable in one generation or historical period may not be so in another.

(4) *Cultural differences affect students' achievement.* These factors include different learning styles, communication styles, behavioral styles, values, attitudes, and priorities that may conflict with those of the mainstream. Educators working with gifted Black students should understand two facts: First, by virtue of being gifted, Black students exhibit characteristics of giftedness (e.g., creativity, inventiveness, high level of abstraction, critical thinking) to varying degrees; and second, Black students' frames of reference may be markedly different from that of the predominant culture. When Black students are identified as gifted, attention must be given to how their cultural and social backgrounds influence their achievement. In essence, schools and gifted programs must acknowledge and affirm student diversity and individuality.

(5) *Curricular modifications must reflect pluralism.* If educators, reformers, and decision makers take proactive, strong stances in adopting multiculturalism as a model of curriculum and instruction, then positive educational outcomes will increase for minority students. Multiculturalism promises to redress many of the current inadequacies in gifted education — the underrepresentation of minority students, the lack of diversity among teachers, monocultural curriculum and instruction, biased and standardized identification and assessment practices, teachers who are inadequately prepared in cultural diversity, and policies that reinforce (directly or indirectly) these problems.

In essence, we cannot give lip service to multicultural concerns in education. There must be a commitment to translate ethical principles and standards into practice. Monocultural and ethnocentric practices are increasingly becoming a form of maladjustment. Monoculturalism acts as an invisible veil that prevents people from seeing education as a potentially biased system (Sue et al., 1992). Accordingly, educators need to become culturally aware and competent; education needs to become culturally responsive and responsible to its constituents.

PREVENTION AND INTERVENTION ISSUES

Most efforts in schools are intervention oriented rather than prevention oriented. That is, they are directed at older students, and their timing is such that the problems they seek to eliminate already exist. Optimal strategies must be prevention oriented. Thus, research and practice would seek to prevent underachievement, to keep students from experiencing school failure, educational disengagement, and educational suicide (Renzulli et al., 1994). Preventive strategies include early and ongoing assessment of gifted and potentially gifted Black students; developing reliable, valid assessment tools and strategies for young minority students; developing gifted programs and services at the preschool and early elementary school levels; educating teachers and families for empowerment; and understanding minority child development holistically by addressing academic, affective, and psychological needs.

Prevention and intervention must also examine peer pressures to resist academic achievement. Negative peer pressures and poor peer relations contribute to the poor representation of Black students in gifted programs. Gifted or achieving Black students may be accused of "acting White" and rejecting the Black culture when they achieve in school. Black students may intentionally underachieve to avoid being ostracized by peers. Because peers play a powerful role in students' lives, intervention efforts must be directed not only at gifted Black students but also at their peers. Promising practices should be schoolwide, and interventions must include group counseling, peer counseling, conflict resolution programs, and initiatives aimed at enhancing Black students' self-esteem, self-confidence, racial identity, and self-efficacy. Working with gifted Black students in isolation from their peers is fruitless; environmental factors, as discussed throughout this book, can wreak havoc on the achievement and motivation of gifted and highly able Black students.

Family-school partnerships are equally important for ensuring the success of gifted and potentially gifted Black students. Oppressive environmental forces influence how Black parents live and rear their children. Black parents may be distrustful of the educational process and view it as an instrument of the predominant culture that strips Blacks of their own cultural values, beliefs, norms, and attitudes. Those parents who hold this point of view may resist placing their children in gifted programs. Similarly, due to lack of understanding, educators may have unfounded stereotypes of Black parents and families. We will continue to see very capable Black students poorly represented in gifted education if we do not narrow or close the credibility gap between schools and Black families.

This gap can be narrowed and eventually closed when educators and families become partners working in behalf of students. As discussed in Chapter 9, educators require training and continuing professional education and development to work more effectively with Black parents and to increase the roles and rights of families in the educational process. Similarly, parents and significant others may require training to work effectively with schools to understand and exercise their rights relative to identification and assessment, placement decisions, curriculum and instruction, and school involvement. Decreasing and eliminating negative environmental and social forces in schools is essential for Black students' success. Despite legislation, racism and discrimination persist in school settings. As stated by Boykin (1986):

> Poor performance relative to mainstream children and a high incidence of school dropout are still the rule rather than the exception for these children, despite two decades of national concern. We must ask why there has been so little progress toward solving this problem, in spite of the apparent best of intentions and the commitment of very considerable resources. (p. 57)

The problems continue because we have not adequately addressed the correlates of academic underachievement within this population. This book is offered as a contribution to the limited data available relating social, cultural, and psychological factors to underachievement among gifted and potentially gifted Black students. Research that seeks to understand and then address social, psychological, and cultural barriers to academic achievement is in great demand in our schools and gifted programs.

Gifted underachievers are among the most misunderstood and educationally neglected students in schools; no other group of students, except Black students, has suffered so much from lack of interest in them as persons (Whitmore, 1980). It has been reiterated here and elsewhere that for gifted Black students to receive an equal educational opportunity, there must be early identification, with attention to special needs; careful programming in light of their strengths, characteristics, and learning styles; intelligent and caring teaching that is free of limiting expectations; comprehensive counseling programs and services; and family and community support services.

DIRECTIONS FOR FUTURE RESEARCH

Learning Environments

Academic achievement is dependent on more than individual abilities and aspirations. The social environment in which learning takes place can enhance or diminish the behaviors that lead to optimal achievement. The school is a microcosm of the society. Therefore, the racial and gender-role stereotypes and biases that are prevalent in society find their way into schools. Black students' feelings of disconnection occur because schools foster conformity and assimilation akin to the melting pot phenomenon. Educators must examine the classroom climate relative to its ecology (physical and material aspects that are external to individuals, such as school and classroom size), milieu (characteristics of people and groups), social system (relationships of people and groups), and culture (belief systems and values).

Several educational reform reports in the last decade (e.g., Boyer, 1984; Goodlad, 1984; Sizer, 1984) stressed that students' social and psychological development is more critical today than ever before. The reports emphasized that students need opportunities to develop their talent and potential, to learn about and understand their potential, to increase their self-esteem, to set personal goals, to make informed decisions, to persevere, and to see differences as good and desirable. These recommendations suggest that schools cannot be places where only academics are taught. Humanistic and affective education recognizes the cause–effect relationship between students and their social circumstances and the importance of educating the whole child. Stated differently, gifted young minds also have feelings, emotions, and perceptions that influence when and how the mind functions. According to Childers and Fairman (1986):

> Schools have an obligation to provide a healthy organizational climate that is conducive to optimal personal-social and academic learning. Environments that provide individuals with a feeling of significance, a sense of competence, and a belief that they have some control over important aspects of their environment will enable these individuals to feel more comfortable, feel greater self-worth and, consequently, take more risks. The lack of these elements in public school is a predominant cause of student failure. (p. 332)

Affective, humanistic educators place students at the center of learning. They recognize that students have individual psychological and socioemotional needs; that schools can help students identify, integrate, and balance their socioemotional, psychological, and academic needs; and that students gain more from an academic curriculum when their socioe-motional and psychological needs are concurrently met. Gifted Black students must be exposed to teachers who hold high expectations; who are empathetic, accepting, child oriented, interested, understanding, and genuine; and who foster a "curriculum of caring" (Bronfenbrenner, 1979). With this supportive and nurturing environment, teachers can expect gains in gifted Black students' academic achievement, self-concept, intrinsic motivation, attendance and class participation, and feelings of belonging and ownership. Affective education promotes confidence, connectedness, compassion, and choosing in children. Boy and Pine (1988) lamented:

> We may never know the untold number of boys and girls who could have achieved optimum benefits from their educational experience, but did not because their emotional problems prevented them from doing so. (p. 223)

In other words, classroom climates for gifted Black students must be characterized by empathetic understanding, acceptance, sensitive listening, authenticity, presence, immediacy, equity, and equality. In this environment, teachers are acknowledging that gifted students' hearts are as important as their heads.

Family Research

In 1978, Allen described the limited applicability of theories of Black family life. Too often, it was argued, theories and research fail to capture the strengths and uniqueness of Black people. They do not focus on the dynamic, change-oriented, adaptive perspectives of Black family life. Ethnocentric research, whether on Black students or on their families, reflects findings of the larger predominant society. For example, income, occupational status, family structure, and parents' educational levels are considered the primary determinants of family functioning and the quality of family life. When Black families deviate from the prevailing or acceptable norms, they are viewed as abnormal or pathological. Focusing only on gifted students in nuclear families and ignoring racial variables in research promises to yield fruitless data—information that carries little external validity and generalizability in this multicultural society.

While behavioral scientists frequently operate from value-laden perspectives, research is not a neutral process. In many ways, the study of Black students and their families is very personal, despite researchers' beliefs that they approach their subjects with great objectivity (Dilworth-Anderson & McAdoo, 1988). Stated differently, the theoretical and conceptual perspectives of researchers are influenced by their personal life history, family of origin, value orientations, and group identification. One's social position, class, generation, occupation, values, and ethos all affect the production of knowledge (Dilworth-Anderson & McAdoo, 1988). The baggage that researchers bring to their work is packed with group and personal ideologies and experiences. Theoretical perspectives reflect the basic value assumptions of researchers themselves rather than logical fact-finding. Value-laden research compromises and threatens the conceptual and theoretical integrity of a science or a discipline.

If gifted Black students are to prosper in school and in life, educators and researchers cannot continue to promote a knowledge base that is culturally insensitive and irresponsible. Future research must consider the multitude of variables that are important in the lives of Black families, including achievement orientations, beliefs, and values.

Recruitment and Retention Philosophy

When Black students enter gifted programs, they may need to make significant personal and social adjustments, particularly if they come from racially heterogeneous settings. Future research must be devoted to those factors that promise to increase the goodness of fit between gifted, potentially gifted, and underachieving Black students and gifted education programs.

Black students are often expected to adapt to gifted programs. The greater the compatibility between the gifted program and Black students, the more positive students' social integration (e.g., feeling connected to peers, teachers, faculty; the overall social life of the program), and the greater the probability that Black students will persist in the gifted program.

Retention efforts are likely to be successful when educators set clear expectations for gifted Black students, enhance their school competencies, and increase their opportunities for affiliation and support. School personnel who are committed to the identification and placement of Black students in gifted programs must take a proactive and preventive stance by beginning the identification process early. Educators must also set clear expectations for gifted Black students; increase their self-awareness relative to areas of giftedness, strengths, shortcomings, and learning styles; enhance their school competence (e.g., research, test-taking, study, and interpersonal communication skills); establish mentorships and cohort or affinity groups; provide comprehensive academic counseling services; provide vocational and career counseling; and provide personal and group counseling services.

As described below, other important strategies for successful recruitment and retention include developing a student and community needs assessment, identifying allies in the Black community, working within the fields of gifted and urban education, working with businesses and professional organizations in the Black community, and allocating sufficient resources to increase service options offered to gifted Black students:

(1) *Assess needs.* Although the poor representation of Black students may be visually evident, school personnel should also examine the extent and nature of the underrepresentation. For instance, although Black students in general may be underrepresented in gifted education, the problem may be most acute among Black students who are economically disadvantaged, male, or at the secondary level.

(2) *Identify allies in the Black community.* If recruitment and retention efforts are to be successful, educators must communicate with Black students on an interpersonal level. Building such a relationship requires attending community events and celebrations, finding the "pulse" of the Black community (usually church and religious leaders, retired teachers, business leaders), and showing interest in understanding Black students as individuals and cultural beings.

(3) *Work within and outside of gifted education.* It is important to reach beyond the literature in gifted education to work with Black students. Most organizations in urban education, psychology, and counseling, for example, have newsletters and journals with theoretical and empirical data on educational, psychological, and socioemotional issues relative to working with Black students. Although the information may not be specific to gifted Black students, it is nonetheless relevant and informative.

(4) *Allocate resources.* For recruitment and retention to be successful, educators must be willing and able to commit time and fiscal resources. For instance, economically disadvantaged Black students may require scholarships to participate in summer enrichment programs, to take private lessons in their talent areas, to take college admissions examinations, to attend test-taking workshops and courses, and to participate in other services offered to gifted students. Dollars must also be allocated for the continuing professional education and development of teachers in both gifted education and multicultural education.

A FINAL WORD

The issues discussed and recommendations offered in this book are meant to guide teachers, counselors, administrators, and other educational personnel in their work with gifted, potentially gifted, and underachieving Black students. Although some of the issues presented are unique to Black students, others are not; they are also experienced by other students of color and by gifted and nongifted students.

We must pay closer attention to the many factors that affect Black students' representation in gifted programs. Encouraging the potential and talents of all children requires a broadened vision of giftedness that reflects an understanding that talent varies markedly with cultural, racial, economic, and linguistic backgrounds (Hadaway & Marek-Schroer, 1992). Accordingly, professionals in gifted education must ensure that programs are equitable and defensible, that they are inclusive rather than exclusive, and that minority, economically disadvantaged, and underachieving gifted students have an equal opportunity to learn in a nurturing and stimulating educational environment.

The recommendations for increasing and maintaining the representation of Black students in gifted education programs are not exhaustive; rather, they offer a point from which to begin to ensure the success of all gifted students, particularly those who have yet to reveal their capabilities. To continue relying on unidimensional rather than multidimensional assessment strategies, to ignore contemporary theories of intelligence, and to perceive cultural difference and diversity as inconsequential to learning and academic success is to contribute to Black students' poor achievement and representation in gifted programs.

To be successful in gifted programs, Black students must feel empowered. Educators can do much to empower Black students. This empowerment comes from having a sense of belonging and connectedness with the gifted program, with students, with teachers, and with the curriculum. Empowerment comes from having teachers who understand and respect cultural diversity and who promote multiculturalism. It comes from enriching and diversifying the demographics of the gifted program relative to students, teachers, and other personnel who can serve as mentors, role models, and advocates. Empowering gifted Black students requires having comprehensive support services in place—supportive peer groups, school counselors, psychologists, and other school personnel who are trained to work with both gifted and minority students and who are sensitive to the issues that attend being both gifted and a racial minority. Empowering and, thus, retaining Black students in programs for the gifted also necessitates encouraging substantive family involvement, welcoming families and significant others into the formal learning process at all grade levels.

In general, our efforts to recruit Black students into gifted programs have increased in recent years. However, more concerted efforts must be aimed at the retention of these students once they are placed. In this way, we ensure that underachieving, gifted, and potentially gifted Black students receive the education to which they are entitled, that their educational rights are not violated, and that they participate in all opportunities that promise to discover and then nurture their abilities.

Legal, Social, and Ethical Issues in Measurement with Minority Students: Sample Court Cases

Hobson v. Hansen (1967)

COMPLAINT. In this District of Columbia case, minority groups questioned the constitutionality of using group IQ and achievement measures in placing children in special educational tracks. Black students were overrepresented in low-ability tracks (particularly educably mentally retarded [EMR] classes), and White students were placed disproportionately in upper-ability tracks (especially college preparatory classes).

RULING. The court prohibited the use of tests for purposes of grouping, holding that the tests had been standardized on primarily White, middle-class populations; therefore, the tests yielded biased results when administered to minority students.

Diana v. California State Board of Education (1970)

COMPLAINT. Plaintiffs on behalf of nine Latin American students charged that the children were inappropriately placed in EMR classes as a result of scores on IQ tests that assumed equality of the examinees' linguistic and cultural backgrounds. When the students were permitted to take the test in their primary language, there was an average increase of 15 IQ points.

RULING. The case led to an out-of-court settlement stipulating that children from non-English-speaking homes would be tested in their native language and to subsequent out-of-court settlements specifying that IQ tests used for special education placement must be normed on culturally and linguistically relevant groups and contain no culturally unfair content.

Larry P. v. Wilson Riles (1979)

COMPLAINT. Plaintiffs were six Black parents who claimed that their children had been placed wrongly in EMR classes because the standardized IQ tests used for placement were racially and culturally biased. The case first appeared in 1971 against the San Francisco Unified School District. After several years of injunctions and appeals, the case finally came to trial in 1979.

RULING. The court rendered a decision in favor of the plaintiffs. Noting that disproportionate numbers of Black students were placed in EMR classes (Black students constituted 27% of the total student population but over 60% of the EMR population), the court found: "There is less than one in a million chance that the over-representation of Black children and the under-enrollment of non-Black children in the EMR classes in 1967–1977 would have resulted under a color-blind system of placement" (cited in Anderson, Stiggins, & Gordon, 1980, p. 19). The state of California appealed the decision. In 1984, an appellate court upheld the court's decision (Worthen, Borg, & White, 1993).

References

Allen, W. (1978). The search for applicable theories of Black family life. *Journal of Marriage and the Family, 40*, 117–131.

Allington, R. C. (1980). Teacher interruption behaviors during primary grade oral reading. *Journal of Educational Psychology, 72*, 371–377.

Allport, G. (1979). *The nature of prejudice*. Reading, MA: Addison-Wesley.

Alvino, J. (1991). An investigation into the needs of gifted boys. *Roeper Review, 13*(4), 174–180.

American Association of Colleges for Teacher Education. (1990). *Teacher education pipeline II: Schools, colleges, and departments of education enrollments by race and ethnicity*. Washington, DC: Author.

American Association of Colleges for Teacher Education Commission on Multicultural Education. (1973). No one model American. *Journal of Teacher Education, 24*(4), 264–265.

American Association of University Women. (1992). *How schools shortchange girls*. Washington, DC: National Education Association Professional Library.

American Educational Research Association, American Psychological Association, & National Council on Measurement in Education. (1985). *Standards for educational and psychological testing*. Washington, DC: American Psychological Association.

American Federation of Teachers, National Council on Measurement in Education, & National Educational Association. (1990). Standards for teacher competence in educational assessment of students. *Educational Measurement: Issues and Practices, 9*(4), 30–32.

American heritage dictionary of the English language. (1973). New York: Houghton Mifflin.

Anderson, K. L., & Allen, W. R. (1984). Correlates of extended household structure. *Phylon, 45*(2), 144–157.

Anderson, B. L., Stiggins, R. J., & Gordon, D. W. (1980). *Educational testing facts and issues: A layperson's guide to testing in the schools*. Portland, OR: Northwest Regional Educational Laboratory and California State Department of Education.

Applebee, A. (1989). *A study of book-length works taught in high school English courses*. Albany, NY: Center for the Learning and Teaching of Literature, State University of New York, School of Education.

Archambault, F. X., Westberg, K. L., Brown, S. W., Hallmark, B. W., Zhang, W., & Emmons, C. L. (1993). Classroom practices used with gifted third and fourth grade students. *Journal for the Education of the Gifted, 16*(2), 103–119.

Arnold, K. D. (1993). Undergraduate aspirations and career outcomes of academically talented women: A discriminant analysis. *Roeper Review*, *15*(3), 169–175.

Atkinson, D. R., Jennings, R. G., & Liongson, L. (1990). Minority students' reasons for not seeking counseling and suggestions for improving services. *Journal of College Student Development*, *31*, 342–350.

Au, K. H., & Kawakami, A. J. (1994). Cultural congruence in instruction. In E. R. Hollins, J. E. King, & W. C. Hayman (Eds.), *Teaching diverse populations: Formulating a knowledge base* (pp. 5–23). New York: State University of New York Press.

Aylward, G. P. (1994). *Practitioner's guide to developmental and psychological testing*. New York: Plenum Medical Book.

Baldwin, A. Y. (1989). The purpose of education for gifted Black students. In C. J. Maker & S. W. Schiever (Eds.), *Critical issues in gifted education: Defensible programs for cultural and ethnic minorities* (Vol. 2, pp. 237–245). Austin, TX: ProEd.

Baldwin, A. Y. (1994). The seven plus story: Developing hidden talent among students in socioeconomically disadvantaged environments. *Gifted Child Quarterly*, *38*(2), 80–84.

Banks, J. A. (1979). *Teaching strategies for ethnic studies* (2nd ed.). Boston: Allyn and Bacon.

Banks, J. A. (1988). *Multiethnic education: Theory and practice*. Boston: Allyn & Bacon.

Banks, J. A. (1993). Approaches to multicultural curriculum reform. In J. A. Banks and C. A. M. Banks (Eds.), *Multicultural education: Issues and perspectives* (2nd ed., pp. 195–214). Boston: Allyn & Bacon.

Banks, J. A. (1994). Multicultural education: Historical development, dimensions, and practice. In L. D. Darling-Hammond (Ed.), *Review of research in education* (pp. 3–49). Washington, DC: American Educational Research Association.

Banks, J. A., & Banks, C. A. M. (Eds.). (1993). *Multicultural education: Issues and perspectives* (2nd ed.). Boston: Allyn & Bacon.

Baptiste, H. P., Jr. (1992). Conceptual and theoretical issues. In H. C. Waxman, J. Walker de Felix, J. E. Anderson, & H. P. Baptiste Jr. (Eds.), *Students at risk in at-risk schools: Improving environments for learning* (pp. 11–16). Newbury Park, CA: Corwin Press.

Bartley, R. (1980). *An analysis of secondary students' educational aspiration, school satisfaction and self satisfaction in the Seattle public schools* (Report No. 80-9). Seattle: Washington Department of Planning, Research, and Evaluation. (ERIC Document Reproduction Service No. ED 209 399)

Beidel, D. C., Turner, M. W., Marquette, W., & Trager, K. N. (1994). Test anxiety and childhood anxiety disorders in African American and White school children. *Journal of Anxiety Disorders*, *8*(2), 169–179.

Bempechat, J., & Ginsburg, H. P. (1989). *Underachievement and educational disadvantage: The home and school experience of at-risk youth*. New York:

ERIC Clearinghouse on Urban Education. (ERIC Document Reproduction Service No. ED 315 195)

Benbow, C. P., & Arjmand, O. (1990). Predictors of high academic achievement in mathematics and science by mathematically talented students: A longitudinal study. *Journal of Educational Psychology, 82*, 430–441.

Bennett, C. I. (1990). *Comprehensive multicultural education: Theory and practice* (2nd ed.). Boston: Allyn & Bacon.

Bennett deMarrais, K., & LeCompte, M. D. (1995). *The way schools work: A sociological analysis of education* (2nd ed.). White Plains, NY: Longman.

Berk, R. A. (1983). Learning disabilities as a category of underachievement. In L. S. Fox, L. Brody, & D. Tobin (Eds.), *Learning disabled/gifted children: Identification and programming* (pp. 51–76). Baltimore: University Park Press.

Binet, A., & Simon, T. (1905). Methodes nouvelles pour le diagnostic du niveau intellectual des anormaux. *Annee Psychologique, 11*, 191–244.

Bitting, P. F., Cordeiro, P. A., & Baptiste, H. P., Jr. (1992). Philosophical and conceptual issues related to students at risk. In H. C. Waxman, J. Walker de Felix, J. E. Anderson, & H. P. Baptiste Jr. (Eds.), *Students at risk in at-risk schools: Improving environments for learning* (pp. 17–32). Newbury Park, CA: Corwin Press.

Bloom, B. S. (1964). *Stability and change in human characteristics.* New York: John Wiley.

Bloom, B. S. (Ed.). (1985). *Developing talent in young people.* New York: Ballantine.

Board of Education of Hendrick Hudson Central School District v. Rowley, 458 U.S. 176 (1982).

Borland, J. H., & Wright, L. (1994). Identifying young, potentially gifted, economically disadvantaged students. *Gifted Child Quarterly, 38*(4), 164–171.

Bourdieu, P. (1977). Cultural reproduction and social reproduction. In J. Karabel & A. Halsey (Eds.), *Power and ideology in education* (pp. 487–510). New York: Oxford University Press.

Bowie, R. L., & Bond, C. L. (1994). Influencing future teachers' attitudes toward Black English: Are we making a difference? *Journal of Teacher Education, 45*(2), 112–118.

Bowles, S., & Gintis, H. (1976). *Schooling in capitalist America.* New York: Basic Books.

Boy, A. V., & Pine, G. J. (1988). *Fostering psychosocial development in the classroom.* Springfield, IL: Charles C. Thomas.

Boyer, E. L. (1984). *High school: A report on secondary education in America.* New York: Harper & Row.

Boykin, A. W. (1986). The triple quandary and the schooling of Afro-American children. In U. Neisser (Ed.), *The school achievement of minority children* (pp. 57–92). Hillsdale, NJ: Erlbaum.

Boykin, A. W. (1994). Afrocultural expression and its implications for schooling. In E. R. Hollins, J. E. King, & W. C. Hayman (Eds.), *Teaching diverse populations: Formulating a knowledge base* (pp. 225–273). New York: State University of New York Press.

Bricklin, B., & Bricklin, P. (1967). *Bright child, poor grades.* New York: Delacorte Press.

Britton, G., & Lumpkin, M. (1983). Females and minorities in basal readers. *Interracial Books for Children Bulletin, 14*(6), 4–7.

Bronfenbrenner, U. (1979). Beyond the deficit model in child and family policy. *Teachers College Press, 81,* 95–104.

Brophy, J. (1988). Research on teacher effects: Uses and abuses. *Elementary School Journal, 89*(1), 3–22.

Brown v. Board of Education of Topeka, Kansas, 347 U.S. 483 (1954).

Bullivant, B. M. (1993). Culture: Its nature and meaning for educators. In J. A. Banks & C. A. M. Banks (Eds.), *Multicultural education: Issues and perspectives* (2nd ed., pp. 29–47). Boston: Allyn & Bacon.

Burstein, N. D., & Cabello, B. (1989, September/October). Preparing teachers to work with culturally diverse students: Another educational model. *Journal of Teacher Education, 540*(5), 9–16.

Burt, C. (1972). The inheritance of general intelligence. *American Psychology, 27,* 175–190.

Butler, R. O. (1975). Psychotherapy: Implications of a Black-consciousness process model. *Psychotherapy: Theory, Research and Practice, 12,* 407–411.

Butler-Por, N. (1987). *Underachievers in school: Issues and interventions.* New York: John Wiley & Sons.

Byrnes, D. A. (1984). Social isolates and the teacher. *Educational Forum, 48*(3), 373–381.

Callahan, C. M. (1991). An update on gifted females. *Journal for the Education of the Gifted,* 14, 284–311.

Campbell, C. A. (1991). Group guidance for academically under-motivated children. *Elementary School Guidance & Counseling,* 25, 302–306.

Carnegie Corporation of New York. (1984/1985). Renegotiating society's contract with the public schools. *Carnegie Quarterly, 29/29,* 1–4, 6–11.

Carroll, A., Gurski, G., Hinsdale, K., & McIntyre, K. (1977). *Culturally appropriate assessment: A sourcebook for practitioners.* Los Angeles: Regional Resource Center.

Carter, K. (1984). Do teachers understand principles for writing tests? *Journal of Teacher Education, 35*(6), 57–60.

Carter, T. P., & Chatfield, M. L. (1986). Effective bilingual schools: Implications for policy and practice. *American Journal of Education, 95*(1), 200–234.

Cassidy, J., & Hossler, A. (1992). State and federal definitions of the gifted: An update. *Gifted Child Quarterly, 15*(1), 46–53.

Childers, J. H., & Fairman, M. (1986). The school counselor as a facilitator of organizational health. *The School Counselor, 33*(5), 332–337.

Citizens Policy Center for Oakland. (1984). *Voices from the classroom. Students and teachers speak out on the quality of teaching in our schools. A report of the Students for Quality Teaching Project.* San Francisco: Rosenberg Foundation.

Clance, P. R., & Imes, I. M. (1978). The imposter phenomenon in high achieving women: Dynamics and therapeutic intervention. *Psychotherapy: Theory, Research and Practice, 15,* 241–245.

Clark, B. (1992). *Growing up gifted* (4th ed.). Columbus, OH: Merrill.

Clark, L., DeWolf, S., & Clark, C. (1992). Teaching teachers to avoid having culturally assaultive classrooms. *Young Children, 47*(5), 4–9.

Clark, R. (1983). *Family life and school achievement: Why poor Black children succeed and fail.* Chicago: University of Chicago Press.

Clawson, T. W., Firment, C. K., & Trower, L. L. (1981). Test anxiety: Another origin for racial bias in standardized testing. *Measurement and Evaluation in Guidance, 13*(4), 210–215.

Clawson, T. W., Firment, C. K., & Trower, L. L. (1989). Text anxiety: Another origin for racial bias in standardized testing. *Measurement and Evaluation in Guidance, 13,* 210–215.

Colangelo, N. (1988). Families of gifted children: The next ten years. *Roeper Review, 11*(1), 16–18.

Colangelo, N. (1991). Counseling gifted students. In N. Colangelo & G. A. Davis (Eds.), *Handbook of gifted education* (pp. 273–284). Needham Heights, MA: Allyn & Bacon.

Colangelo, N., & Davis, G. A. (Eds.). (1991). *Handbook of gifted education.* Boston: Allyn & Bacon.

Colangelo, N., & Dettman, D. F. (1983). A review of research on parents and families of gifted children. *Exceptional Children, 50,* 22–27.

Colangelo, N., & Exum, H. A. (1979, January/February). Educating the culturally diverse gifted: Implications for teachers, counselors, and parents. *G/C/T, 6,* 22–23, 54–55.

Colangelo, N., Kerr, B. A., Maxey, J., & Christensen, P. (1992). Characteristics of academically talented minority students. *Journal of Counseling and Development, 70,* 606–609.

Coleman, J. S. (1987). Families and schools. *Educational Researcher, 16,* 32–38.

Coleman, J. S., Campbell, E. Q., Hobson, C. J., McPartland, J., Mood, A. M., Weinfeld, F. D., & York, R. L. (1966). *Equality of educational opportunity.* Washington, DC: U.S. Government Printing Office.

Coleman, M. J., & Fults, B. A. (1985). Special-class placement, level of intelligence, and the self-concepts of gifted children: A social comparison perspective. *Remedial and Special Education, 6*(1), 7–11.

College Entrance Examination Board. (1985). *Quality and excellence: The educational status of Black Americans.* New York: Author.

Cooley, M. R., Cornell, D. G., & Lee, C. (1991). Peer acceptance and self concept of Black students in a summer gifted program. *Journal for the Education of the Gifted, 14*(2), 166–177.

Council for Exceptional Children. (1994). Statistical profile of special education in the United States, 1994. Suppl. to *Teaching Exceptional Children, 26*(3), 1–4.

Cox, J., Daniel, N., & Boston, B. (1985). *Educating able learners.* Austin, TX: University of Texas Press.

Crocker, L., Schmitt, A., & Tang, L. (1988). Test anxiety and standardized achievement test performance in the middle school years. *Measurement and Evaluation in Counseling and Development, 20*(4), 149–157.

Cross, W. E., Jr. (1971, July). Toward a psychology of Black liberation: The Negro-to-Black conversion experience. *Black World, 20,* 13–27.

Cross, W. E., Jr. (1995). The psychology of Nigrescence: Revising the Cross model. In J. G. Ponterotto, J. M. Casas, L. A. Suzuki, & C. M. Alexander (Eds.), *Handbook of multicultural counseling* (pp. 93–122). Thousand Oaks, CA: Sage.

Csikszentmihalyi, D. R., & McCormack, J. (1986). The influence of teachers. *Phi Delta Kappan, 67,* 415–419.

Curry, R. L. (1961). Certain characteristics of underachievers and overachievers. *Peabody Journal of Education, 39,* 41–45.

Damico, S. B. (1983). The two worlds of school: Difference in the photographs of Black and White adolescents. *The Urban Review, 17*(3), 210–222.

Darling-Hammond, L. D. (Ed.). (1994). *Review of research in education.* Washington, DC: American Educational Research Association.

Davis, G. A., & Rimm, S. B. (1994). *Education of the gifted and talented* (3rd ed.). Boston: Allyn & Bacon.

Davis, W. E., & McCall, E. J. (1990). *At-risk children and youth: A crisis in our schools and society.* Orono, ME: University of Maine.

Delisle, J. R. (1992). *Guiding the social and emotional development of gifted youth: A practical guide for educators and counselors.* New York: Longman.

DellaValle, J. C. (1984). *An experimental investigation of the relationship between preference for mobility and the word-pair recognition scores of seventh-grade students to provide supervisory and administrative guidelines for the organization of effective instructional environments.* Unpublished doctoral dissertation, St. Johns University, Jamaica, NY.

Demo, D. H., & Acock, A. C. (1988). The impact of divorce on children. *Journal of Marriage and the Family, 50*(3), 619–648.

deVaul, S., & Davis, J. (1988, September 30). *Whole family: Whole child. Broken family.* Paper presented at the conference of the West Virginia Association for Gifted and Talented, Parkersburg, WV. (ERIC Document Reproduction Service No. ED 305 776)

Dewey, J. (1963). *Experience and education.* New York: Collier.

Diana v. California State Board of Education, No. C-70-37 RFP, District Court of Northern California, 1970.

Diener, C. I., & Dweck, C. S. (1980). An analysis of learned helplessness II: The processing of success. *Journal of Personality and Social Psychology, 39,* 940–952.

Dilworth-Anderson, P., & McAdoo, H. P. (1988). The study of ethnic minority families: Implications for practitioners and policymakers. *Family Relations, 37,* 265–267.

Dirkes, M. A. (1985). Anxiety in the gifted: Pluses and minuses. *Roeper Review, 8*(1), 13–15.

Dorr-Bremm, D. W., & Herman, J. L. (1986). *Assessing student achievement: A profile of classroom practices*. Los Angeles: Center for the Study of Evaluation, University of California.

Dovidio, J. F., & Gaertner, S. L. (Eds.). (1986). *Prejudice, discrimination, and racism*. Orlando, FL: Academic Press.

Dunn, R., Beaudry, J. A., & Klavas, A. (1989). Survey of research on learning styles. *Educational Leadership, 46*(6), 50–58.

Dunn, R., DeBello, T., Brennan, P., Krimsky, J., & Murrain, P. (1981). Learning style researchers define differences differently. *Educational Leadership, 38*(5), 372–375.

Dusek, J. B. (1980). The development of test anxiety in children. In I. G. Sarason (Ed.), *Test anxiety: Theory, research and applications*. Hillsdale, NJ: Erlbaum.

Eato, L. E., & Lerner, R. M. (1981). Relations of physical and social environment perceptions to adolescent self esteem. *Journal of Genetic Psychology, 139*, 143–150.

Eccles, J. (1985). Why Jane doesn't run: Sex differences in educational and occupational patterns. In F. D. Horowitz & M. O'Brien (Eds.), *The gifted and talented: Developmental perspectives* (pp. 251–295). Washington, DC: American Psychological Association.

Eccles, J. (1989). Bringing young women to math and science. In M. Crawford & M. Gentry (Eds.), *Gender and thought: Psychological perspectives*. New York: Springer-Verlag.

Edelman, M. W. (1985). The sea is so wide and my boat is so small: Problems facing Black children today. In H. P. McAdoo & J. L. McAdoo (Eds.), *Black children: Social, educational, and parental environments* (pp. 72–84). Newbury Park, CA: Sage.

Edmonds, R. (1979). Effective schools for the urban poor. *Educational Leadership, 37*, 15–23.

Edmonds, R. (1986). Characteristics of effective schools. In U. Neisser (Ed.), *The school achievement of minority children* (pp. 93–104). Hillsdale, NJ: Erlbaum.

Education Commission of the States Task Force on Education for Economic Growth. (1983). *Action for excellence*. Denver, CO: Author.

Education for All Handicapped Children Act, 20 U.S.C. §1401 *et seq.* (1975).

Eisenberg, S., & O'Dell, F. (1988). Teaching children to trust in a non-trusting world. *Elementary School Guidance & Counseling, 22*, 264–267.

Erikson, E. (1968). *Identity, youth and crisis*. New York: Norton.

Exum, H. (1983). Key issues in family counseling with gifted and talented black students. *Roeper Review, 5*(3), 28–31.

Fantini, M., & Weinstein, G. (1968). *Making urban schools work*. New York: Holt, Rinehart, & Winston.

Farquhar, W. W., & Payne, D. A. (1964). A classification and comparison of techniques used in selecting under- and over-achievers. *Personnel and Guidance Journal, 42*, 874–884.

Feingold, A. (1988). Cognitive gender differences disappearing. *American Psychologist, 43*, 95–103.

Feldhusen, J. F. (1994). A case for developing America's talent: How we went wrong and where we go now. *Roeper Review, 16*(4), 231–233.

Festinger, L. (1954). A theory of social comparisons. *Human Relations, 2*, 117–140.

Filla, T., & Clark, D. (1973). *Human relations resource guide on in-service programs.* St. Paul, MN: Minnesota Department of Education.

Fine, B. (1967). *Underachievers: How they can be helped* (1st ed.). New York: Dalton.

Fine, M. (1986). Why urban adolescents drop into and out of public high school. In G. Natriello (Ed.), *School dropouts: Patterns and policies* (pp. 52–69). New York: Teachers College Press.

Fine, M. J., & Pitts, R. (1980). Intervention with underachieving gifted children: Rationale and strategies. *Gifted Child Quarterly, 24*, 51–55.

Finney, B. C., & Van Dalsem, E. (1969). Group counseling for gifted underachieving high school students. *Journal of Counseling Psychology, 16*(1), 87–94.

Fleming, M., & Chambers, B. (1983). Teacher-made tests: Windows on the classroom. In W. E. Hathaway (Ed.), *Testing in the schools: New directions for testing and measurement* (pp. 29–38). San Francisco: Jossey-Bass.

Ford, B. A. (1992). Multicultural education training for special educators working with African-American youth. *Exceptional Children, 59*(2), 107–114.

Ford, D. Y. (1992). Determinants of underachievement among gifted, above-average, and average Black students. *Roeper Review, 14*(3), 130–136.

Ford, D. Y. (1993a). Black students' achievement orientation as a function of perceived family achievement orientation and demographic variables. *Journal of Negro Education, 62*(1), 47–66.

Ford, D. Y. (1993b). An investigation into the paradox of underachievement among gifted Black students. *Roeper Review, 16*(2), 78–84.

Ford, D. Y. (1993c). Support for the achievement ideology and determinants of underachievement as perceived by gifted, above-average, and average Black students. *Journal for the Education of the Gifted, 16*(3), 280–298.

Ford, D. Y. (1994a). An exploration of perceptions of alternative family structures among university students. *Family Relations, 43*(1), 68–73.

Ford, D. Y. (1994b). Nurturing resilience in gifted Black students. *Roeper Review, 17*(2), 80–85.

Ford, D. Y. (1994c). *The recruitment and retention of Black students in gifted programs.* Research-Based Decision Making Series. Storrs, CT: National Research Center on the Gifted and Talented, University of Connecticut.

Ford, D. Y. (1995). *Correlates of underachievement among gifted and non-gifted Black students: Technical report.* Storrs, CT: National Research Center on the Gifted and Talented, University of Connecticut.

Ford, D. Y., & Harris, J. J., III. (1991). On discovering the hidden treasure of gifted and talented African-American children. *Roeper Review, 13*(1), 27–33.

Ford, D. Y., & Harris, J. J., III. (1994). Promoting achievement among gifted Black students: The efficacy of new definitions and identification practices. *Urban Education, 29*(2), 202–229.

Ford, D. Y., & Harris, J. J. (1995a). Underachievement among gifted African-American students: Implications for school counselors. *The School Counselor, 42*(3), 94–106.

Ford, D. Y., & Harris, J. J. (1995b). University counselors' perceptions of factors incident to achievement among gifted Black and gifted White students. *Journal of Counseling and Development, 73*(4), 443–450.

Ford, D. Y., & Harris, J. J. (in press). Attitudes and perceptions of Black students toward school, achievement, and other educational variables. *Child Development*.

Ford, D. Y., Harris, J. J., III, & Schuerger, J. M. (1993). Racial identity development among gifted Black students: Counseling issues and concerns. *Journal of Counseling and Development, 71*(4), 409–417.

Ford, D. Y., Harris, J. J., Turner, W. L., & Sandidge, R. F. (1991). The extended African-American family: A pragmatic strategy to blunt the blades of injustice. *The Urban League Review Policy Research Journal, 14*(2), 1–13.

Ford, D. Y., Harris, J. J., Webb, K. S., & Jones, D. (1994). Rejection or confirmation of cultural identity: A dilemma for high-achieving Blacks? *Journal of Educational Thought, 28*(1), 7–33.

Ford, D. Y., Harris, J. J., & Winborne, D. G. (1990). The coloring of IQ testing: A new name for an old phenomenon. *The Urban League Review Policy Research Journal, 13*(1/2), 99–111.

Ford, D. Y., Schuerger, J. M., & Harris, J. J. (1991). Meeting the socio-psychological needs of gifted Black students. *Journal of Counseling and Development, 69*(6), 577–580.

Ford, D. Y., & Webb, K. S. (1994). Desegregation of gifted educational programs: The impact of *Brown* on underachieving children of color. *Journal of Negro Education, 63*(3), 358–375.

Ford, D. Y., Winborne, D. G., & Harris, J. J. (1991). Determinants of underachievement among gifted Black students: Learning to underachieve. *Journal of Social and Behavioral Sciences, 35*(3), 145–162.

Ford, M. A. (1989). Students' perceptions of affective issues impacting the social emotional development and school performance of gifted/talented youngsters. *Roeper Review, 11*(3), 131–134.

Fordham, S. (1988). Racelessness as a strategy in Black students' school success: Pragmatic strategy or pyrrhic victory? *Harvard Educational Review, 58*(1), 54–84.

Franklin, J. H. (1988). A historical note on Black families. In H. P. McAdoo (Ed.), *Black families* (2nd ed., pp. 23–26). Newbury Park, CA: Sage.

Frantz, C. S., & Prillaman, D. (1993). State certification endorsement for school counselors: Special education requirements. *The School Counselor, 40*, 375–379.

Fraser, B. J. (1994). Research on classroom and school climate. In D. Gabel (Ed.), *Handbook of research on science teaching and learning* (pp. 493–541). New York: Macmillan.

Fraser, B. J., & Fisher, D. L. (1982). Predicting students' outcomes from their perceptions of classroom psychosocial environment. *American Educational Research Journal, 19,* 498–518.

Frasier, M. (1989). A perspective on identifying Black students for gifted programs. In C. J. Maker & S. W. Schiever (Eds.), *Critical issues in gifted education: Defensible programs for cultural and ethnic minorities* (Vol. 2, pp. 213–255). Austin, TX: ProEd.

Frasier, M. M., & Passow, A. H. (1994). *Toward a new paradigm for identifying talent potential.* Storrs, CT: National Research on the Gifted and Talented, University of Connecticut.

Frasier, M. M., Garcia, J. H., & Passow, A. H. (1995). *A review of assessment issues in gifted education and their implications for identifying gifted minority students.* Storrs, CT: National Research on the Gifted and Talented, University of Connecticut.

Frederico, P. A., & Landis, D. B. (1980). *Are cognitive styles independent of ability and aptitude?* Paper presented at the annual conference of the American Psychological Association.

Freeman, J. (1983). Emotional problems of the gifted child. *Journal of Child Psychology and Psychiatry, 24,* 66–70.

Freire, P. (1993). *Pedagogy of the oppressed.* New York: Continuum.

Gagne, F. (1989). Peer nomination as a psychometric instrument: Many questions asked but few answered. *Gifted Child Quarterly, 33,* 53–58.

Galbraith, J. (1985). The eight great gripes of gifted kids: Responding to special needs. *Roeper Review, 8*(1), 15–17.

Gallagher, J. J. (1979). Issues on the education for the gifted. In A. H. Passow (Ed.), *The gifted and talented: Their education and development.* Chicago: University of Chicago Press.

Gallagher, J. J., & Gallagher, S. A. (1994). *Teaching the gifted child* (4th ed.). Needham Heights, MA: Allyn & Bacon.

Gallagher, J. J., & Kinney, L. (Eds.). (1974). *Talent delayed — talent denied: A conference report.* Reston, VA: Foundation for Exceptional Children.

Gallup poll finds public support for programs for gifted students. (1992, December 9). *Education Week,* p. 2.

Garcia, R., & Walker de Felix, J. (1992). The dropout issue and school reform. In H. C. Waxman, J. Walker de Felix, J. E. Anderson, & H. P. Baptiste Jr. (Eds.), *Students at risk in at-risk schools. Improving environments for learning* (pp. 43–60). Newbury Park, CA: Corwin Press.

Gardner, H. (1983). *Frames of mind: The theory of multiple intelligences.* New York: Basic Books.

Gay, G. (1990). Achieving educational equality through curriculum desegregation. *Phi Delta Kappan, 72*(1), 56–72.

Gay, G. (1993). Ethnic minorities and educational equality. In J. A. Banks and C. A. M. Banks (Eds.), *Multicultural education: Issues and perspectives* (2nd ed., pp. 171–194). Boston: Allyn & Bacon.

Gay, J. E. (1978). A proposed plan for identifying Black gifted children. *Gifted Child Quarterly, 22,* 353–359.

Gelbrich, J. A., & Hare, E. K. (1989). The effects of single parenthood on school achievement in a gifted population. *Gifted Child Quarterly, 33*(3), 115–117.

Gerler, E. R., Jr., Kinney, J., & Anderson, R. F. (1985). The effects of counseling on classroom performance. *Humanistic Education and Development, 23,* 155–165.

Gifted and Talented Children Act, 20 U.S.C. § 3311 (1978).

Giroux, H. (1983). Theories of reproduction and resistance in the new sociology of education. *Harvard Educational Review, 52,* 257–293.

Glasser, W. (1986). *Control theory in the classroom.* New York: Harper & Row.

Goddard, H. H. (1912). *The Kallikak family, a study in the heredity of feeble-mindedness.* New York: Macmillan.

Gollnick, D. M., & Chinn, P. C. (1994). *Multicultural education in a pluralistic society* (4th ed.). New York: Merrill.

Goodlad, J. I. (1984). *A place called school: Prospects for the future.* New York: McGraw-Hill.

Governors' Commission on Socially Disadvantaged Black Males. (1989). *Call to action* (vol. 2). Columbus, OH: Author.

Gowan, J. C. (1957). Intelligence, interests, and reading ability in relation to scholastic achievement. *Psychology Newsletter, 15/16,* 22–36.

Granat, D., Hathaway, P., Saleton, W., & Sansing, J. (1986). Blacks and Whites in Washington: How separate? How equal? A special report. *Washingtonian, 22,* 152–182.

Green, K., Fine, M. J., & Tollefson, N. (1988). Family systems characteristics and underachieving gifted adolescent males. *Gifted Child Quarterly, 32*(2), 267–272.

Gross, M. U. M. (1989). The pursuit of excellence or the search for intimacy? The forced-choice dilemma of gifted youth. *Roeper Review, 11,* 189–193.

Gubbins, E. J., Siegle, D., Renzulli, J. S., & Brown, S. W. (Fall, 1993). Assumptions underlying the identification of gifted and talented students. *The National Research Center on the Gifted and Talented Newsletter,* pp. 3–5.

Gullickson, A. R., & Ellwein, M. C. (1985). Post hoc analysis of teacher-made tests: The goodness of fit between prescriptions and practice. *Educational Measurement: Issues and Practice, 4*(1), 15–18.

Hadaway, N., & Marek-Schroer, M. F. (1992). Multidimensional assessment of the gifted minority student. *Roeper Review, 15*(2), 73–77.

Hale-Benson, J. (1986). *Black children: Their roots, culture, and learning styles* (2nd ed.). Baltimore: Johns Hopkins University Press.

Hall, E. (1983). Recognizing gifted underachievers. *Roeper Review, 5,* 23–25.

Hall, E. T. (1959). *The silent language.* New York: Anchor Books.

Hammill, D. D. (1990). On defining learning disabilities: An emerging consensus. *Journal of Learning Disabilities, 23,* 74–91.

Hargis, C. H. (1989). *Teaching low achieving and disabled students.* Springfield, IL: Charles C. Thomas.

Harris, J. J., & Ford, D. Y. (1991). Identifying and nurturing the promise of gifted Black students. *Journal of Negro Education, 60*(1), 3–18.

Harry, B. (1992). Restructuring the participation of African-American parents in special education. *Exceptional Children, 59*(2), 123–131.

Haynes, N. M., Hamilton-Lee, M., & Comer, J. P. (1988). Differences in self-concept among high, average, and low achieving high school sophomores. *The Journal of Social Psychology, 128*(2), 259–264.

Hebert, T. (1991). Meeting the affective needs of bright boys through bibliotherapy. *Roeper Review, 13*(4), 207–212.

Hebert, T. (1993). *Ethnographic descriptions of the high school experiences of high ability males in an urban environment.* Storrs, CT: University of Connecticut.

Heid, C. A. (Ed.). (1988). *Multicultural education: Knowledge and perspectives.* Bloomington, IN: Indiana University Center for Urban and Multicultural Education.

Hembree, R. (1988). Correlates, causes, effects, and treatment of test anxiety. *Review of Educational Research, 58*, 47–77.

Herskovitz, M. J. (1958). *The myth of the Negro past.* Boston: Beacon Press.

Hill, K. T. (1984). Debilitating motivation and testing: A major educational problem, possible solutions, and policy applications. In R. Ames & C. Ames (Eds.), *Research on motivation in education: Student motivation.* New York: Academic Press.

Hill, K. T., & Wigfield, A. (1984). Test anxiety: A major educational problem and what can be done about it. *The Elementary School Journal, 85*(1), 105–126.

Hitchcock, M. E., & Tompkins, G. E. (1987). Are basal reading textbooks still sexist? *The Reading Teacher, 41*, 288–292.

Hobson v. Hansen, 269 F. Supp. 401 (D.D.C. 1967), off'd sub nom. Smuck v. Holson, 408 F. 2d 175 (D.C. Cir. 1969).

Hodgkinson, H. (1988). An interview with Harold Hodgkinson: Using demographic data for long-range planning. *Phi Delta Kappan, 70*(2), 166–170.

Hollinger, C., & Fleming, E. (1992). Project CHOICE: The emerging roles and careers of gifted women. *Roeper Review, 15*(3), 156–160.

Hollingworth, L. S. (1926). *Gifted children: Their nature and nurture.* New York: Macmillan.

Hollingworth, L. S. (1942). *Children above 180 IQ (S-B).* Yonkers-on-Hudson, NY: World Book Company.

Horowitz, F., & O'Brien, M. (Eds.). (1985). *The gifted and talented: Developmental perspectives.* Washington, DC: American Psychological Association.

Hoy, W. K., & Tarter, C. J. (1992). Measuring the health of the school climate: A conceptual framework. *NASSP Bulletin, 76*(517), 71–79.

Hundeide, K. (1992). Cultural constraints on cognitive development. In P. S. Klein & A. J. Tannenbaum (Eds.), *To be young and gifted* (pp. 52–69). Norwood, NJ: Ablex.

Hutchinson, R. L., & Reagan, C. A. (1989). Problems for which seniors would seek help from school counselors. *The School Counselor, 36*, 271–280.

Irvine, J. J. (1991). *Black students and school failure: Policies, practices, and prescriptions.* New York: Praeger.

Jackman, M. R. (1977). Prejudice, tolerance, and attitudes toward ethnic groups. *Social Science Research, 6*, 145–169.

Jacobs, J. C. (1971). Effectiveness of teacher and parent identification of gifted children as a function of school levels. *Psychology in the Schools, 8*, 140–142.

Janos, P. M., & Robinson, N. M. (1985). Psychological development in intellectually gifted children. In F. D. Horowitz & M. O'Brien (Eds.), *The gifted and talented: Developmental perspectives* (pp. 149–195). Washington, DC: American Psychological Association.

Jenkins, L. E. (1989). The Black family and academic achievement. In G. L. Berry & J. K. Asamen (Eds.), *Black students: Psychological issues and academic achievement* (pp. 138–152). Newbury Park, CA: Corwin Press.

Jensen, A. R. (1969). How much can we boost IQ and scholastic achievement? *Harvard Educational Review, 39*, 1–123.

Jensen, A. R. (1979). *Bias in mental testing.* New York: Free Press.

Jones, R. L. (1988). *Psychoeducational assessment of minority group children: A casebook.* Berkeley, CA: Cobb & Henry.

Kahle, J. B. (1986). *Equitable science education: A discrepancy model.* Perth, Western Australia: Science and Mathematics Education Center, Curtin University of Technology.

Kahle, J. B., & Meece, J. (1994). Research on gender issues in the classroom. In R. Gabel (Ed.), *Handbook on research in science education* (pp. 542–557). New York: Macmillan.

Karnes, F. A., & Whorton, J. E. (1991). Teacher certification and endorsement in gifted education: Past, present, and future. *Gifted Child Quarterly, 35*(3), 148–150.

Kaufmann, F. A. (1981). The 1964–1968 presidential scholars: A follow-up study. *Exceptional Children, 48*, 164–169.

Kaufmann, F. A., & Sexton, D. (1983). Some implications for home-school linkages. *Roeper Review, 6*(1), 49–51.

Keirouz, K. S. (1990). Concerns of parents of gifted children: A research review. *Gifted Child Quarterly, 34*(2), 56–63.

Kerr, B. A. (1991). *A handbook for counseling the gifted and talented.* Alexandria, VA: American Counseling Association.

Kessler, J. W. (1963). My son, the underachiever. *PTA Magazine, 58*, 12–14.

Kinder, D. R. (1986). The continuing American dilemma: White resistance to racial change 40 years after Myrdal. *Journal of Social Issues, 42*, 151–171.

King, S. H. (1993). The limited presence of African-American teachers. *Review of Educational Research, 63*, 115–149.

Kitano, M. K. (1991). A multicultural educational perspective on serving the culturally diverse gifted. *Journal for the Education of the Gifted, 15*(1), 4–19.

Klausmeier, K., Mishra, S. P., & Maker, C. J. (1987). Identification of gifted learners: A national survey of assessment practices and training needs of school psychologists. *Gifted Child Quarterly, 31*(1), 135–137.

Kline, B. E., & Short, E. B. (1991). Changes in emotional resilience: Gifted adolescent boys. *Roeper Review, 13*(4), 118–121.

Korman, M. (1974). National conference on levels and patterns of professional training in psychology: Major themes. *American Psychologist, 29*, 301–313.

Kowitz, G. T., & Armstrong, C. M. (1961). Under-achievement: Concept or artifact? *School and Society, 89,* 347–349.

Kunjufu, J. (1993, February 5). "Maximizing African-American male academic achievement." Paper presented at the fifth annual Equal Educational Opportunity Conference, Louisville, KY.

Labov, W. (1985). The logic of nonstandard English. In P. P. Giglioli (Ed.), *Language and social context.* New York: Viking Penguin.

Ladson-Billings, G. (1990a). Culturally relevant teaching: Effective instruction for Black students. *The College Board Review, 155,* 20–25.

Ladson-Billings, G. (1990b). Like lightning in a bottle: Attempting to capture the pedagogical excellence of successful teachers of Black students. *Qualitative Studies in Education, 3*(4), 335–344.

Ladson-Billings, G. (1994). Who will teach our children: Preparing teachers to successfully teach African American students. In E. R. Hollins, J. E. King, & W. C. Hayman (Eds.), *Teaching diverse populations: Formulating a knowledge base* (pp. 129–158). New York: State University of New York Press.

Langdon, C. A. (1991). Comment. So long, June and Ward. *Educational Horizons, 69*(4), 170.

Larry P. v. Riles, 343 F. Supp. 1306 (N.D. Cal. 1972) (preliminary injunction), affirmed, 502 F. 2d 963 (9th Cir. 1974), opinion issued No. C-71-2270 RFP (N.D. Cal. October 16, 1979).

Lee, C. (1984). An investigation of psychosocial variables related to academic success for rural Black adolescents. *Journal of Negro Education, 53*(4), 424–433.

Levin, H. M. (1990). The educationally disadvantaged are still among us. In J. G. Bain & J. L. Herman (Eds.), *Making schools work for underachieving minority students* (pp. 3–11). New York: Greenwood.

Lewin, K. (1936). *Principles of topological psychology.* New York: McGraw.

Li, A. K. F. (1988). Self-perception and motivational orientation in gifted children. *Roeper Review, 10*(3), 175–180.

Lightfoot, S. (1983). *The good high school.* New York: Basic Books.

Locke, D. C. (1989). Fostering the self-esteem of African-American children. *Elementary School Guidance & Counseling, 23,* 254–259.

Locke, D. C. (1992). *Increasing multicultural understanding: A comprehensive model.* Newbury Park, CA: Sage.

Mackler, B. (1970). Blacks who are academically successful. *Urban Education, 5,* 210–237.

MacLeod, J. (1987). *Ain't no makin' it: Leveled aspirations in a low-income neighborhood.* Boulder, CO: Westview Press.

Mahoney, A. R., & Seeley, K. R. (1982). *A study of juveniles in a suburban court* (Tech. Rep.). Washington, DC: U.S. Department of Justice.

Maker, J. C., & Schiever, S. W. (Eds.). (1989). *Critical issues in gifted education: Defensible programs for cultural and ethnic minorities* (Vol. 2). Austin, TX: ProEd.

Manaster, G. J., & Powell, P. M. (1983). A framework for understanding gifted adolescents' psychological maladjustment. *Roeper Review, 6*(2), 70–73.

Mandel, H. P., & Marcus, S. I. (1988). *The psychology of underachievement: Differential diagnosis and differential treatment*. New York: Wiley.

Marion, R. L. (1980). Communicating with parents of culturally diverse exceptional children. *Exceptional Children, 46*(8), 616–623.

Marion, R. L. (1981). Working with parents of the disadvantaged or culturally different gifted. *Roeper Review, 4*(1), 32–34.

Marland, S. (1972). *Education of the gifted and talented: Report to the Congress of the United States by the U.S. Commissioner of Education*. Washington, DC: U.S. Government Printing Office.

Maslow, A. H. (1954). *Motivation and personality*. New York: Harper & Row.

Maslow, A. H. (1968). *Toward a psychology of being* (2nd ed.). Princeton, NJ: Van Nostrand.

Matter, D. E., & Matter, R. M. (1985). Children who are lonely and shy: Action steps for the counselors. *Elementary School Guidance & Counseling, 20*, 129–135.

McAdoo, H. P. (Ed.). (1988). *Black families* (2nd ed.). Newbury Park, CA: Sage.

McAdoo, H. P. (Ed.). (1993). *Family ethnicity: Strength in diversity*. Newbury Park, CA: Sage.

McCall, R. B., Applebaum, M., & Hogarty, P. (1973). *Developmental changes in mental performance* (Society for Research in Child Development Monograph Series 150[3]).

McCall, R. B., Evahn, C., & Kratzer, L. (1992). *High school underachievers: What do they achieve as adults?* Newbury Park, CA: Sage.

McLeod, J., & Cropley, A. (1989). *Fostering academic excellence*. New York: Pergamon Press.

McLoyd, V. C. (1990). The impact of economic hardship on Black families and children: Psychological distress, parenting, and socioeconomic development. *Child Development, 61*, 311–346.

Mercer, D. C. (1986). Learning disabilities. In N. G. Haring & L. McCormick (Eds.), *Exceptional children and youth* (4th ed., pp. 119–159). Columbus, OH: Charles E. Merrill.

Mickelson, R. A. (1984). *Race, class, and gender differences in adolescents' academic achievement attitudes and behaviors*. Unpublished dissertation, Department of Education, University of California, Los Angeles.

Milgrim, R. M. (Ed.). (1993). *Counseling gifted and talented children: A guide for teachers, counselors, and parents*. Norwood, NJ: Ablex.

Moynihan, D. (1965). *The Negro family: The case for national action*. Washington, DC: U.S. Department of Labor, Office of Planning and Research.

Murray, H. (1938). *Explorations in personality*. New York: Oxford University Press.

Nairn, A. (1980). *The reign of ETS: The corporation that makes up minds*. Washington, DC: Ralph Nader.

National Center for Health Statistics. (1983). *Advanced report of final natality statistics: 1978* (Monthly Vital Statistics Rep. 31[8]). Washington, DC: U.S. Government Printing Office.

National Coalition of Advocates for Students. (1985). *Barriers to excellence: Our children at risk*. Boston: Author.

National Coalition of Advocates for Students. (1988). *New voices: Immigrant students in U.S. Public Schools.* Boston: Author.

National Commission on Excellence in Education. (1983). *A nation at risk: The imperative for educational reform.* Washington, DC: U.S. Department of Education.

National Defense Education Act of 1958, Pub. Law 97–35 (September 13, 1981).

National Opinion Research Center. (1980). *General social surveys, 1972–1980: Cumulative codebook.* Storrs, CT: Roper Public Opinion Research Center, University of Connecticut.

Neill, D. M., & Medina, N. J. (1989). Standardized testing: Harmful to educational health. *Phi Delta Kappan, 70*(9), 688–697.

Newman, C. I., Dember, C. F., & Krug, O. (1973). He can but he won't: A psychodynamic study of so-called "gifted underachievers." *Psychoanalytic Study of the Child, 28,* 83–129.

Noble, K. D. (1987). The dilemma of the gifted woman. *Psychology of Women Quarterly, 11,* 367–378.

Noble, K. D. (1989). Living out the promise of high potential: Perceptions of 100 gifted women. *Advanced Development, 1,* 57–75.

Oakes, J. (1988). Tracking: Can schools take a different route? *National Education Association,* 41–47.

Ogbu, J. U. (1983). Minority students and schooling in pluralistic societies. *Comparative Education Review, 27*(2), 168–190.

Ogbu, J. U. (1988). Human intelligence testing: A cultural-ecological perspective. *Phi Kappa Phi Journal, 68,* 23–29.

Ogbu, J. U. (1994). From cultural differences to differences in cultural frame of reference. In P. M. Greenfield & R. R. Cocking (Eds.), *Cross-cultural roots of minority child development* (pp. 365–391). Hillsdale, NJ: Erlbaum.

Ohlsen, M. M., & Gazda, G. M. (1965). Counseling underachieving bright pupils. *Education, 86,* 78–81.

Ordovensky, P. (1988, April 13). Test bias aids boys in scholarship. *USA Today,* p. 10.

Parham, T. A. (1989). Cycles of psychological nigrescence. *The Counseling Psychologist, 17*(2), 187–226.

Parham, T. A., & Helms, J. E. (1985). Relation of racial identity attitudes to self-actualization and affective states of Black students. *Journal of Counseling Psychology, 32*(3), 431–440.

Payne, B. D. (1984). The relationship of test anxiety and answer-changing behavior: An analysis by race and gender. *Measurement and Evaluation in Guidance, 16*(4), 205–210.

Pearson, J. L., Hunter, A. G., Ensminger, M. E., & Kellam, S. G. (1990). Black grandmothers in multi-generational households: Diversity in family structure and parenting involvement in the Woodlawn community. *Child Development, 61*(2), 434–442.

Pegnato, C. W., & Birch, J. W. (1959). Locating gifted children in junior high school: A comparison of methods. *Exceptional Children, 25,* 300–304.

Pelligrini, A. D., & Glickman, C. D. (1990). Measuring kindergartners social competence. *Young Children, 45*(4), 40–44.

Peterson, J. S. (1990). Noon-hour discussion: Dealing with the burdens of capability. *GCT, 13*(4), 17–22.

Piorkowski, G. K. (1983). Survivor guilt in the university setting. *The Personnel and Guidance Journal, 61*(10), 620–622.

Plake, B. S., Ansorge, C. J., Parker, C. S., & Lowry, S. R. (1982). Effects of item arrangement, knowledge of arrangement, test anxiety and sex performance. *Journal of Educational Measurement, 19*(1), 49–57.

Ponterotto, J. G., & Pedersen, P. B. (1993). *Preventing prejudice: A guide for counselors and educators.* Newbury Park, CA: Sage.

Prom-Jackson, S., Johnson, S. T., & Wallace, M. B. (1987). Home environment, talented minority youth, and school achievement. *Journal of Negro Education, 56*(1), 111–121.

Raph, J. B., Goldberg, M. L., & Passow, A. H. (1966). *Bright underachievers.* New York: Teachers College Press.

Rathvon, N. W. (1991). Effects of a guidance unit in two formats on the examination performance of underachieving middle school students. *The School Counselor, 38,* 294–304.

Read, C. R. (1991). Achievement and career choices: Comparisons of males and females. *Roeper Review, 13*(4), 188–193.

Reis, S. M. (1987). We can't change what we don't recognize: Understanding the special needs of gifted females. *Gifted Child Quarterly, 31,* 83–89.

Reis, S. M. (1991). The need for clarification in research designed to examine gender differences in achievement and accomplishment. *Roeper Review, 13*(4), 193–198.

Reis, S. M., & Callahan, C. M. (1989). Gifted females: They've come a long way — or have they? *Journal for the Education of the Gifted, 12,* 99–117.

Rensberger, B. (1984). Margaret Mead: An indomitable presence. In A. L. Hammond (Ed.), *A passion to know: 20 profiles in science* (pp. 37–38). New York: Charles Scribner's Sons.

Renzulli, J. S. (1978). What makes giftedness? Reexamining a definition. *Phi Delta Kappan, 60*(3), 180–184.

Renzulli, J. S. (1986). The three-ring conception of giftedness: A developmental model for creative productivity. In R. J. Sternberg & J. E. Davidson (Eds.), *Conceptions of giftedness* (pp. 53–92). New York: Cambridge University Press.

Renzulli, J. S., Reis, S. M., Hebert, T. P., & Diaz, E. I. (1994). The plight of high ability students in urban schools. In M. C. Wang & M. C. Reynolds (Eds.), *Making a difference for students at risk* (pp. 61–98). Thousand Oaks, CA: Corwin.

Ridley, C. R. (1989). Racism in counseling as an adverse behavioral process. In P. B. Pedersen, J. G. Draguns, W. J. Lonner, & J. E. Trimble (Eds.), *Counseling across cultures* (3rd ed., pp. 55–77). Honolulu, HI: University of Hawaii Press.

Rimm, S., & Lowe, B. (1988). Family environments of underachieving gifted students. *Gifted Child Quarterly, 32*(4), 353–359.

Rogers, C. R. (1951). *Client-centered therapy: Its current practice, implications, and theory.* Boston: Houghton Mifflin.

Rogers, C. R. (1961). *On becoming a person: A therapist's view of psychotherapy.* Boston: Houghton Mifflin.

Rosenthal, K., & Jacobson, L. (1968). *Pygmalion in the classroom: Teacher expectation and pupil intellectual development.* New York: Holt, Rinehart, & Winston.

Roth, R. M. (1970). *Underachieving students and guidance.* New York: Houghton Mifflin.

Ruben, A. M. (1989). Preventing school dropouts through classroom guidance. *Elementary School Guidance & Counseling, 24*, 21–29.

Rumberger, R. W. (1987). High school dropouts: A review of issues and evidence. *Review of Educational Research, 57*(2), 101–121.

Rutter, M. (1990). Psychosocial resilience and protective mechanisms. In J. Rolf, A. Masten, D. Cichetti, K. Nuechterlein, & S. Weintraub (Eds.), *Risk and protective factors in the development of psychopathology* (pp. 181–214). New York: Cambridge University Press.

Ryan, J. S. (1983). Identifying intellectually superior Black children. *Journal of Educational Research, 76*(3), 153–156.

Sadker, M., & Sadker, D. (1982). *Sex equity handbook for schools.* New York: Longman.

Sadker, M., Sadker, D., & Long, L. (1993). Gender and educational equality. In J. A. Banks & C. A. M. Banks (Eds.), *Multicultural education: Issues and perspectives* (2nd ed., pp. 111–128). Boston: Allyn & Bacon.

Samuda, R. J., Kong, S. L., Cummins, J., Lewis, J., & Pascual-Leone, J. (1991). *Assessment and placement of minority students.* Lewiston, NY: Hogrefe and ISSP.

Saracho, O. N. (1989). Cognitive style in the play of young children. *Early Childhood Development and Care, 51*, 65–76.

Saracho, O. N., & Gerstl, C. K. (1992). Learning differences among at-risk minority students. In H. C. Waxman, J. Walker de Felix, J. E. Anderson, & H. P. Baptiste Jr. (Eds.), *Students at risk in at-risk schools. Improving environments for learning* (pp. 105–136). Newbury Park, CA: Corwin Press.

Sarason, S. B., Davidson, K. S., Lighthall, F. F., Waite, R. R., & Ruebush, B. K. (1960). *Anxiety in elementary school children.* New York: Wiley.

Saurenman, D. A., & Michael, W. B. (1980). Differential placement of high-achieving and low-achieving gifted pupils in grades four, five, and six on measures of field dependence–field independence, creativity, and self-concept. *Gifted Child Quarterly, 24*, 81–86.

Sax, G. (1989). *Principles of educational and psychological measurement and evaluation* (3rd ed.). Belmont, CA: Wadsworth.

Schlosser, L. K. (1992). Teacher distance and student disengagement: School lives on the margin. *Journal of Teacher Education, 43*(2), 128–140.

Schmitz, C. C., & Galbraith, J. (1985). *Managing the social and emotional needs of the gifted: A teacher's survival guide.* Minneapolis, MN: Free Spirit.

Seeley, K. R. (1984). Giftedness and juvenile delinquency in perspective. *Journal for the Education of the Gifted, 8,* 59–72.

Serwatka, T. S., Deering, S., & Stoddard, A. (1989). Correlates of the under-representation of Black students in classes for gifted students. *Journal of Negro Education, 58*(6), 520–530.

Shade, B. J. (1978). Social-psychological characteristics of achieving Black children. *Negro Educational Review, 29*(2), 80–87.

Shade, B. J. (1994). Understanding the African American learner. In E. R. Hollins, J. E. King, & W. C. Hayman (Eds.), *Teaching diverse populations: Formulating a knowledge base* (pp. 175–189). New York: State University of New York Press.

Shade, B. J., & Edwards, P. A. (1987). Ecological correlates of the educative style of Afro-American children. *Journal of Negro Education, 56*(1), 88–99.

Shade, B. J., & New, C. A. (1993). Cultural influences on learning: Teaching implications. In J. A. Banks & C. A. M. Banks (Eds.), *Multicultural education: Issues and perspectives* (2nd ed., pp. 317–331). Boston: Allyn & Bacon.

Shapiro, J. P., Loeb, P., & Bowermaster, D. (1993). Separate and unequal: Examining special education. *U.S. News & World Reports, 115*(23), 46–60.

Shaull, R. (1993). Foreword. In P. Freire, *Pedagogy of the oppressed* (pp. 11–16). New York: Continuum.

Shavelson, R. J., Bolus, R., & Keesling, J. W. (1980). Self-concept: Recent developments in theory and methods. In D. A. Payne (Ed.), *Recent developments in affective measurement.* San Francisco: Jossey-Bass.

Shaw, M. C., & McCuen, J. T. (1960). The onset of academic underachievement in bright children. *Journal of Educational Psychology, 51*(3), 103–108.

Silverman, L. K. (1989). Invisible gifts, invisible handicaps. *Roeper Review, 12,* 37–42.

Silverman, L. K. (Ed.). (1993). *Counseling the gifted and talented.* Denver, CO: Love.

Sinclair, R. L., & Ghory, W. J. (1987). *Reaching marginal students: A primary concern for school renewal.* Berkeley, CA: McCutchan.

Sinclair, R. L., & Ghory, W. J. (1992). Marginality, community, and the responsibility of educators for students who do not succeed in school. In H. C. Waxman, J. Walker de Felix, J. E. Anderson, & H. P. Baptiste Jr. (Eds.), *Students at risk in at-risk schools: Improving environments for learning* (pp. 33–42). Newbury Park, CA: Corwin Press.

Sizer, T. (1984). *Horace's compromise: The dilemma of the American high school.* Boston: Houghton Mifflin.

Slaughter, D. T., & Epps, E. G. (1987). The home environment and academic achievement of Black American children and youth: An overview. *Journal of Negro Education, 56*(1), 3–20.

Slaughter, D. T., & Kuehne, V. S. (1988). Improving Black education: Perspectives on parent involvement. *Urban League Review, 11*(1–2), 59–75.

Sleeter, C. E., & Grant, C. A. (1993). *Making choices for multicultural education* (2nd ed.). New York: Merrill.

Smith, J., LeRose, B., & Clasen, R. E. (1991). Underrepresentation of minority students in gifted programs: Yes! It matters! *Gifted Child Quarterly, 35*(2), 81–83.

Smitherman, G. (1983). Language and liberation. *Journal of Negro Education, 52*(1), 15–23.

Snyderman, M., & Rothman, S. (1987). Survey of expert opinion on intelligence and aptitude testing. *American Psychologist, 42*(2), 137–144.

Spearman, C. (1927). *The abilities of man.* New York: Macmillan.

Sternberg, R. J. (1985). *Beyond IQ: A triarchic theory of human intelligence.* Cambridge, England: Cambridge University Press.

Sternberg, R., & Davidson, J. E. (Eds.). (1986). *Conceptions of giftedness.* Cambridge, England: Cambridge University Press.

Sternberg, R. J., & Detterman, D. K. (1986). *What is intelligence: Contemporary viewpoints on its nature and definition.* Norwood, NJ: Ablex.

Sternberg, R. J., & Kolligian, J. (Eds.). (1990). *Competence reconsidered.* New Haven, CT: Yale University Press.

Sternberg, R. J., & Wagner, R. (1985). *Practical intelligence.* New York: Cambridge University Press.

Stockard, J., & Mayberry, M. (1992). *Effective educational environments.* Newbury Park, CA: Sage.

Sue, D. W., Arrendondo, P., & McDavis, R. J. (1992). Multicultural counseling competencies and standards: A call to the profession. *Journal of Counseling and Development, 70,* 477–486.

Sue, D. W., & Sue, D. (1990). *Counseling the culturally different: Theory & Practice* (2nd ed.). New York: Wiley & Sons.

Supplee, P. L. (1990). *Reaching the gifted underachiever: Program strategy and design.* New York: Teachers College Press.

Taguiri, R., & Litwin, G. H. (Eds.). (1968). *Organizational climate: Explorations of a concept.* Boston: Harvard University Press.

Tannenbaum, A. J. (1983). *Gifted children: Psychological and educational perspectives.* New York: Macmillan.

Tannenbaum, A. J. (1992). Early signs of giftedness: Research and commentary. In P. S. Klein & A. J. Tannenbaum (Eds.), *To be young and gifted* (pp. 3–32). Norwood, NJ: Ablex.

Taylor, C. W., & Ellison, R. L. (1968). *Manual for Alpha Biographical Inventory.* Salt Lake City, UT: Institute for Behavioral Research in Creativity.

Taylor, J. B. (1983). Influence of speech variety on teachers' evaluation of reading comprehension. *Journal of Educational Psychology, 75*(5), 662–667.

Terman, L. M. (1925). *Genetic studies of genius: Vol. 1. Mental and physical traits of a thousand gifted children.* Stanford, CA: Stanford University Press.

Text of Carnegie Report. (1986). *Education Week, 5,* 11–18.

Thorndike, R. L. (1963). *The concepts of over- and under-achievement.* New York: Teachers College Press.

Title IV, Part B [Jacob K. Javits Gifted and Talented Students Education Act of

1988], Elementary and Secondary Education Act, 20 U.S.C. § 3061 *et seq.* (1988).

Tittle, C. K. (1978). *Sex differences in testing: A review with policy recommendations.* (ERIC Document Reproduction Services No. ED 164 623)

Tittle, C. K., & Zytowski, D. G. (Eds.). (1978). *Sex-fair in testing and measurement: Research and implications.* Washington, DC: National Institute of Education.

Tomlinson, T. (1992). *Issues in education. Hard work and high expectations: Motivating students to learn.* Washington, DC: U.S. Department of Education, Office of Educational Research and Improvement.

Torrance, E. P. (1977). *Discovery and nurturance of giftedness in the culturally different.* Reston, VA: Council on Exceptional Children.

Tran, M. T., Young, R. L., & Di Lella, J. D. (1994). Multicultural education courses and the student teacher: Eliminating stereotypical attitudes in our ethnically diverse classroom. *Journal of Teacher Education, 45*(3), 183–189.

Turner, B. G., Beidel, D. C., Hughes, S., & Turner, M. W. (1993). Test anxiety in African-American school children. *School Psychology Quarterly, 8*(2), 140–152.

Tuttle, F. B., Becker, L. A., & Sousa, J. A. (1988). *Characteristics and identification of gifted and talented students* (3rd ed.). Washington, DC: National Education Association.

U.S. Bureau of the Census. (1970). Household and family characteristics: March, 1969. In *Current Population Reports* (Series P-20, No. 200). Washington, DC: U.S. Government Printing Office.

U.S. Bureau of the Census. (1982). *Characteristics of the population below poverty level: 1980* (Current Population Rep. p-60). Washington, DC: U.S. Government Printing Office.

U.S. Bureau of the Census. (1983). *Money, income, and poverty status of families and persons in the United States: 1982 advanced report* (Current Population Rep. p-60 [140]). Washington, DC: U.S. Government Printing Office.

U.S. Bureau of the Census. (1984). *Persons in institutions and other group quarters: 1980 census of populations, PC 80-2-40.* Washington, DC: U.S. Government Printing Office.

U.S. Bureau of the Census. (1985a). Household and family characteristics: March, 1984. In *Current Population Reports* (Series P-20, No. 398). Washington, DC: U.S. Government Printing Office.

U.S. Bureau of the Census. (1985b). Marital status and living arrangements: March, 1984. In *Current Population Reports* (Series P-20, No. 399). Washington, DC: U.S. Government Printing Office.

U.S. Bureau of the Census. (1990). *Summary of population and housing characteristics, West Virginia* (U.S. Department of Commerce Bureau of the Census Publication No. 1990 CPH-1-50). Washington, DC: U.S. Government Printing Office.

U.S. Congress. (1970, April). Public Law 91-230.

U.S. Congress. (1988, April). Public Law 100-297.

U.S. Department of Education. (1990). *To assure the free appropriate public education of all handicapped children*. Twelfth annual report to Congress on the implementation of the Education of the Handicapped Act. Washington, DC: Author.

U.S. Department of Education. (1993). *National excellence: A case for developing America's talent*. Washington, DC: Office of Educational Research and Improvement.

U.S. Department of Education. (1994). *Javits gifted and talented students education program. Grants projects abstracts, 1992–1993*. Washington, DC: Office of Educational Research and Improvement, Programs for the Improvement of Practice.

U.S. Department of Education, Office of Special Programs. (1993). *Fifteenth annual report to Congress on the implementation of the Individuals with Disabilities Education Act*. Washington, DC: Author.

VanTassel-Baska, J. (1989). The role of the family in the success of disadvantaged gifted learners. *Journal for the Education of the Gifted, 13*(1), 22–36.

VanTassel-Baska, J., Patton, J., & Prillaman, D. (1989). Disadvantaged gifted learners at-risk for educational attention. *Focus on Exceptional Children, 22*(3), 1–16.

VanTassel-Baska, J., & Willis, G. (1988). A three year study of the effects of income on academically able students. *Gifted Child Quarterly, 31*(4), 169–173.

Vogt, L. A., Jordan, C., & Tharp, R. G. (1987). Explaining school failure, producing school success: Two cases. *Anthropology & Education Quarterly, 18*, 276–286.

Waetjen, W. B. (1977, September). *Sex differences in learning: Some questions*. Paper presented at the fourth annual meeting of the International Society for the Study of Behavioral Development, Pavia, Italy.

Wagner, M. (1991, September). *Drop outs with disabilities: What do we know? What can we do?* Menlo Park, CA: SRI International.

Walker de Felix, J. (1992). Issues confronting at-risk students. In H. C. Waxman, J. Walker de Felix, J. E. Anderson, & H. P. Baptiste Jr. (Eds.), *Students at risk in at-risk schools: Improving environments for learning* (pp. 61–64). Newbury Park, CA: Corwin Press.

Wang, M. S., Haertel, G. D., & Walberg, H. J. (December/January 1993/94). Synthesis of research: What helps students learn? *Educational Leadership*, pp. 74–79.

Waxman, H. C. (1992). Reversing the cycle of educational failure for students in at-risk school environments. In H. C. Waxman, J. Walker de Felix, J. E. Anderson, & H. P. Baptiste Jr. (Eds.), *Students at risk in at-risk schools: Improving environments for learning* (pp. 1–10). Newbury Park, CA: Corwin Press.

Webb, J. T., Meckstroth, E. A., & Tolan, S. S. (1982). *Guiding the gifted child*. Dayton, OH: Ohio Psychology Press.

Welch, I. D., & McCarroll, L. (1993). The future role of school counselors. *The School Counselor, 41*(1), 48–53.

Wellesley College Center for Research on Women. (1992). *How schools short-change girls*. Washington, DC: American Association of University Women Educational Foundation.

Wesman, A. G. (1968). Intelligence testing. *American Psychologist, 27*, 267–274.

West, J. D., Hosie, T. W., & Mathews, F. N. (1989). Families of academically gifted children: Adaptability and cohesion. *The School Counselor, 37*, 121–127.

Whalen, R. E. (1984). Secondary education: Student flows, course participation, and state requirements. In V. Plisko (Ed.), *The condition of education* (pp. 149–182). Washington, DC: U.S. Government Printing Office.

Whitmore, J. R. (1980). *Giftedness, conflict, and underachievement*. Boston: Allyn & Bacon.

Whitmore, J. R. (1986). Understanding a lack of motivation to excel. *Gifted Child Quarterly, 30*(2), 66–69.

Willig, A. C., Harnisch, D. L., Hill, K. T., & Maehr, M. L. (1983). Sociocultural and educational correlates of success-failure attributions and evaluation anxiety in the school setting for Black, Hispanic, and Anglo children. *American Educational Research Journal, 20*(3), 385–410.

Wilson, M. N. (1989). Child development in the context of the Black extended family. *Child Development, 44*(2), 380–385.

Winne, P. H., Woodlands, M. J., & Wong, B. Y. (1982). Comparability of self-concept among learning disabled, normal, and gifted students. *Journal of Learning Disabilities, 15*(8), 470–475.

Wittmer, J., & Myrick, R. D. (1989). *The teacher as facilitator*. Minneapolis, MN: Educational Media Corporation.

Wolfle, J. A. (1991). Underachieving gifted males: Are we missing the boat? *Roeper Review, 13*(4), 181–183.

Worthen, B. R., Borg, W. R., & White, K. R. (1993). *Measurement and evaluation in the schools*. New York: Longman.

Zill, N. (1983). *Happy, healthy, and insecure*. New York: Doubleday.

Zuccone, C. F., & Amerikaner, M. (1986). Counseling gifted underachievers: A family systems approach. *Journal of Counseling and Development, 64*, 590–592.

Index

About the Author

Donna Y. Ford is an assistant professor of educational psychology at the University of Virginia. She teaches in the gifted education program and is a researcher with the National Research Center on the Gifted and Talented. Professor Ford has published numerous articles and book chapters on gifted Black students in the areas of identification and assessment, underachievement, counseling, family studies, child development, and multicultural and urban education.